against
the grain

(extraordinary gluten-free recipes
made from real, all-natural ingredients)

against
the grain

NANCY CAIN

PHOTOGRAPHS BY JENNIFER MAY

CLARKSON POTTER/PUBLISHERS
NEW YORK

CLARKSON POTTER is a trademark and POTTER with colophon
is a registered trademark of Random House LLC.

"Against The Grain" is a trademark of Against The Grain Gourmet Foods, LLC

Library of Congress Cataloging-in-Publication Data
Cain, Nancy.
Against The Grain: extraordinary gluten-free recipes made from real, all-natural
ingredients/Nancy Cain; photographs by Jennifer May.
Pages cm
Includes index.
1. Gluten-free diet—Recipes. 2. Baking. I. May, Jennifer, photographer. II. Title.
RM237.86.C33 2015
641.81′5—dc23   2014008646

ISBN 978-0-385-34555-2
eISBN 978-0-385-34556-9

Printed in China

Prop styling by Raina Kattleson
Food styling by Kendra McKnight
Book and cover design by Ashley Tucker
Cover photography by Jennifer May

10 9 8 7 6 5 4 3 2 1

First Edition

To the guys in my life:
Tom, Alex, Marty,
and, yes, Chester

contents

PINEAPPLE DREAM CAKE

1 Duncan Hines Pineapple
Supreme Cake Mix
½ cup Crisco Oil
1 vanilla or pineapple
instant pudding mix
4 eggs - 1 cup water

DEEP CHOCOLATE DREAM CAKE

1 Duncan Hines Deep Chocolate
Cake Mix
½ cup Crisco Oil
1 chocolate instant pudding
mix
4 eggs - 1 cup water

DUNCAN HINES DREAM

DIRECTIONS FOR ALL CA

Blend all ingredients, then beat at med
minutes. Bake in greased and floured 10
350° for 45 to 55 minutes. Cool in pan (
15 minutes.

GLAZE - Mix 1 cup sifted confect
milk. Spread over

going against the grain

MY IDEA TO START MY GLUTEN-FREE BREAD COMPANY, Against The Grain, began, as many other gluten-free companies do, in our kitchen and with a familiar story. A family member is diagnosed with celiac disease; the mom (and it is almost always the mom) goes into high gear to create baked goods the whole family can enjoy. Before she knows it, she is baking for her family, gluten-intolerant neighbors, local restaurants, and farmer's markets. But the moment I truly knew gluten-free baking was *my* mission, however, happened at The Weeping Rock Gas Dock and Café in Thousand Island Park, New York.

A seasonal gathering spot for summer residents on the St. Lawrence River, The Weeping Rock was a modern-day Alice's Restaurant, built into the ledge at water's edge around a massive, perennially wet, granite boulder. It was run by Donna, a scrappy guitar-picking singer with an uncanny ability to make almost anything taste delicious. For many, the day began with coffee and conversation on the dock at The Weeping Rock. By noon, it was a hangout for hungry fishermen, sunbathing teenagers, and those traveling through by boat, and Donna fed them all.

Both pastry and pizza doughs made without gums can be rolled out in a variety of thicknesses and are easy to handle.

Our family of four was at our river cottage, as usual, for my older son Alex's sixteenth birthday. My husband, Tom, and my younger son, Marty, had both been diagnosed with celiac disease the previous fall. Early on we had made the decision that the entire family would eat gluten-free, so for Alex's birthday party I had developed a new gluten-free pizza recipe. No one could believe it was gluten-free, and when several guests suggested that I should sell my pizzas commercially, I found it an intriguing idea. Having zero knowledge of the food business, I asked Donna if she would be willing to bake up a few pizzas and give out free samples to her customers in exchange for feedback. Donna was game, so I delivered two pizzas and some general baking instructions and waited for the response. That evening, Donna came by my cottage with two big, white, slightly grease-splattered paper plates, autographed with glowing customer comments. Over a dozen customers tried and raved about the pizza. Most of the taste testers were teenagers, and not one of them was gluten-intolerant. This was before "gluten-free" was a household word, and if asked, most of the pizza's fans wouldn't have had a clue what it meant. For me, this was the realization that I had a product that was not just "good for gluten-free" but also appealed to a mainstream audience. A year and a half later, we began shipping our first products out of my house in Vermont, and Donna had moved to Vermont to become our first employee.

gluten-free: a parallel baking universe

Pizza was the very first gluten-free thing I attempted to bake. It was a Friday night, two days after Marty's celiac diagnosis— pizza night. In the pre-celiac era, I prided myself on my homemade pizza, and I liked the Friday night ritual: I would whip up our favorite crust with unbleached flour, knead out all the week's hassles, let it rest, shape it, spread it with my homemade pizza sauce, and top it with whatever struck my fancy—leftovers, local Vermont cheeses, pepperoni, marinated artichokes, or black olives.

Expectations and anxiety were running high that first gluten-free pizza night. We were still reeling from the celiac diagnosis; gluten, we realized, was everywhere. We had just finished emptying our pantry and refrigerator, thrown away our toaster, the bread maker, assorted pots and pans, and started over. The kids were eagerly anticipating their Friday night pizza, but after only forty-eight hours' experience with gluten-free products, I was dubious. But I was determined to keep our ritual, so I did the unthinkable. I bought a gluten-free pizza crust mix—the box certainly made it sound appetizing and effortless.

I dumped the mix in the bowl and carefully followed the directions. I might as well have been working with Flubber; it looked lumpy and smelled like dirty socks. I figured if I worked the dough a little more, it would turn into something I could knead. Instead, I got a quivering pudding texture. Convinced that I had missed something in the directions, I plopped the entire sorry mess into the trash. Little did I know that I wasn't supposed to knead at all. In regular bread making, kneading is key—it disperses the yeast and facilitates gluten formation, and oh yeah, that's what we were trying to avoid. Instead of gluten, the mix contained xanthan gum, a stabilizer that most bakers—professional and amateur—still believe is necessary. I had entered a parallel baking universe, and I had to learn a whole new set of baking skills.

So I ditched the mixes and started working from scratch. I bought rice flour, tapioca starch, and cornstarch—the big three of gluten-free at the time—plus xanthan gum after reading over and over how it was required to "add back the elasticity." No matter how I combined the ingredients, it was always the same—just okay. I tried substituting sorghum flour and potato starch with not much improvement. By that time, I could make rich and fudgy brownies and chocolate cake that fooled the

Glazed Yeast Doughnuts (page 127) made from scratch are fried into light and fluffy breakfast treats.

most discriminating palates, but acceptable bread and pizza crust eluded me. I began to seek out every *flourless* baking recipe I could find to try to understand why they worked. I looked at the ingredients, examined the techniques, and paid attention to the proportions of fats to starches, proteins, and liquids. Among lots of other things, I learned that I had been working with a very narrow definition of flour. "Flour" didn't necessarily have to be milled and poured from a bag—flourless recipes worked because some other ingredient *acted* like flour. I also learned that starch is insoluble in cold water. Yikes, no wonder it felt like I was baking with Flubber: I was trying to make bread out of a non-Newtonian fluid thickened by xanthan gum, the same Oobleck that my kids had made in preschool with cornstarch and water to simulate the action of quicksand. Xanthan gum is a pseudoplastic substance, its thickening properties dependent on the force it receives. Mix it at high speeds, it thins. Let it rest, it thickens—really thickens. No wonder it vexes bakers so, and no wonder it is so overused.

Eventually, I had to go back to the basics of kitchen chemistry, to understand how fats, carbohydrates, protein, and water affect the taste, texture, aroma, and shelf life of both wheat-based and gluten-free baked goods. The first thing I did was dispense with xanthan gum altogether. The culmination of all that knowledge was the birthday pizza, and the beginning of Against The Grain Gourmet.

thinking against the grain

Our company is called Against The Grain because we take a different approach to gluten-free baking. We believe that it is entirely possible to bake gluten-free using the natural properties of real foods. We don't use processed ingredients that simulate the effects of gluten like xanthan gum, modified starches, or things you can't pronounce that really mean water-soluble polymers derived from spruce tree cellulose.

Many gluten-free bread doughs are more batter-like and require high-walled pans. Heavy gauge, dimpled pans help to circulate the air during baking and brown the bread more evenly.

Dough won't rise? Bread too dry? We don't go to food chemists to solve the problem—we look for real food solutions that come from your local grocery store. We ask ourselves: "What foods will act as dough enhancers? What foods will naturally facilitate moisture retention?"

When you bake with real food, gluten-free is not about foreign-tasting additives: It's about using ingredients in inventive ways. It's about adapting time-honed baking techniques to work in ways you never imagined. And most fundamentally, it's about never having to lower your expectations or make excuses. We have built a company whose products are purchased by both gluten-free and mainstream consumers. Many people buy our pizza because it is gluten-free, but every day many tell us it's also the best frozen pizza on the market.

Over the years I've learned a lot about how ingredients function in gluten-free baking—not just about their properties, but also that *how* I use ingredients can be as important as the ingredients themselves. Creaming the butter and sugar in a recipe, for example, will produce a light and airy cake; using melted butter in the same recipe will produce a dense, flat cake. Both use butter, but creaming is a process that physically incorporates tiny air pockets around the sugar in the butter. When baked, these tiny air pockets expand to produce a light crumb. This is not a technique unique to gluten-free baking; it is an established mixing technique to incorporate air in a batter, and it becomes even more important when working with gluten-free flours.

In many ways gluten-free baking is liberating. There are so many varieties of flours to choose from, so many opportunities to improve the flavor and nutritional profile of baked goods. You just have to find the right combination of ingredients and methods. I absolutely love creating new ways to solve old problems, and I invite you into my kitchen to bake alongside me. My approach will change not only the way you view gluten-free baked goods but also the way you bake.

A silky batter for Madeleines (page 309) is made by melting and then cooling the butter. Before baking, the batter is thoroughly chilled to harden the butter and lighten the crumb.

the fundamentals
of gluten-free baking

Gluten-free baking is kind of like having a new baby: There is no lack of unsolicited opinions about what you *should* be doing.

"That baby ought to be wearing socks" was a common one I got when carrying around my newborn years ago in New York City during the summertime. *Socks? Really? It's like 100 degrees on this pavement.* My favorite *erroneous* gluten-free "should" is "You must use xanthan or guar gum in gluten-free doughs to give them structure." Or, as some of the most well-known gluten-free bakers might say, "Xanthan gum is a critical component of most gluten-free baking," and "Every baked item requires some xanthan gum for optimum texture." Xanthan gum is one of the main reasons that so many gluten-free baked goods have an off, chemical taste. It is an industrial ingredient, an additive stabilizer used in sauces, salad dressings, and ice creams, but totally unnecessary in gluten-free baked goods.

All you need to produce great-tasting and reliable gluten-free baked goods are real ingredients and a good understanding of the fundamentals of gluten-free baking. And here they are:

gluten-free flours are not created equal

Wheat-based flours are very consistent. For example, if you buy a bag of King Arthur Unbleached Bread Flour, it will have a protein content of 12.7% and will be milled from hard red spring wheat in the northern Great Plains. I had the occasion to visit a wheat mill in Manhattan, Kansas, the fall of 2013, and was truly amazed by the very specific characteristics that can be milled into flour. That 12.7% protein is pretty specific, and whenever and wherever you break open a bag of King Arthur flour, you know exactly what a cup will weigh and how it will perform.

This couldn't be further from the truth when it comes to gluten-free flours. Some flours come from grains; some come from nuts and seeds; and some come from legumes. So it is not surprising that gluten-free flours have different weights and absorption rates, not to mention different flavors. But there are also many varieties of the same flour, and they differ from brand to brand. And, even within the same flour type, the way it's grown and milled greatly affects its weight and its baking properties. Major brands of wheat-based flours are milled in the same way; this is not the case for most gluten-free flours. And, when multiple gluten-free flours are combined in an all-purpose mix, it is virtually impossible to find consistency across brands.

We purchase truckloads of tapioca starch from the same supplier. Every different lot comes with a material specifications sheet, and there is always a range of moisture content. Extracted from the tuber cassava, the amount of tapioca starch yielded varies with the weather, the soil, the temperature, and the age of the plant. In short, as no two cassavas are alike, no two batches of tapioca are ever the same, and so no two brands of the same gluten-free flour that use tapioca are ever the same either. For the most part, the subtle variations don't make a huge difference in baked goods in which gluten traditionally has a negligible role, like quick breads, muffins, cakes, pies, pancakes, and cookies. But for bread baking, where the ratio of liquid to dry ingredients is so critical, substituting one flour for another is not a simple matter. Different flours weigh different amounts. A cup of tapioca starch, for example, weighs far less than a cup of potato starch. So if you seriously want to make the best bread possible, you need to invest in a kitchen scale. (See "Some Basic Tools," page 25.)

Gluten-free flours also have different protein and fiber contents. Most pure starches—tapioca, arrowroot, potato, and cornstarch—are pretty much interchangeable by weight, but a number of other flours are not. Coconut flour, for example, absorbs four times the liquid of other flours. Adding ¼ cup (30g) of coconut flour to a recipe is like adding 1 cup (160g) of rice flour or sorghum. (See more on this subject on page 44.)

most gluten-free flours work better in a mixture

All around Vermont we have stone walls that have lasted for a century or more. If you look closely, you'll see there is no mortar holding the walls together, and there are big stones and little stones. If you try to build a stone wall of identically sized stones, your wall won't stand without mortar. The structure of baked goods is a lot like those walls: When baking with wheat, gluten is the mortar. In the absence of gluten, you want flours with different-size granules to improve your structure. Of course, there are some exceptions like pancakes and crepes, in which a single gluten-free flour performs just fine. But for the most part, mixing at least two different flours with different granule sizes—one of those two a pure starch—will significantly improve the structure and integrity of your baked goods. Even if you are baking with something like rolled oats, the structure is vastly improved if you include some oatmeal flour, to fill in the spaces between the whole oats. If you look at commercial gluten-free flour mixes, most contain three or more different flours for this exact reason.

gluten-free hydration ratios are surprisingly high

Bread bakers often refer to the ratio of liquid to flour by weight as the hydration ratio. Liquids include not just water but also ingredients like milk, vegetable oil, juice, and whole eggs (which are about 75% water). Typically, the hydration ratios for wheat-based breads range from 50% to 80%, depending on the type of flour and baked good. Since one cup of liquid weighs ½ pound, this means that a 2-pound loaf of bread contains two to over three cups of liquid. For wheat-based baking, high hydration ratios are used for breads like focaccia and ciabatta, with loose, open crumb structures. On the lower hydration end are dense breads like bagels.

Gluten-free breads require much higher hydration ratios, typically with a ratio of more than 100%. These are very loose doughs, and kneading many gluten-free doughs is more akin to folding the dough over and over with a spatula. Hydration ratios in the recipes in this book tend to be in the 110% range. In practice, high hydration ratios mean that gluten-free breads tend to lose their shape unless baked in high-wall pans or pans that support their structure. Rolls were perhaps the most vexing to me, but the Hot Cross Buns (page 79) and Biscuits (page 76) are two examples of recipes that demonstrate that anything is possible. The presence of more water or liquids in gluten-free breads also means that baking times are typically longer.

non-gluten protein builds structure

Most gluten-free bakers believe that the structure in baked goods comes from gluten. Gluten certainly contributes to the structure, but other proteins play a similar role and are just as important. Oddly enough, although gluten is a protein, most gluten-free bakers don't look to protein sources for a substitute. Rather, they look to gums like xanthan and guar and high-fiber binders like psyllium husks.

Typical wheat flour for bread baking is almost 13% protein. Very few gluten-free flours contain that much protein, and those that do would typically be used in a mixture of two or more flours. During the baking process, proteins, whether they come from the flour or added protein sources like eggs, milk, nuts, and seeds, thicken the dough or batter and add structure. There are many reasons why gluten-free baked goods rise beautifully and then fall, but chief among them is inadequate protein. As a dough begins to heat up and bake, there has to be sufficient protein to set and form the walls; otherwise the dough will flatten or not create a resilient enough structure to hold in gases.

the contribution of starch is as important as that of gluten

Pure starches get a bad rap when it comes to gluten-free baking, yet they are probably the least understood component of gluten-free baked goods. Like protein, starches are essential to the structure of gluten-free baked goods. All traditional flours, whether from cereals or grains, are at least 70% starch, and starch is made up of chains of sugar molecules. These chains may be either straight or branched, and the percentage of each type varies according to the type of starch.

Pure starch is insoluble in cold water, and unless starch granules are broken down by heat, the shearing action of mixing, or enzymes (as in fermentation with yeast), they are dead weight in gluten-free dough. Starch becomes soluble in water when heated and forms an elastic gel as the starch granules absorb water and swell. It is this gel that can help build structure, contribute to the crumb, and aid in moisture retention.

gums are not necessary

If starch acts as an elastic gel, why do you need binders like xanthan or guar gums or other gels? *You don't.* Too often xanthan gum is thrown in as a security blanket because bakers think that a gluten replacement is a requirement of gluten-free baking, and yes, gums can often be used to mask shortcomings in a recipe. Put in enough xanthan gum and it will hold most anything together. The only case in which you may need a nonstarch gel or binder is as an egg replacer—in this situation, my go-to is a chia seed or flaxseed slurry. Chia and flax are not only natural binders, but they are packed with protein and fiber, so unlike xanthan and guar gums, they add protein and improve the nutritional profile of any baked good.

Starch granules expand when gluten-free flours are allowed to absorb heated liquids and fats prior to mixing the dough.

part I: **building blocks**

Baking is an interesting interplay between ingredients and how we use them. How we mix them, bake them, and cool them all determine how the final product rises, how it browns, and whether it is light or dense, moist or crumbly. Since gluten-free baked goods often involve multiple flours and some compensation for the absence of gluten, subtle differences can have a major impact on a recipe's success.

Fundamentally, baked goods are made up of proteins, carbohydrates, fats, and leavening agents. Understanding the role these ingredients play in the baking process is the key to successful gluten-free baking and, especially, problem solving and making substitutions. For example, with this knowledge you'll understand why a solid shortening like butter should be replaced with a solid shortening like coconut oil or palm oil. Or how an egg substitute like a chia slurry may be a good binder but result in a pale crust.

fats and oils

Fats may be solids or liquids. They may come from animal sources like cream and butter or from vegetable sources like coconut oil, palm oil, sunflower oil, and canola oil. The choice of fat, whether it is solid or liquid, and its melting point (the temperature at which a solid turns to liquid) have a significant impact on a baked good. Some of the functions of fats and oils:

LEAVEN: The temperature at which a solid fat begins to melt and the amount of water and air in the fat contribute to the leavening of baked goods. The fat may naturally contain water, as in butter (about 20% water). As the temperature increases during baking, solid fats melt, the water in them becomes steam, and the steam leavens the baked good. The later the fat melts in the bake cycle, the more the fat contributes to the rise. This is because the leavening effect of the fat has a chance to work in tandem with the development of the baked good's structure.

TENDERIZE: Tenderizing is the opposite of building structure. Although fats leaven, they tend to work against structure development and tenderize baked goods. By coating the proteins and starch granules, fat prevents these two structure builders from coming together. Butter, for example, has a low melting point—it melts very quickly after being heated, at about body temperature—so it makes for an excellent tenderizer. Often recipes will direct you to refrigerate a dough containing butter before baking to extend its melting point to allow for structure development. Cookies are a prime example of this: By refrigerating the dough before baking, you *reduce* the amount they spread and puff.

MOISTEN: Unlike water, liquid fats such as oil don't evaporate in the baking process and thus moisten a baked good. For this reason, cakes and muffins made with butter tend to rise more but are drier. Cakes made with oil tend to be the moistest.

CARRY FLAVOR: There is nothing like fat to carry flavor, both by coating the various elements in a baked good and by creating a pleasant mouthfeel that delivers the optimum amount of flavor. Applesauce, for example, can be a good, low-calorie oil substitute in a muffin, but you may find that you have to increase the amount of flavoring to achieve the same depth of taste.

starches

All flours, even nut and seed flours, contain starch. Wheat flour, for example, is about 75% starch, coconut flour is 14%, and even almond flour is 7%. Pure starches, like tapioca starch and potato starch, look like fine powder but are actually made up of granules—tiny, layered balls of starch. The most significant property of starch in gluten-free baking is that it is insoluble in cold water. When you mix pure starch and water together, the starch doesn't dissolve but becomes sus-pended in the water and creates a pseudo-plastic substance (i.e., a slurry). Though untreated pure starches are insoluble in cold water, some starches are "modified," which means that most are chemically treated so they absorb cold water and remain stable under a variety of mixing, baking, freezing, and thawing conditions. But starch can also be modified physically through cooking and drying to stabilize it. Functions of starch, whether it is pure starch or a component of a higher-protein flour:

REINFORCE STRUCTURE: As the starch heats during the baking process, the starch granules begin to absorb moisture and swell. This is the process of gelatinization, in which the starch granules swell and thicken into a gel, trapping air bubbles and adding volume and structure to the baked good. Pregelatinizing the starch (heat-treating it before mixing) increases the elasticity of the dough prior to putting it in the oven and, to some degree, mimics the action of gluten in trapping air bubbles.

CREATE CRUMB OR TEXTURE: Yeast feeds on sugar during the fermentation process, and the starch, when it comes in contact with water, releases enzymes that break the starch down into sugar. As the yeast eats the sugar, it produces carbon dioxide and alcohol. The CO_2 leavens the bread and gives it its crumb and bubble-like texture. Meanwhile the alcohol evaporates during proofing or is burned off during baking. Starch in nonyeast breads also adds to the crumb by gelling and trapping air and water in the dough, as described above.

AID IN MOISTURE RETENTION: When starch granules are heated, they swell and absorb liquids, infusing the dough with moisture. As the bread cools, the gel created by water absorption begins to return to its granular state. When stale bread is reheated in an oven, the starch once again absorbs water and gelatinizes, improving its taste.

protein

Gluten, which we are all avoiding, is protein. Proteins are chains of amino acids, which are the building blocks of life. Proteins are also the building blocks of baked goods, both wheat-based and gluten-free. Xanthan and guar gums are routinely used as gluten replacements, yet neither contains a measurable amount of protein. Some gluten-free flours are high in protein, which certainly can help, but they often are included as a percentage of an overall flour mixture and often require some type of binder like eggs or starch gels to retain moisture. Flours made from rolled oats (14%) and flax meal (23%) are high in protein and have good binding properties.

Ingredients like eggs, dried milk powder, and whey protein are often added to gluten-free bread recipes. (For the dairy-free recipes in this book—they're flagged with this icon ⒹⒻ—it may be coconut milk.) These are all good sources of protein and act as building blocks in developing structure. This section describes the function of protein in general; eggs, which have very specific functions, are described in the section that follows. Functions of protein in baked goods:

BUILD STRUCTURE: Proteins do the opposite of tenderizers. They toughen the dough and build the framework for the structure of baked goods. Remember in the old gluten-heavy days when high-protein wheat flour worked great for breads, but made tough, rubbery pie crusts? That is because of the high protein content. After many years of baking gluten-free, I've found we definitely have the advantage when it comes to pie crusts and other tender baked goods.

ENHANCE BROWNING: During the final stages of baking, when the crust has reached a high enough temperature, the carbohydrates (in the form of sugar) and the amino acids (in the protein) combine to brown the crust and produce the aroma we associate with baked bread. This process, known as the Maillard reaction, is also responsible for the browning and flavor of roasted meats. Baked goods like cakes and muffins will remain pale and not develop a crusty, flavorful exterior with low-protein gluten-free flours.

eggs

Eggs are proteins in a category all their own when it comes to baking, particularly gluten-free baking. Eggs are the basis of many flourless recipes, custards, meringues, and angel food and sponge cakes, and are an excellent multipurpose source of protein that, depending on the recipe, binds, tenderizes, moisturizes, dries, and/or leavens baked goods. Whole eggs are good for certain recipes; some recipes call for just yolks or whites; and some call for both, but added separately.

WHOLE EGGS: Egg proteins in their natural state are separate little coils. When exposed to heat, when vigorously mixed, or when in contact with acidity, the coils unwind, attach themselves to other proteins, and form a web. This is how liquid raw eggs become solid and how egg whites are whipped into a meringue. These webs are the reason eggs are not only superb leavening agents and binders but also an important source of structure in gluten-free baked goods. Eggs provide steam for leavening and moisture for starches—yolks are half water and whites are almost all water. Eggs improve the flavor, texture, and color of baked goods, and contribute necessary protein to browning. Egg washes, for example, often facilitate the browning of baked goods such as brioche.

EGG YOLKS: The yolk contains all of the fat in an egg, and it is also a natural source of lecithin. You may recognize soy lecithin as an ingredient in almost all commercially avail-able chocolate bars—that is because lecithin is an emulsifier that binds together ingredients that wouldn't normally stick together. In chocolate it binds cocoa and sugar solids with cocoa butter. Egg lecithin is indispensable for emulsifying oil and water in foods like mayonnaise and hollandaise sauce. Since starch is insoluble in cold water, egg yolks play a central role in pulling together gluten-free doughs and batters.

EGG WHITES: Also known as albumen, egg whites are made up of mostly water and a little more than half of the egg's proteins. When beaten, the proteins in egg whites unwind, and a protein film forms around air bubbles. This is the basis of foams that provide both lightness and structure in baked goods like meringues, sponge cakes, fluffy pancakes, and soufflés. I use egg whites in many pie doughs to both bind the dough into a workable consistency and to make it flakey. Although most proteins are round, egg whites contain fibrous proteins similar to gluten. Is it any surprise that egg whites are so useful here? Egg whites play many other roles: as drying and crisping agents in recipes like crackers, as a shiny glaze for adhering seeds to the top of breads, and as an effective way to provide protein but lower fat.

part II: **some basic tools**

I grew up in simpler times. In our country home, there was no Internet and just a few TV channels, and summers were spent outdoors exploring. Our favorite pastime was building tree forts in the woods: Our dad gave us access to all the lumber we needed, a handsaw, and a hammer and nails. The challenge was to design and build a tree fort the old-fashioned way, to meet our expectations of a structure befitting Tarzan. It was a lesson that I have carried with me my entire life: You can build some pretty amazing structures with very little to work with, but it becomes a lot easier if you have the right tools to do the job.

For a professional baker, I have a pretty minimalist kitchen—no stand mixer, no bread machine, and I think cast-iron skillets are the best. But I have learned that some tools may make gluten-free baking a whole lot easier.

small appliances

For my style of gluten-free baking, my most indispensable gadget is my *food processor*. I inherited my first one from my late dad, who ironically was a gadget freak. Yes, it is a bit more complicated to clean than a bowl, but it makes dough creation much faster. Now I can whip up a pie crust to the perfect consistency and have it rolled out in less than 15 minutes

every time I bake. Besides that, I also use a very basic *hand mixer* for batters, plus a *tortilla machine*. The latter certainly isn't a necessity—you can make do with a cast-iron skillet and a little improvisation—but my tortilla recipe tends to be batter-like, and homemade wraps are an all-time favorite in our household.

baking aids

I'm not sure I even knew there was such a thing as *parchment paper* until I began baking gluten-free. Because I work with sometimes hard-to-handle, challenging-to-roll, and sticky dough that adheres to pans like Velcro, parchment paper may be the one thing I could not do without. *Plastic wrap* makes pie crusts a snap because it is so flexible: I always direct you to roll out pie crusts and pastry dough between two pieces of plastic wrap. And what a great invention *sealable storage bags* are, for both extruding batter-like dough and decorating with icing. Just fill the bag, snip off a bottom corner to the diameter you desire, and you have an instant, disposable pastry bag.

bread pans

We all know that gluten adds structure, but in gluten-free baking, pans are a big component.

LOAF PANS: The first time I tried to bake my own gluten-free sandwich bread, I used a 5 × 9-inch glass loaf pan. The bread tasted okay, but it was a perfect 5 × 9-inch brick, and I couldn't get over the skinny, rectangular slices. Gluten-free bread needs a pan with high walls, like a climbing rose needs a trellis, to train the loaf up, not out. Bread loaf pans can be incredibly expensive, or fairly inexpensive. What works best is a 4½ × 8-inch steel or aluminum blend pan with corrugated or dimpled sides. This pan makes a perfect loaf of approximately 1.5 pounds. (If you add up the ingredients in grams in the sandwich bread recipes, you will find they total approximately 1.5 pounds or 700 +/– grams.) The sides of these pans make for better air circulation, which means better browning and more even baking. The textured walls also allow the finished loaf to release quite easily from the pan.

Norpro Dimpled Nonstick Bread Pans, which are inexpensive, work as well as any other. They are 3 inches deep (great for rising dough), measure 4½ inches across, and come in 8-, 10-, and 12-inch lengths. The smallest size makes a perfect 1½-pound loaf. It may seem attractive to bake longer sandwich loaves like the ones found in the grocery store. However, only two additional inches in pan length means a 25% increase in dough amount. To figure out how much dough to fill a pan, you need to calculate the cubic volume (height × length × width) of the pan and adjust the size of the recipe according to the following table.

PAN SIZE (IN.)	CUBIC VOLUME (IN.)	RECIPE INCREASE
4½ × 8 × 3	108	0%
4½ × 10 × 3	135	25%
4½ × 12 × 3	162	50%

For example, if you want to bake a 12-inch loaf in one of these pans, you need to increase the weight of the ingredients in the recipe by 50% (just multiply the gram amounts by 1.5). It is possible to scale up the recipe by volume (cup, tablespoon, and teaspoon) amounts by adding one-half more of every ingredient, but it is a bit less precise.

PERFORATED FRENCH BREAD PAN: The secret to making good gluten-free baguettes is a perforated baguette pan that allows air to circulate around the entire baguette and allows moisture to escape. It will produce a loaf that is crusty on the outside and chewy on the inside. I'm not sure why perforated baguette pans for home bakers have such wide channels—typically they are 3 inches across and are not ideal for gluten-free baguettes. Gluten-free dough contains significantly more liquid, and because it spreads you end up with baguettes that look like an Italian loaf or, worse, a Yule log. I have had pretty good success by taking a 2-channel pan, pushing the sides together some to round the bottom, and bending the side walls toward the center, to create a channel more like 2½ inches wide. And since gluten-free dough is more hydrated, you must line the baguette pan with parchment paper to avoid dough

The natural sugars in sweet potatoes feed the yeast in this Sweet Potato Bread (page 64) and produce an exceptionally moist bread with a good rise. This is a recipe you'll want to scale up to a 10-inch or 12-inch loaf.

seepage into the perforations. But air still circulates and browns the baguette evenly.

other pans and tools

I'm not sure whether a *kitchen scale* qualifies as a small appliance or a tool, but along with parchment paper, it is probably the most important addition to my gluten-free kitchen. I tend to use teaspoons and tablespoons for volumetric measures and sometimes cup measures for liquids, but I weigh all the rest of my ingredients. I can't tell you the number of times that I've thrown out inconsistent, overly wet, or overly dry baked goods, all due to imprecisely measured ingredients. It wasn't until I started using a scale that I started getting predictable results from recipes. Given the high cost of most gluten-free flours and mixes, I honestly believe the payback in buying a scale is a no-brainer.

For muffins, cakes, bars, and other sweet and savory dishes, you can use just about any of the pans you may already own. You only have to grease and line the pans with parchment paper to ensure easy release. My very favorite pans include removable-bottom tart pans (both large and individual ones) and springform pans. Shallow tart pans allow you to arrange your fillings artfully and create a freestanding golden-brown shell. With a freestanding tart, the slices come out clean and stunning, which is significant for more fragile gluten-free pastries.

Other pans used in the following recipes include:

- Baking sheets (also known as cookie sheets)
- Bundt pan
- 9 × 13-inch glass baking dish
- 8 × 8-inch glass baking dish
- Deep-dish pie plate
- Individual brioche molds

There are a few kitchen tools that make mixing, spread, rolling, and transferring gluten-free dough easier. We joke at the factory that *butter knives* are our "all-purpose tools" for spreading, smoothing, and shaping breads. In my home kitchen, the "all-purpose tool" has to be a *dinner fork* (although I use butter knives a lot, too). I use forks all the time—for tasks like whisking hot and cold ingredients, beating eggs, hand-creaming butter and icings, dipping chocolate, and making docking holes in crackers. Of course, you can buy all sizes and shapes of whisks and pastry blenders, but a regular kitchen fork will do. Some other tools you may need or want include:

- Dough scraper (also known as a bench scraper or dough divider)
- Pastry brush
- Pastry or pizza cutter
- Rolling pin
- English muffin rings
- Cast-iron skillet
- Ingredient bins
- Biscuit and/or cookie cutters
- Flexible silicone or nylon spatula
- Flexible metal spatula
- Candy thermometer

part III: the naturally gluten-free pantry

EGGS: Eggs are the perfect ingredient for gluten-free baked goods, and have many properties that are essential to the baking process. They are important sources of protein for structure, steam for leavening, and moisturizers for starch-dense recipes. They are also thickeners and add fat for mouthfeel and elasticity, and they hold flours together and contribute to a smooth, creamy texture. Typically a large egg without the shell (what I use in this book) weighs between 48 and 50 grams.

Egg yolk is where the fat and lecithin (the emulsifier) as well as almost 50% of the protein are located. Yolks thicken, smooth, and moisturize baked goods; they also add a richness of color. Most important, they bind ingredients together, particularly the water and fats in any recipe. Egg whites are mostly water, contain no fat, and are about 12.5% protein, in the form of albumin and ovalbumin. When pure egg whites are beaten, the albumin protein forms a stable foam, which is essential to meringues. When egg whites are folded into a batter and heated, as in an angel food cake, the ovalbumin protein forms its own structure.

MILK: In gluten-free baked goods, milk protein acts much like the protein in flour: It adds flavor and texture, and contributes to structure.

Milk also adds fats and sugars, which carry the flavor. I use whole milk and 2% milk interchangeably in the recipes in the book. Whole milk and skim milk do not differ significantly in the amount of protein or sugar—only in the fat content. If you choose to use skim milk in these recipes, you may obtain different results because of the significant difference in fat content.

CHIA SEEDS: If you are vegan or can't eat eggs, the best substitute is a chia seed slurry, a combination of chia seeds and water whisked together. Chia is a culinary variety of *Salvia hispanica*, a member of the mint family, and is commonly referred to as a superfood for its high nutritional value. Chia is rich in omega-3 fatty acids, with almost three times the amount in flaxseeds. Chia also packs a ton of protein and fiber for such a small seed. It is sometimes confused with Salba; although they are similar, the culinary chia seed is black, and Salba, an heirloom form of chia, is white, but they are interchangeable in recipes.

Chia seeds swell and form a tasteless gel when they absorb moisture; they have many of the culinary properties of both eggs and xanthan gum. They absorb seven to nine times their weight in water, making them an effective binder, emulsifier, and thickener.

Chia does not contribute to leavening, however, so it must be used with chemical leavening agents like baking powder and baking soda. The typical formula for replacing one egg is 1 tablespoon of seeds to 3 tablespoons of water.

FLAXSEEDS: Flaxseeds are oily and distinctly flavored, with a seed coating that contains a gum. Like chia, when combined with water, flax forms a gel that can be used as a substitute for the emulsifying, binding, and thickening properties of eggs. (The typical formula for replacing one egg is 1 tablespoon of seeds to 3 tablespoons of water.) However, unlike chia, flax must be ground in order for its complete nutritional benefits to be released. And given its distinct taste, it is best used in doughs and batters with other prominent flavors. My favorite applications are whole seeds added to a bread dough or as the gelatinous basis for flourless crackers.

The flaxseed is 40 to 45% oil, so it can also be used as a healthy and fibrous substitution for other oils or shortening in a recipe. For gluten-free formulations, the gelatinous nature of flaxseeds contributes the benefit of adding to the overall structure of the baked good while providing a healthier form of fat. Typically, flax meal is substituted for oil in a 3:1 ratio (e.g., 1 cup flax meal to replace ⅓ cup oil). However, because flaxseeds can easily absorb up to 75% of their weight in water, flax drastically increases the water absorption properties of dough and significantly affects its handling characteristics.

SUNFLOWER SEEDS: To call them sunflower "seeds" is technically a misnomer, because they are the fruit of the sunflower and are properly referred to as "kernels." Sunflowers are grown for their kernels and their oil. I once biked past miles of sunflower fields in southern Ontario, and it was the closest I've come to seeing plants sing to the sun. It is not surprising how they got their name.

Most home bakers don't realize that sunflower seeds are an important source of lecithin and may be used much like eggs as emulsifiers, binders, and thickening agents. They impart a nutty taste while bringing together oil and water in doughs and sauces. In fact, we use sunflower seeds to make our Nut-Free Pesto Pizzas.

Sunflower seeds, because they are over 40% protein with high fiber content, also function splendidly as flour in many flourless recipes. Grinding sunflower seeds in a food processor to create sunflower meal is a quick process. You can also make your own sunflower seed butter in a food processor or take a shortcut and buy commercial sunbutter. Commercial sunbutter is very much like peanut butter in how it works in recipes. (If I do buy sunbutter, I tend to buy the organic version, since it does not include additional sugar, oils, salt, and preservatives.) It should be noted that one drawback to baking with sunflower seeds is that the chlorophyll in the seeds may react with baking soda and turn light-colored baked goods green. Adding a teaspoon of an acidic ingredient like lemon juice or white vinegar will reverse that effect.

PUMPKIN AND PUMPKIN SEEDS: What's really cool about pumpkins is that you can use both the pulp and the seeds to enhance your baked goods. I first started using pumpkin seeds as a walnut substitute—Against The Grain is a nut-free facility, and I wanted to share baked goods at work. But once I started using pumpkin seeds in my recipes, I learned that they work very much like sunflower seeds. They are ideal for making naturally gluten-free products, and they increase the nutritional profile of baked goods while acting like a binder and thickener.

Like purees made from sweet vegetables (e.g., sweet potato, carrot, and beets), pumpkin puree adds flavor and moistness to baked goods and often staves off potential dryness. Pumpkin puree also may be added in place of up to 50% of the fat in a recipe. As an egg replacer, ¼ cup of fruit or vegetable puree is the equivalent of one egg, and depending on the recipe, you may have to add ½ teaspoon of baking soda to compensate for the leavening effect of eggs.

SESAME SEEDS: Sesame is more than a garnish sprinkled on bagels and hamburger buns: It has one of the highest oil contents of any seed and is the basis for many plant-based oils. Ground up, it becomes sesame tahini, which performs much like a nut butter in baked goods. Sesame seeds by themselves function as flour in flourless recipes for crackers, cakes, and wafers. And as a flavoring, toasted sesame oil gives a richness and depth to savory breads and crackers. Sesame has the added advantage of being about 25% protein, so it adds protein to any gluten-free flour mixture. Like other seeds, sesame is a good source of dietary fiber.

NUTS AND NUT BUTTERS: Ground nuts and nut butters (which are essentially ground nuts processed until they release their oils and become creamy) are certainly not low-calorie ingredients, but they add a richness to baked goods along with structure. In short, they act like high-fat, but nevertheless nutritious, flour. Using them in cakes, cookies, bars, and even quick breads eliminates the need to use butter or other shortening. Typically, nut butters are sweetened with sugar or other sweeteners like honey or bananas and held together with either whole eggs or simply egg whites. Many flourless baked goods feature cashews, almonds, pecans, and walnuts, to name a few.

COCOA: Chocolate flavor makes everything taste better, and that is particularly the case with gluten-free baked goods made with less palatable flours. Cocoa powder, which typically is 10 to 20% fat, acts like flour in baked goods and can function as flour, flavor, and fat, all rolled into one ingredient.

In order to maintain an ideal dry to liquid ratio when baking with cocoa powder you have to include it in your dry weight or risk creating an overly dry baked good. Cocoa powder comes in two forms: natural and Dutch process. Natural cocoa powder, which is what I use for my recipes, is an acidic ingredient and requires neutralizing with baking soda.

The natural sweetness and binding properties of coconut have a magical effect on these moist and intensely chocolate Cocobean Cupcakes (page 268).

Dutch process cocoa is cocoa that has been chemically treated to reduce its acidity.

COCONUT: I really can't say enough about coconut, one of my go-to ingredients for making sweet gluten-free baked goods and creating healthier as well as dairy-free products. The first thing you should know about coconut is that it is not a nut. It is a fruit that comes in many forms: coconut flour (which is four times as absorptive as wheat flour), coconut milk, coconut water (the fluid inside a green coconut), dried coconut, coconut oil, coconut cream, and coconut butter (also sometimes sold as creamed coconut). With the exception of coconut water and coconut milk, all of these forms are solid at room temperature. At Against The Grain, we began using organic coconut milk commercially when we developed our dairy-free line of rolls and bagels. That was my first introduction to the remarkable properties of coconut.

- **Coconut milk (full-fat)** can be substituted for dairy milk in just about any sweet recipe, and is the basis of rich, dairy-free custards, ganaches, and pastry creams. If used in savory recipes, you can lessen the coconut taste by neutralizing the coconut milk with ⅛ teaspoon of baking soda per 13.5-ounce can.

- **Coconut oil** is an excellent substitute for butter, although one should use 20% less coconut oil than butter because butter is 80% fat and 20% water. Coconut oil is primarily saturated fat that is very heat stable. Unlike coconut butter and coconut milk, the oil does not impart a discernible taste.

- **Dried, flaked coconut** is an excellent addition to baked goods, giving them texture and binding together gluten-free flours and sweeteners. Dried coconut is also the base of simple, flourless macaroon-type cookies that are held together and leavened with only egg whites.

- **Coconut butter** can easily be made by grinding dried coconut in a food processor (see recipe, page 143), much as peanuts are ground into peanut butter. Unlike coconut oil, coconut butter also includes the coconut solids. It is solid at room temperature but softens as it is warmed (it melts above 76°F). It is used as the basis for sweet or savory spreads, for smoothies and sauces; hardened, it is an excellent foundation for bars, fudges, and fillings.

- **Coconut cream** is the solid cream that rises to the top of canned full-fat coconut milk. The fastest way to collect coconut cream is to chill a can of coconut milk for several hours. The cream solidifies and can then be skimmed off. Simply beat the cream on high, add a little sweetener and vanilla, if desired, and you have a superb dairy-free whipped topping. Cocoa powder can easily be added to the cream to create a chocolate cream or ganache. Whipped coconut cream freezes well.

MOLASSES AND HONEY: Molasses and honey are both liquid sugars, but they are also the key to tenderizing gluten-free baked goods. Both are hygroscopic, which means they absorb water from the environment, a huge benefit for avoiding dry gluten-free baked goods. During the baking process, honey and molasses tenderize by delaying structure formation and robbing the protein and starch of water. This has the effect of both slowing down the speed at which the protein sets and delaying the gelling of the starches in the flours. So, instead of rubbery, gummy baked goods, you get tender ones. On the other hand, if you add too much liquid sweetener, you get the opposite effect: No structure ever forms, so breads are either flat or rise and collapse. Baked goods like cookies that are too sweet will spread and fall flat.

Like other sweeteners, molasses and honey contribute to browning through the caramelization of the sugars at high temperatures. And, if enough honey or molasses is used, the sugars act as a preservative and increase a baked good's shelf life by retaining water, thereby slowing down the staling process. They also have the effect of reducing the water activity that promotes microbial growth. It should be noted that both honey and molasses are highly acidic, so they need to be neutralized or offset by an alkaline ingredient like baking soda. Too much acidity will coagulate or set the protein way too early in the

baking process and prevent the product from rising.

Whereas dry sugars are typically added early in the mixing process to promote leavening (e.g., creaming sugar and butter to facilitate air pockets), liquid sugars should be added as close to the end of the mixing process as possible, so as not to overtenderize the dough.

RAISINS: Raisins can improve the flavor, texture, volume, color, and shelf life of breads, cookies, and bars. Like molasses and honey, raisins are hygroscopic and absorb water from the environment. But they also contain a compound that is a natural inhibitor of microbial growth. Indeed, the raisin's inhibitor is so effective that it has been used in beef jerky formulations as a preservative. Raisins may be added whole, chopped, or in the form of raisin juice.

One of the most interesting forms of raisins is raisin juice, which you can prepare in your own kitchen (see page 69). It is produced by boiling raisins in water without sugar or any other additives. The result, when boiled down sufficiently, is a brown liquid much like molasses. I have added raisin juice to yeast-leavened bread dough and found it produces one of the tastiest, moistest loaves I have developed. It should also be noted that raisins, pureed in a food processor, are an excellent sweetener with superb binding capabilities.

DATES: Like raisins, dates are a naturally sweet, whole fruit that can be chopped or pureed and added to bind flours and starches, to increase the moisture content, and to add dietary fiber. (Dates contain approximately 80% sugar, 2 to 5% protein, 6 to 10% fiber, and 5% water, if fresh rather than dried.) They are also the basis for many sweetened raw foods and pair particularly well with cranberries and coconut.

CINNAMON: Cinnamon is as much about smell as it is about taste. Like cocoa, it is an excellent mask for strong-tasting gluten-free flours like quinoa and garbanzo bean. It also can be used effectively paired with chocolate to enhance flavor. Cinnamon is a natural preservative that inhibits mold growth, and for that reason it can slow yeast growth. Thus, it is best to leave it out of fermenting dough and only add it during the final kneading and dough formation process. Cinnamon is a great flavor, but a little cinnamon goes a long way; too much leaves the baked good tasting kind of dusty.

APPLE BUTTER AND PECTIN: Apple butter, an excellent source of pectin, thickens and gels gluten-free bread doughs, moisturizes them, increases loaf volume, and softens the texture. It also may be used as a fat substitute in baked goods, and is a source of dietary fiber.

Pectin is found both in the cell walls of fruit and between the cells. It is the substance, for example, that makes apples hard and crisp. As an apple ripens, enzymes naturally present in fruit break down the pectin, and the apple softens and becomes mushy. Commercially, the most common sources of pectin are apples and citrus fruits. You can buy one of several brands, but they contain other ingredients like dextrose. Or, you can make your own pectin by boiling 2 cups of water for every pound of unpeeled apple slices, straining the mixture, and then further reducing the liquid.

BEANS AND BEAN FLOURS: Beans are one of those vegetables that can be added to gluten-free baked goods either as a flour or as whole beans that have been pureed. Commercially available bean flours include soy, garbanzo (chickpea), fava, garfava (a mixture of the previous two), black bean, and navy bean. Typically, bean flours are added to gluten-free flour blends as 20 to 25% of the mixture. Since many gluten-free flour mixtures are light on protein, bean flours increase the protein content to more closely match that of wheat flour. Beans also contain a good amount of pectin. Many bakers find that the combination of increased protein content and the binding, moisturizing properties of pectin provide more wheat-like texture to gluten-free breads. But not everyone likes the taste of bean flour in breads, and I am one of them. What I have found, however, is that I really like the effect of whole, pureed beans in brownies and bars. Not only do they function as a fat substitute, but they improve the glycemic index and dietary fiber profile for those avoiding more highly refined starches. You can puree either canned beans or dried ones that have been soaked. Soaking beans allows them to slowly absorb moisture, soften, and break down some of the complex sugars that cause gas.

POTATOES: Like beans, potatoes—both regular and sweet potatoes—can be added to gluten-free breads and baked goods either as a component of the flour mixture or as mashed whole potatoes. Also like beans, potatoes contain a significant amount of pectin, which contributes to their gelling and moisturizing properties. Potato flour (made from both the peel and the flesh) tends to result in dense, moist baked goods, whereas potato starch has properties akin to the light, binding effect of tapioca starch and arrowroot. Compared to beans, potatoes have a very neutral, almost sweet flavor that can be made into traditional white bread. I first learned about adding potatoes to bread from Peter Reinhart's *Whole Grain Breads*. I had to do a lot of ingredient and procedural adaptations, and there were a lot of failures along the way. But from the outset, I was convinced that potato water and potatoes are some of the best additions to yeast-based gluten-free loaf breads.

BANANAS AND AVOCADOS: Bananas and avocados are unique fruits for their rich, creamy texture that thickens and moisturizes baked goods. Bananas and avocados are good replacements for fats, particularly in gluten-free baked goods, because there is no gluten to become tough and chewy. They are a highly effective substitute for eggs because their texture captures air bubbles and acts as a leavening agent. Bananas are also an excellent substitute for refined sugar.

VINEGAR: In gluten-free breads, vinegar is used in two ways. First, it is added along with baking soda in quick breads to create lots of bubbles to expand during the baking process and increase volume. Second, it is used as a dough conditioner to create a higher, fluffier loaf. Dough conditioners are commonly used in the commercial production of gluten-free sandwich breads, but they are typically derived from some industrial concoction. You can simply add vinegar to your recipe in a volume equal to the yeast (e.g., 1 tablespoon vinegar to 1 tablespoon yeast) to strengthen the dough so that it can expand without collapsing.

Commercial dough enhancers or conditioners are typically used with lower-gluten flours like whole wheat, and they are more than just vinegar or acetic acid. They often contain additional starch, along with vital wheat gluten (which boosts the protein content of the flour). In gluten-free breads, we always seem to have ample starch, but our flours are gluten-challenged. If you are attempting a basic gluten-free yeast bread with or without eggs, you might try one or more of the following additions to "condition" the dough:

- Potato flakes: 1/8 cup per loaf
- Distilled white vinegar: equal to the amount of the yeast
- Unflavored, pure whey protein (such as The Organic Whey): 1 tablespoon per cup of flour
- Pure, soy-free whey powder is expensive, so you can always try substituting powdered instant milk as your conditioner

SOUR CREAM: Sour cream is an acid, a protein, and a fat, all rolled into a single ingredient. It is cream that is "cultured" by adding bacteria, which causes the protein to thicken into a gel. (Some commercial manufacturers add gums and starches to thicken it and to keep the liquid whey from separating, but it is possible to buy pure sour cream.) The culture acts as an emulsifier, pulling together starches, oil, and liquids in gluten-free batters and doughs. And the milk sugars and fat in sour cream tenderize, moisturize, flavor, and add richness to gluten-free baked goods. As an acidic ingredient, sour cream also combines with baking soda in a recipe to increase the production of carbon dioxide. One added benefit is that sour cream tends to trap air bubbles more effectively than acidic ingredients such as vinegar and lemon juice.

If you are on a dairy-restricted diet, you can replace sour cream with full-fat, whipped coconut milk that has vinegar added to it (1 teaspoon per cup). Also, reduce the other liquids in the recipe accordingly to retain the proper ratio of dry to liquid ingredients.

BAKING SODA AND BAKING POWDER: These chemical leavening agents produce gas when added to recipes in the presence of moisture and/or heat. Generally speaking, 1 teaspoon of baking powder or ¼ teaspoon of baking soda is adequate for leavening 1 cup of flour. I have noticed that many gluten-free recipes increase the amount of chemical leavening agents, probably to compensate for lack of gluten. But when gluten-free baking recipes are hydrated adequately, the baked goods will not have a problem rising.

Baking soda, or sodium bicarbonate, is always paired with one or more naturally acidic ingredients like vinegar, citrus juice, sour cream, molasses, honey, chocolate, brown sugar, or buttermilk. Baking soda is four times as powerful as baking powder. When combined with acid and moisture, baking soda immediately begins releasing most of its gas,

These healthy Sunrise Warming Muffins (page 159), which contain baking soda, baking powder, and sour cream, are tender and moist.

although a little more is released when it is heated. When working with the compromised structure of gluten-free baked goods, you want to add baking soda as one of your final ingredients, and you want to get your creation in the oven as soon as possible to retain as many of the bubbles as you can. Too much baking soda will make baked goods taste soapy, with a kind of chemical taste. If there aren't enough acidic ingredients in a batter or dough to neutralize the baking soda, it also can interact with the chlorophyll in sunflower seeds, berries, and some types of buckwheat, turning golden baked goods greenish. That is normal, but you may want to use spices and/or cocoa to disguise the color in those recipes.

Baking powder contains baking soda, one or more dry acid salts, and starch or filler to separate the soda from the acid. The acid salts release acid when they come in contact with liquids, and when the acid combines with the baking soda in the powder, it produces carbon dioxide.

ORANGE PULP: After buying a home juicer and seeing the mountain of pulp pile up, I went to the Internet to search for a use besides our composter. Among juicer fanatics, I found recipes using fruit and vegetable pulp in quick breads—dried orange pulp is often used to retain moisture and serve as a fat substitute (up to 5%) in shelf-stable and frozen baked goods. Those properties sounded like they were designed for gluten-free baked goods. Orange pulp definitely adds moisture as well as structure, and I have added it to my arsenal of natural ingredients. I haven't yet tried drying the pulp in my dehydrator, but you can probably guess that's in my future.

part IV: the varieties of gluten-free flours

Unlike wheat flours, gluten-free flours include many whole grains, nuts, seeds, and pseudocereals (nongrains that function like grain flours). Everyone's taste is different, but it is generally agreed that many gluten-free flours have nutty, earthy overtones. Sampling many different flours and brands is the best way to find your favorite flour combinations. I had been baking gluten-free for more than five years before I discovered *light buckwheat*—I discovered it by chance, nestled in among wheat flours at my local supermarket. For years, I had dismissed buckwheat as a heavy, earth-flavored flour, suitable for pancakes but not much else. Now it is my favorite all-purpose flour, essential to these recipes and suitable for all types of baked goods. I purchase my light buckwheat flour directly from Bouchard Family Farms, which grows and mills it in Maine (www.ployes.com), but it is also available online and in the bulk bins of most co-ops and natural foods stores.

flavor

The bran coats of whole grains and some seeds often have a bitter taste. This is nature's adaptation to prevent birds and other animals from eating all the seeds or grains that would otherwise be germinated. The challenge in gluten-free baking is to take advantage of the high protein, high fiber, and nutritional benefits of whole grains while minimizing the bitterness. A number of techniques, including toasting, boiling, and fermentation, reduce the bitterness, and the addition of acidic sweeteners like molasses, brown sugar, and maple syrup works to mask the bitter effect.

Most neutral-tasting gluten-free flours are predominantly starches, since protein and fat both give flour a more distinctive taste. However, starches used alone are not sufficient substitutes for wheat, and they need to be combined with higher-protein flours and other sources of protein. The most neutral-tasting flour is rice flour, and it is not surprising that it is the predominant starch in most commercial gluten-free baked goods and pastas. Though taste is important, gluten-free flour can't be chosen by flavor alone. It is also important to consider the binding properties of the flours, their ability to absorb and hold water, and the texture they impart to baked goods.

some commonly available gluten-free grains

Grains are members of the grass family. They are classified as monocots because they have a single seed leaf inside the seed coat.

CORNSTARCH is produced by soaking and fermenting corn in water. The process washes the starch out, which is then dried. Cornstarch is used as a thickener in both sauces and baked goods, and it is the most common anticaking additive in products like shredded cheeses and powdered sugar.

MILLET is a small-seeded grain, once mostly thought of as birdseed in the United States. However, in the rest of the world, it has long been an important food crop. Millet flour has a neutral to slightly bitter taste and a protein content similar to that of wheat flour. Among gluten-free flours, it is considered to be one of the easiest to digest.

OATS are high in protein and have the most soluble fiber of any grain. The outer hull of the oat grain is removed to expose the groat (the outer hull is an excellent source of insoluble fiber known as oat fiber). Steel-cut oats are whole oat groats cut into smaller sizes. The groats can also be flaked and steamed into rolled oats and instant oats.

BROWN RICE is the rice grain with just the outer husk removed. It can be ground to varying degrees of coarseness, and the texture varies considerably among brands. Although it is a relatively low-protein flour, it is an effective substitute for sorghum, buckwheat, and millet in small amounts.

WHITE RICE has the outer husk layer as well as the bran and germ layers stripped away.

It is a very neutral-tasting flour good for light cakes.

SORGHUM is a high-protein grain grown in tropical and subtropical climates. Sorghum is the third leading cereal crop in the United States and is grown for both human and animal consumption. It is also used in the production of sorghum molasses and some beers. Many people believe the taste of sorghum flour is closest to wheat flour. Sorghum flour is perhaps the best substitution for light buckwheat flour in recipes, since it has a very similar protein and fiber profile.

TEFF is a tiny, high-protein, high-calcium grain. It may be dark, red, or ivory. It is considered to be a lower-carb grain because up to 40% of teff grains can be fiber. Teff is often used as a solo flour in flatbreads, and it can be substituted for buckwheat.

some commonly available gluten-free nongrains

Nongrains include nuts, seeds, legumes, roots, tubers, and pseudocereals. They are classified as dicots because they have two seed leaves inside the seed coat.

ALMOND FLOUR is the blanched nuts ground into high-protein, high-fat flour or meal. Almond flour (also known as almond meal) is available commercially, but it is easy to grind the almonds yourself. It is a very popular flour with those following a low-carbohydrate diet.

AMARANTH FLOUR comes from amaranth seeds, which are from a plant in the beet and spinach family. The seeds are considered a pseudograin because they have properties of grains. Amaranth flour has a distinctive, earthy taste and is high in protein and fiber. Amaranth seeds also can be popped and have a gelatinous consistency much like quinoa when cooked.

ARROWROOT STARCH is made from the arrowroot plant tuber. It is mostly carbohydrates and has a gel-like consistency and thickening properties when heated. It is related to the ornamental prayer plant as well as ginger and banana plants.

BUCKWHEAT FLOUR is milled from a fruit seed closely related to wild rhubarb and sorrel. There are many types of buckwheat, from dark to light. It can be used as a substitute for teff, millet, quinoa, sorghum, and brown rice flours. I use a light, silver-hulled Acadian buckwheat grown exclusively in northern New England and Canada. It has a fine texture, and it may be the most neutral-tasting gluten-free flour with a decent protein content.

CHICKPEA FLOUR, also known as garbanzo bean flour, is milled from a light-flavored, rounded member of the bean family. It is commonly used in Indian food and is also called gram flour and besan. It is an excellent choice for batters to be fried.

COCONUT FLOUR is produced from the fruit of the coconut palm tree and is made by drying out and grinding the leftover pulp from coconut milk production. It has a high-fiber content and is the most highly absorptive of all gluten-free flours, absorbing four times more fluid than other gluten-free flours. Added to a batter with adequate hydration, it produces a very moist baked good. Coconut flour has a distinctive and slightly sweet coconut taste.

FAVA FLOUR is milled from fava beans, which are also called broad beans and are in the legume family. Fava beans are related to lima beans, but they are not true beans; they are really a large-seeded vetch, a ground cover crop that is grown as forage in pastures and for soil improvement. Fava beans are high in protein, soluble fiber, and carbohydrates. The high protein content of fava flour produces baked goods with a very wheat-like texture, but the distinct bean flavor is not for everyone.

FLAX MEAL comes from the seeds of the flax plant, which is both a food and fiber crop (the foliage is made into linen). Flaxseeds may be dark or golden, and are chewy, due to their high oil content. Flax meal is high in fat and protein with a good omega-3 profile. It is also very high in dietary fiber. Flaxseeds also have a coating that attracts and absorbs water, creating a gel that is commonly used as an egg replacer; thus, flax meal works well as a thickener and binder.

POTATO FLOUR is ground from cooked, dehydrated whole potatoes. It is a heavy flour, as opposed to the lightness of potato starch. Potato flour absorbs lots of moisture in baked goods. A small amount in bread adds moisture and makes very tender loaves. It is also excellent for fried batters since it crisps up rapidly in hot oil.

POTATO STARCH is a very light starch produced from the root tubers of the potato plant. To make the starch, potatoes are pulverized until the starch leaches out. Then the starch is washed out with water and dried into a white, tasteless powder. Low in both protein and fat, potato starch is a good thickener and gelling agent. Substitutes for potato starch are tapioca starch and arrowroot starch.

QUINOA FLOUR comes from a seed that acts like a cereal. Like amaranth, it is related to beets and spinach. It is a good source of fiber and protein. Because the bitter seed coating produces a taste that some people find off-putting they prebake the flour to reduce its bitterness. Quinoa can also be dehydrated into flakes (the flakes come from seeds that are prewashed to remove bitterness and then steam rolled).

SOY FLOUR is milled from soybeans, which are not considered true beans. Soybeans can be ground into a high-protein fine flour or made into oil. Like bean flours, soy flour creates a moist wheat-like crumb in breads and baked goods, but leaves a distinctive beany taste.

Soy flour is also favored for low-glycemic diets because only about 35% of soybeans are carbohydrates, with the rest being protein, oil, and water.

TAPIOCA FLOUR, which is also called cassava flour, is basically tapioca starch but with the fiber included. The flour is produced by cooking, drying, grinding, and milling the cassava root into a fine powder. Like tapioca starch, it is a neutral flour that improves the texture of baked goods, but it has a far greater fiber content (7 to 12%). Unfortunately, tapioca flour is still not as accessible as other gluten-free flours to the home baker.

TAPIOCA STARCH comes from the root of the cassava, or manioc, plant. The fibrous root is ground to a pulp to release the starch. The starch is then separated from the pulp and dried. It is a low-protein, low-fat, and high-carbohydrate starch, but it redeems itself as an ideal thickener that forms a gel when heated. As a gluten-free flour, it is flavorless and adds a chewiness to baked goods. Tapioca starch is great for freezing and thawing because unlike other gluten-free flours it doesn't leach out water. Like other starches, it is insoluble in cold water unless physically or chemically modified.

how to adjust for weight differences in flours

The only way to really control for differences between brands of gluten-free flours is to

Tapioca starch doesn't just provide structure for open-crumb breads. When combined with light buckwheat and molasses in these Yankee Ginger Snaps (page 211), it produces big, chewy cookies like those you find in a bakery.

weigh your ingredients. If you do not have a scale, you need to become a critical nutrition label reader. For the particular flour you are using, look on the top of the nutrition label for the serving size and the weight in grams. For example, the label may read:

Nutrition Facts

Serving size ¼ cup (30g)	Servings Per Container 20.00

Then you know that a full cup of your flour weighs 4 × 30 grams, or 120 grams. If the recipe you are using calls for 1 cup (140g) and you are using a cup measure, then you have to adjust the amount (volume) of flour you add to make it equivalent in weight, as shown below.

1. Determine the weight of 1 cup of your flour using the Nutrition Facts on the label.
   e.g., 1 cup weighs 120g
2. Check the weight of 1 cup indicated in the recipe.
   e.g., the recipe calls for 140g
3. Subtract the weight of your flour from the recipe weight.
   e.g., 140 − 120 = 20g
4. Divide the difference by the weight of 1 cup of your flour.
   e.g., 20/120 = ⅙ cup

This means that the recipe weight is one sixth more of a cup than the weight of your flour. Thus, you will have to add ⅙ cup (or 8 teaspoons) of your flour to make it an equivalent amount. Without this adjustment, you are most definitely going to end up with a thinner dough or batter.

If you are measuring out ingredients by volume, you will get the most accurate volume measurements if you use a set of cup measures and level off the top rather than measuring with a single graduated cup. Even if kitchen math is your strong suit, you can see why a scale would save you a lot of work.

variability in the protein content, fiber, and absorption rates of gluten-free flours

One of the beauties of gluten-free flours is that there are so many different sources with different flavors, textures, and nutrition profiles. This does, however, make it a little tricky to substitute one kind of flour for another in a recipe. For example, protein content varies considerably between flours, as shown in the table that follows. Protein content is one of the major determinants of how much water the flour will absorb during the mixing process. It takes more of a low-protein flour to produce dough of the same consistency as high-protein flours. If you try to substitute a low-protein flour for a higher-protein flour, you will end up with a slack dough. Fiber also significantly affects how much water flour will absorb. All-purpose wheat flour has a consistent 2.5% fiber, whereas gluten-free flours have wildly different amounts of fiber. For example, a high-fiber flour like coconut will absorb nearly four times more liquid than regular flours.

percent of protein and fiber for gluten-free flours

FLOUR	PROTEIN (%)	FIBER (%)
Almond	21.4	10.7
Amaranth	13.0	10.0
Arrowroot	0.0	3.1
Brown Rice	7.5	5.0
Buckwheat	13.3	13.3
Coconut	14.3	35.7
Fava	27.0	24.2
Garbanzo	20.0	16.7
Millet	10.0	13.3
Oat	17.5	10.0
Potato Flour	0.1	5.9
Potato Starch	0.0	0.0
Quinoa	13.0	5.9
Sorghum	11.8	8.8
Soy	35.7	10.7
Tapioca Starch	0.0	0.0
Teff	13.0	13.3
White Rice	5.0	2.5

Source of Nutritional Data: Bob's Red Mill

In practical terms, the variability in protein and fiber between different gluten-free flours means that: (1) you should substitute flours by weight and (2) you should choose to substitute flours with similar nutritional profiles. For example, the protein content of Bob's Red Mill Buckwheat and Bob's Red Mill Teff are nearly identical.

As you work with different flours, you will get a feel for the ideal dough or batter consistency. Compensating for differences by adding in a tad more flour or liquid in the final stages of mixing should not have a huge effect on the outcome of your baked goods.

some flour suggestions for light-textured baked goods

Similar to wheat flours, for which there is an ideal bread flour and an ideal cake flour, different gluten-free flour combinations work better in some baked goods than in others. Use the lists below as a basis for fairly neutral-tasting baked goods. In general, you will get the best results with a ratio of 50% flour to 50% pure starch (e.g., potato, tapioca, arrowroot, or cornstarch). My two favorite basic "all-purpose" combinations are 50% light buckwheat flour + 50% tapioca starch and 50% oat flour + 50% tapioca starch. I find these two combinations to have the properties most similar to wheat.

YEASTED BREADS
- Brown rice
- Light buckwheat
- Oat
- Sorghum
- Potato flour (use sparingly)
- Starch: Potato starch, tapioca starch

BISCUITS, WRAPS, PASTRIES

- Light buckwheat
- Oat
- Starch: Potato starch, tapioca starch

CAKES

- Coconut (use sparingly unless compensating with significant increase in liquids)
- Brown rice
- Light buckwheat
- Starch: Tapioca starch, potato starch

QUICK BREADS, MUFFINS, COOKIES, AND BARS (WITH ANY STRONG SPICES OR FLAVORS): For these recipes, you can use a 50/50 flour-to-starch combination using light buckwheat, oat, and brown rice flours. Note when using highly absorptive flours like coconut and almond, you will most likely have to increase the amount of liquid, including eggs.

ACCENT FLOURS FOR INTERESTING FLAVORS AND BOOSTING NUTRITION PROFILES: Most gluten-free flours that contain a significant amount of protein have a very distinctive taste. Although some people like the earthy, almost bitter taste of these cereal and grain flours, most will want to add them into a mix of more neutral-tasting flours and starches. In general, you can substitute any of these flours by weight for about 20% of the flour (as opposed to starch) in these recipes. For example, if a recipe calls for 100g of light buckwheat flour and 200g of tapioca starch, you can substitute 20g of millet flour for some of the buckwheat. The flour/starch mix would then be 20g millet, 80g light buckwheat flour, and 200g tapioca starch. The following flours all have a similar protein and fiber profile to buckwheat flour.

- Amaranth
- Millet
- Teff

part V: gluten-free techniques

Whether you are baking with or without gluten, bread baking is all about technique. The fundamental ingredients can be pretty simple: flour, water, yeast, sugar, salt, and in the case of gluten-free breads, adequate protein. But it is how you combine the ingredients, the sequence in which you perform certain steps, the timing, the proofing environment, and how you use your oven that determine a successful outcome.

Understanding how I approach bread baking will help you understand why the recipes contain certain steps and will increase the likelihood that your results will delight you.

choosing a flour palette

If I've learned one thing in running a commercial bakery, it is that there is no accounting for people's tastes. Years ago, when my mother retired, she started a gift shop called The Cinnamon Tree. It was a highly successful business, and I once asked her how she figured out which merchandise to carry. "Simple," she told me. "I buy 50 percent of the stuff I like and 50 percent I hate." I laughed at the time, but it was a very successful strategy. I feel sort of the same way about gluten-free flours. I dislike anything with bean flour in it, yet so many people rave about it. Quinoa

is one of my favorites, but many people think it tastes like potting soil. Clearly some gluten-free flours are an acquired taste, and everyone seems to be passionate about their preferences.

All of our commercial bread products use a single flour—tapioca starch. We have taken an entirely different approach from other gluten-free bread manufacturers by using the tapioca to bind fresh, whole ingredients in a yeast-free bread.

For yeasted breads and baked goods, tapioca is not sufficient on its own. Much of the baking I do uses some combination of light buckwheat flour and tapioca starch, or a combination of tapioca starch and gluten-free oat flour. What you won't find in any of these recipes is corn or soy flours. In our family, we have intolerance issues with both of them, so it was best to just leave them out. If you choose to use a bread mix, I suggest a xanthan gum–free, all-purpose mix like King Arthur Multi-Purpose Flour.

measuring

All of my recipes include volume measures as well as metric weights for flours, but I can't underscore enough that you will get your best results if you weigh ingredients. It doesn't take many failures with expensive gluten-free flours to justify an inexpensive kitchen scale.

Because I weigh flours and starches to determine their volume equivalent, my technique for volume measures is to spoon the flour into a measuring cup and tap it lightly to even the surface. If you dip your measuring cups in the flour, and then level the tops off, you may be getting several tablespoons more than I do.

pregelatinizing starches

You must be wondering how to create tall loaves of yeasted bread with an open crumb without using xanthan gum or some other binder. The answer lies in understanding the gelling properties of starch. Starch is insoluble in cold water. How, then, do you create a gluten-free bread dough with elasticity that will expand as it proofs, trapping in the carbon dioxide as the yeast ferments?

The first step is to make the starch soluble in water. This is done by adding heat, and its effect on the starch is called "pregelatinization." (This, by the way, is how manufacturers make starch soluble in cold water for instant pudding mixes.) In almost all the yeast-leavened recipes in this book, one of my first steps is to bring the liquid (whether it be milk, water, potato water, or something else) and shortening or fat to a boil, stirring vigorously to emulsify (or blend into one) the two ingredients. I then pour this mixture over the flour and mix it until the flour is just uniformly moistened. Depending on the recipe, the

result may look like moist sand or a kind of rubbery gel.

The heat produced by the boiled mixture causes the starch granules to swell as they absorb the oil and water. It is important not to mix the dough too much at this stage because

Starch gels, produced by blending flour with hot liquid and fat, simulate the effect of gluten, binding the dough and giving bread its characteristic chewiness.

overmixing causes the starch granules to totally fall apart and leach out some of the fluid they absorbed. (If you see the oil start to separate out, you've gone way too far.) As the dough cools, the starch becomes gelatinous. This is not unlike thickening a sauce with a starch—as the sauce heats up, it thickens, and as it cools off, it gets *really* thick. You will always see a cooling period of 15 to 20 minutes in the recipes since it is important not to add yeast or eggs to a hot mixture.

proofing the yeast

While I am waiting for the pregelatinized starch to cool, I proof the yeast. Typically, this involves a small amount of warm water, the yeast, and a small amount of sugar to feed the yeast. I use active dry yeast, and I do not use chlorinated water. I warm the proofing water so that it is just a little warmer than lukewarm, typically in a small ceramic bowl, and place the yeast in a warm place. For the sake of standardization, I allow the yeast to proof for 15 minutes.

mixing

None of these recipes requires a big stand mixer. In fact, I have a little three-speed hand mixer, given to me by a friend over twenty years ago. Of course, if you want to buy a stand mixer, gluten-free baking is as good an excuse as any. But you'll find when you stop using xanthan gum, mixing will become a whole lot easier. For some of the recipes, I use my trusty little hand mixer (and sometimes my hands as a mixer).

My favorite mixer, if you want to call it that, is a food processor. I often use my food processor to incorporate boiled liquids into raw flour and to mix in yeast, eggs, and other ingredients. It is also indispensable to me when making pastry doughs and cookies. Many bakers complain about the time it takes to clean a food processor, but the time it saves on the mixing side way more than offsets the cleanup time. When working with a food processor, it is important to always undermix rather than overmix. I use my "pulse" feature often and watch carefully as I blend ingredients. Too much mixing with a sharp food processor blade can actually shear starch granules and weaken structure, and you certainly don't want to do that.

resting

After scooping the dough into a glass or ceramic bowl, I always give the dough 20 to 30 minutes to rest, covered with plastic wrap, on the counter. A significant amount of fluid absorption and thickening goes on during this stage. Sometimes it is quite dramatic: A dough may be transformed from a pancake batter consistency to a shaggy dough with an obvious web-like structure, just during this rest period. In each recipe I try to give you an idea of the dough consistency to expect at each stage, because it is really easy to think that something may have gone wrong. At the end of this rest period, I use a rubber or silicone spatula to punch down the dough and smooth it into a ball because it is usually pretty sticky. Depending on what I am making, I either divide the dough at that stage into balls for rolls, bagels, and so on; turn it into a prepared loaf pan; or simply keep it in the bowl to proof. If the dough is sticky, I keep a small bowl of water handy and dip my fingers (or the spatula) in the water as needed. Rather than load the dough up with additional flour, I end up adding a little moisture, which can't hurt. If the recipe calls for delayed fermentation (see below), I put the dough directly in the refrigerator.

proofing the dough

Living in a cold climate has made me very creative when it comes to finding a warm environment in which to let the dough rise. If it is pretty cold in the house, I cover the bowl and use the microwave oven as a proofing box. I first microwave a 2-cup glass measuring cup full of water until it boils and then slide it to the back corner of the microwave. Then I place the bowl of dough in the microwave and leave the door shut for the prescribed amount of time. I have also had excellent results putting the bowl of dough uncovered under a plastic cake cover/dome and leaving it in a sunny location and/or humid location. I don't give you rising times here, as the duration of the proofing time varies with the ingredients in the recipe, and it may vary slightly with your home baking environment. You should keep a close eye on your dough to ensure that

it does not over-rise, but if your dough has not risen after an hour, it can't hurt to let it rise a little longer.

kneading

It is a common misconception that kneading is only for gluten-based bread baking because the purpose of kneading is to increase the formation of gluten. But kneading after a period of rest also helps disperse the yeast, which contributes to a better rise, and it seems to improve the texture and reduce the crumble factor in finished breads. And it depends on the type of gluten-free bread you are making. If you are making Bagels (page 82) or Sourdough Soft Pretzels (page 91), for example, the recipes call for kneading the dough. If I am dealing with pretty wet dough, I tend to knead my dough right in the bowl, often using a rubber spatula. Some of the recipes call for kneading in a small amount of flour, and typically I have noted this as a range (for example, up to ¼ cup) to account for any variability in your baking conditions.

delayed fermentation

With a typical yeast bread, most of the flavor comes from the yeast. But if you delay the fermentation process, more complex flavors emerge. Delayed fermentation refers to the process of refrigerating yeast dough overnight—when the dough is refrigerated, the yeast and the bacteria are effectively inactivated, allowing enzymes (proteins that

Kneading gluten-free dough requires a light touch. Just enough flour is kneaded into the Sourdough Soft Pretzel (page 91) dough to let you form the pretzels. Adding too much flour and working the dough too hard will prevent an optimal rise.

facilitate chemical changes) in the flour and yeast to break down complex starches into sugars.

I have found that the long, slow fermentation process does two things that are particularly useful for gluten-free doughs: It gives strength and firmness to otherwise wet doughs, which can be hard to handle; and the delayed fermentation can be used to create a more open and irregular crumb, characteristic of breads like ciabatta. Using conventional rising methods, such crumbs are hard to produce in the absence of gluten. Although flavor is certainly a benefit of delayed fermentation, I use the technique for recipes in which I need a dough that I can manipulate, mold, and shape without sacrificing its moistness.

Baking the Potato Rosemary Bread (page 61) in a heavy gauge pan creates a robust, crusty loaf with a tender, fragrant crumb.

baking

Both the composition and the size of the pan you use for loaves of bread are of critical importance. The rate at which heat is transferred from the oven to the bread is through the walls of the pan. Glass (and stoneware) will result in a softer and lighter crust than a metal pan. It is assumed in these recipes that you are using a metal pan. All of the bread loaf recipes are written for a 4½ × 8-inch loaf pan that is 3 inches deep, which is a standard size for a 1½-pound loaf. Just a slight increase in length and width (5 × 9 × 3-inch) is a standard 2-*pound* loaf, and if you use that, you will end up with a wide, flat loaf. I mention this because 5 × 9-inch pans are what most people have; 4½ × 8-inch loaf pans are harder to come by. In a pinch, you can use disposable aluminum 4½ × 8-inch pans, but they are even less effective in conducting heat than glass loaf pans. If you can find a pan with 4-inch-deep sides, you will produce a taller loaf since a high wall gives the loaf greater structure as it rises and bakes.

Once you get the feel for a recipe, you may

want to experiment with baking on a pizza stone. When I use a pizza stone, I place it on a rack in the lower third of my oven and make sure the oven has been at temperature for at least 30 minutes. You also can experiment with adding steam during the initial 5 to 10 minutes of baking. Using steam during this time period will help keep the crust soft and give the loaf more time to expand before the crust sets. I have not found that steam has a significant effect, but others have reported slightly higher volumes with the technique. A simple way to inject steam into the oven is to place an empty metal baking pan in the bottom of the oven as it preheats and then pour water (or ice cubes) into the pan when you put the loaf in the oven.

Since all ovens vary, you should view the times in these recipes as a guide. It should be noted that bread with a higher sugar content will brown faster. In some recipes, I have suggested that you tent your loaf with foil if you find that it is browning too fast. This simply means to crease a piece of foil and rest it on the top of the loaf. The idea is to permit heat circulation but shield the loaf from the direct conduction of heat. If you consistently find your bread is browning too quickly, try baking it on the rack below the middle of your oven.

cooling

I remove bread from the pan immediately upon taking it out of the oven and lay it on its side on a wire cooling rack. If the bread starts to compress on its side, it is not fully cooked, and you need to place it back in the oven in increments of 5 minutes (the walls of properly cooked bread should be firm and the bottom and sides should sound hollow when tapped with your finger). As tempting as it may seem to slice off an end to see how the bread came out, make sure you let the bread cool fully before slicing.

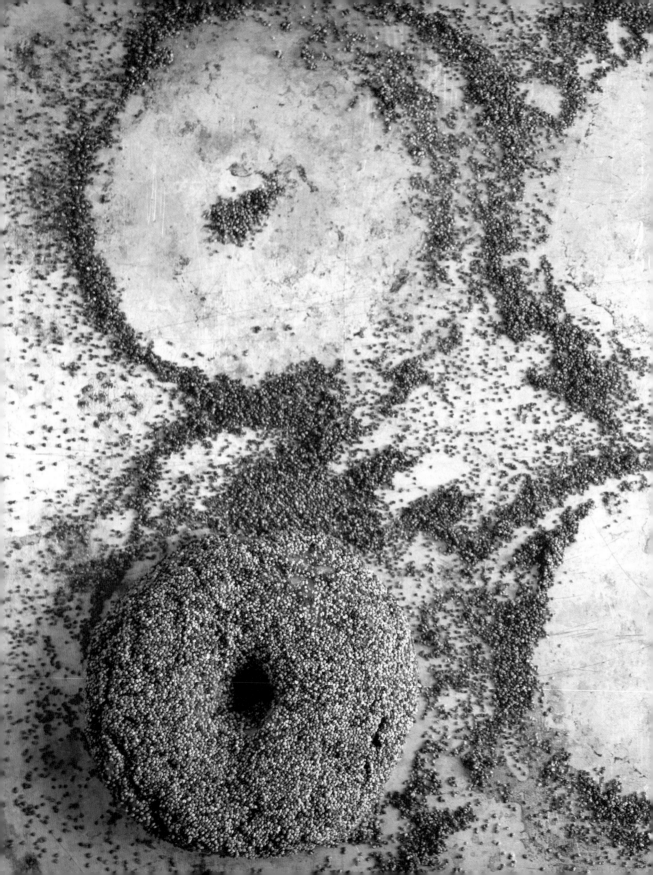

traditional
breads
and
flatbreads

MELISSA CLARK

...ing t...

...d, the St...

...dable and a
...ome cook.

...kitchen equipment in
...ction — the copper gra-
...surize... phon, the mul-
...sion blender — it's the
...I reach for most often.
...a pan I mean: the wide,
...staurant kitchen
...an a staple. It's a work-
...ne cooks, it offers one of
...convenient, inexpensive
...age-old kitchen conun-
...quickest and easiest way
...ti...ely homemade dinner
...u have sheet pans, then
...supremely tasty supper
...rotein, starch, green veg-
...n all at once, with a mini-
...very little cleanup.
...you have at least one of
...onal-grade, heavy-duty
...accurate, that you have a
...which, measuring 18 by 13
...st option for home ovens.)
...sized for commercial ov-
...unwieldy for home use.)

**Chicken with mustard
bread crumbs cooked o...
a sheet pan as part of a
complete dinner.**

ANDREW SCRIVANI FOR THE NEW ...

If you don't have one, go out and b...
couple immediately. You can get a g...
one for less than $20. If you have one, ...
another. And if y... ke to feed a crow...
consider three. I... m the proud owner o...
four, and I use them constantly for everything from spring asparagus to summer

CONTINUED ON PAGE D2

IF YOU HAVE BEEN fortunate enough to travel to Paris, you can't help but notice the number of people walking with a crusty baguette tucked under their arm around lunchtime. If you are gluten-free, it is pretty much torture. Against The Grain's first product was a gluten-free baguette. Our baguettes are crusty with a very open crumb, yet they are not leavened with yeast.

Bread bakers use all kinds of techniques to produce crusty baguettes, the principal one being steam followed by hot heat. For gluten-free bakers, high heat and steam help, but it is a challenge to retain a nice, tight baguette shape without gluten or some other type of binder. The high liquid-to-flour ratio required for an open and moist crumb results in a slack, spreading dough. In the following recipe, I use light buckwheat sourdough starter instead of active dry yeast. The addition of sourdough naturally binds the dough and makes it more elastic while retaining moisture. The result is an airy, springy texture with a crusty exterior.

Bring on the soft cheese, find a nice shaded park bench, and pretend you are in Paris.

sourdough baguettes

makes two 12-inch-long baguettes

2½ cups (350g) tapioca starch, plus 2 tablespoons to ¼ cup (18g to 35g) for kneading

2 teaspoons salt

1 cup milk

½ cup canola oil

⅔ cup light buckwheat Sourdough Starter (page 58)

1 large egg

1. In a food processor, combine the 2½ cups tapioca starch and the salt. Pulse to blend.

2. In a medium saucepan, bring the milk and oil to a boil, stirring constantly. Immediately pour the hot mixture into the dry mixture and pulse until it is moist with a sand-like texture. Allow the dough to cool for 20 minutes.

3. Add the sourdough starter and egg to the cooled dough and process to combine. The dough will be both sticky and runny, with the consistency of pancake batter.

4. Scrape the dough into a bowl and allow the dough to rest for 20 minutes. It will absorb more of the moisture and become thicker. Line a two-channel perforated baguette pan with parchment paper.

5. Knead another 2 tablespoons to ¼ cup of tapioca starch into the dough—just enough so that it is scoopable and not runny.

6. Position an oven rack in the center of the oven and preheat to 375°F. Spoon the dough into the lined baguette pan. Shape and smooth the dough into two loaves about 10 inches long (they will expand longer as they bake). Allow the baguettes to rise in a warm place for 30 minutes.

7. Bake the baguettes for 55 minutes or until lightly browned. Let cool.

IT WAS VERY LIBERATING FOR ME when I realized that I could make sourdough starters with gluten-free flours that were just as good as wheat-based ones. Wild yeast lives in grains and seeds, including those without gluten. When you provide the right conditions—flour and water at about 80°F—the yeast and naturally occurring lactobacillus bacteria in the flour feed on the sugars in the flour and divide and multiply. The by-product of the bacterial action is lactic acid, which creates the pungent, sour taste. The wild yeast provides the carbon dioxide that leavens the bread.

The combination of a light buckwheat starter and a quinoa flake–based starter both produce excellent results in gluten-free sourdough bread. (The latter gives bread an interesting texture reminiscent of oatmeal breads.) These starters give elasticity to the dough, which tends to hold in carbon dioxide better and create a more open crumb. I find the sourdough starters work best in artisan breads (as opposed to sandwich loaf-type breads) to lend additional structure as well as their characteristic sour, yeasty taste.

sourdough starters

LIGHT BUCKWHEAT STARTER INGREDIENTS:

1½ cups (180g) light buckwheat flour, plus 1 cup (120g) for feeding starter

1½ cups unchlorinated water, plus 1 cup for feeding starter (see Note)

QUINOA STARTER INGREDIENTS:

1 cup (100g) quinoa flakes, plus ⅔ cup (66g) for feeding starter

½ cup (96g) potato starch, plus ⅓ cup (64g) for feeding starter

1½ cups unchlorinated water, plus 1 cup for feeding starter (see Note)

1. Make the initial starter: Measure the initial dry ingredient and water amounts into a glass bowl and stir thoroughly until combined. Allow the starter to sit uncovered at room temperature for 3 days. You may cover the bowl with cheesecloth, if desired. The mixture will begin to bubble, and a thin layer of clear liquid will form on the top.

2. Make the starter food: Thoroughly clean a large canning jar (big enough to hold 2 quarts) with a lid to match, and rinse with boiling water. Stir the starter-feeding amounts of dry ingredient and water into the initial starter mixture, and pour the mixture into the glass jar.

3. Refrigerate the fed starter for 24 hours to ferment the new food. Before using the starter for your first batch of bread, stir vigorously to combine the liquid layer on the top (the hooch) and the remaining starter (often referred to as the "sponge"). Keep the unused starter refrigerated.

NOTE: Chlorinated water tends to slow down fermentation. If you do not have spring water, leave an open jug of water on the counter; in several hours the chlorination will dissipate.

The procedure involves creating the initial starter and then feeding it once after 3 days. Much has been written about speeding up the fermentation process while slowing down the action of the beneficial bacteria by creating an acidic environment. Feel free to increase the acidity of your starter environment by substituting some unsweetened pineapple juice for part of the water.

Wild yeast is a living thing, so ideally sourdough starter is fed on a weekly basis, if possible. When you feed your stored starter, just be sure to discard or use the same amount of starter that you feed it: For example, when you feed it 1 cup of flour and 1 cup of water, you need to remove 2 cups of starter. What better excuse do you need to bake some crusty sourdough baguettes? And make sure you thoroughly stir in the "hooch," the amber liquid that forms on the top of your starter.

I DRAW MY INSPIRATION FOR RECIPES from many different sources. One source, in particular, has been Peter Reinhart's *Whole Grain Breads*, a whole-grain wheat baking book. In Reinhart's words, the gluten in whole-grain breads is compromised by the fiber in the bran. We both have a gluten problem: His breads don't have enough, and mine don't have any.

After reading through many of his whole-grain recipes, I had to try a gluten-free version of his Potato Rosemary Bread, which promised a soft bread with an intense rosemary flavor. My initial attempts resulted in either dry, dense loaves that failed to rise, or puddles of dough with no structure. To create a moist loaf with structure, I went back to my own method of pregelatinizing the starch, substituting potato water for my liquid and adding mashed potatoes to the dough. The result was outstanding, with a dense, moist crumb and a sweet, almost creamy flavor. And it's absolutely sublime in a grilled cheese sandwich.

potato rosemary bread

makes one 8-inch loaf

2 cups (280g) tapioca starch

1½ cups (180g) light buckwheat flour

1 teaspoon salt

⅔ cup cooked and mashed skin-on red potatoes, reserving 1⅓ cups of potato cooking water

⅓ cup canola oil

1 tablespoon active dry yeast

1 teaspoon sugar

2 large eggs

1 teaspoon chopped fresh rosemary

1 teaspoon olive oil

1. In a food processor, combine the tapioca starch, buckwheat flour, and salt and pulse until blended.

2. In a medium saucepan, bring 1 cup of the potato water and the canola oil to a boil, stirring constantly. Immediately pour the hot mixture into the dry mixture and process until it is moist with a sand-like texture. Allow the dough to cool for 20 minutes. In a small bowl, combine the yeast, sugar, and remaining ⅓ cup potato water and proof for 15 minutes.

3. Combine the yeast mixture and potatoes with the dough. Add the eggs and rosemary and blend until the dough is smooth and thick.

4. Scoop the dough into a large bowl, cover it with plastic wrap, and let it rise in a warm area until doubled. Grease a 4½ × 8-inch loaf pan. Use a rubber spatula to punch the dough down and scoop it into the pan. Cover it with well-buttered or oiled plastic wrap and let it rest for 30 minutes.

6. Position a rack in the center of the oven and preheat to 400°F. Brush the top of the dough with olive oil. Bake for 70 minutes, or until the loaf is lightly browned and the loaf sounds hollow when tapped. Turn the bread onto a cooling rack and allow it to cool fully before slicing.

AS A MANUFACTURER OF GLUTEN-FREE BREAD, we attend a lot of food shows and provide samples of our food. One of the best parts of these shows is the opportunity for us to taste new products. You never know what gems you will find. It was at one of these shows that I was attending with my sister, Lynn, that she discovered and provided me with my first taste of gluten-free oatmeal bread.

For a number of years, all oats were contaminated with gluten—oats and wheat are often grown side by side, and farmers rotate fields from oats to wheat on a yearly basis. But a few years back, a number of gluten-free oat producers sprang up to meet the demand for "clean" oats. Although oatmeal is sticky in and of itself, it typically needs the addition of other flours for structure and to retain moisture. This recipe uses oats in almost a 2:1 ratio of flour to starch and relies heavily on the protein in eggs to bind the dough and give it structure. Toasting the oats both gives the bread a nutty, caramelized taste and increases the moisture retention of the dough. This is a bread you can make entirely by hand, and the result is a hearty loaf with a loose crumb and lots of fiber and whole grain.

lynn's lovely oat bread

makes one 8-inch loaf

3½ cups rolled oats

1 tablespoon active dry yeast

1 teaspoon brown sugar

1¼ cups (175g) tapioca starch

1 teaspoon salt

3 large eggs

¼ cup canola oil

2 tablespoons honey

2 tablespoons unflavored, unsweetened apple butter

1. Position a rack in the center of the oven and preheat to 350°F. Spread 3 cups of the oats evenly on a baking sheet and toast for 12 minutes. Remove from the oven and allow them to cool. Turn the oven off. Transfer the toasted oats to a food processor and process until ground into a fine flour.

2. Meanwhile, in a small bowl, combine the yeast, brown sugar, and ½ cup warm water and allow it to proof for 15 minutes.

3. In a large bowl, combine the toasted oat flour, tapioca starch, and salt. Add the yeast mixture, eggs, oil, and honey. Stir the dough until well moistened.

4. Add the apple butter and ¾ cup water. Fold in the remaining ½ cup untoasted oats for texture. The dough will be batter-like. Let the dough rest for 30 minutes. Lightly grease a 4½ × 8-inch loaf pan. Scoop the dough into the loaf pan and let it rise until doubled. Meanwhile, preheat the oven to 350°F.

5. Bake for 30 minutes. Then cover the loaf with a foil tent, if necessary, and bake for 50 to 55 minutes, or until the sides and bottom sound hollow when tapped. Let cool fully.

YEARS AGO IN GRADUATE SCHOOL, we lived on modest teaching assistantships and the best way to economize was to brown-bag our lunch. The least expensive, most filling, and most durable backpack sandwich was peanut butter and jelly. Our favorite bread was a locally baked honey-oat bread. In retrospect, it probably had less whole oats in it than commercial white flour, but after all these years, honey-oat bread is a comfort food that reminds me of simpler times.

On a trip to find my son Marty's first grad school apartment, I packed several peanut butter and raspberry jelly sandwiches on this bread. The day after baking, I prepared the sandwiches on frozen slices of the bread. Wrapped in plastic wrap, the sandwiches stayed fresh and moist through two flights and over ten hours. As Marty begins living on his own, this bread is sure to become a staple that he can turn into sandwiches all week. It is a slightly sweet and oat-y bread with a great crumb and even better mouthfeel. For someone just starting out in a gluten-free kitchen, it really beats the heck out of commercial sandwich bread.

oatmeal bread two

makes one 8-inch loaf

2 cups plus 2 tablespoons rolled oats

1¼ cups (175g) tapioca starch

1½ teaspoons salt

1¼ cups milk

¼ cup canola oil

1 tablespoon active dry yeast

1 teaspoon sugar

1 tablespoon honey

3 large eggs

1. Position a rack in the center of the oven and preheat to 350°F. Spread the oats evenly on a baking sheet and toast for 12 minutes. Remove them and allow them to cool.

2. In a food processor, combine the toasted oats, tapioca starch, and salt and process until the oats are ground to a fine flour.

3. In a medium saucepan, bring the milk and oil to a boil, stirring constantly. Pour the hot mixture into the flours and process until it has a sand-like texture. Allow the dough to cool for 20 minutes.

4. In a small bowl, combine the yeast, sugar, and ⅓ cup warm water and allow it to proof for 15 minutes.

5. Add the yeast mixture and honey to the flour mixture and blend until combined, then add the eggs. The dough will be stiff and sticky with the consistency of thick oatmeal.

6. Turn the dough into a bowl and use your wet hands to smooth the dough into a ball. Cover with plastic wrap and let it rest for 30 minutes. Grease a 4½ × 8-inch loaf pan.

7. Knead the dough in the bowl using a rubber spatula dipped in water. Scoop it into the loaf pan and let it rise until doubled.

8. Preheat the oven to 350°F. Bake for 50 minutes, or until the bread sounds hollow when tapped. Turn the bread out to cool.

ALTHOUGH I RUN AN ARTISAN BAKERY, I'll confess that I find the "News" section of geeky industry e-zines like *Food Business News* a fascinating window into what consumers are eating, or at least what manufacturers think people want to be eating. One day I read an article about how a food service giant was expanding their offerings to include sweet potato rolls. Sweet potato rolls? I had never heard of them, even growing up in the South. Always on the lookout for naturally gluten-free flour substitutions, and just happening to have leftover sweet potatoes from Thanksgiving, I had to give them a try. Otherwise I would never have discovered what wonderfully golden and flavorful toast they would make. This bread has all the softness of potato bread, while being moist and flexible. It makes great cream cheese sandwiches and is a nicely color-coordinated and satisfying toast to accompany your morning scrambled eggs.

This recipe recommends refrigerating the dough overnight to maximize the development of flavors; however, the dough can also be made and baked the same day.

sweet potato bread

makes one 8-inch loaf

2 cups (280g) tapioca starch

1½ cups (180g) light buckwheat flour

1 teaspoon salt

1 cup milk

3 tablespoons salted butter

1 tablespoon active dry yeast

1 teaspoon sugar

2 large eggs

¾ cup mashed sweet potato

1. In a food processor, combine the tapioca starch, buckwheat flour, and salt and pulse until blended.

2. In a medium saucepan, bring the milk and butter to a boil, stirring constantly. Immediately pour the hot mixture into the flours and process until it is moist with a sand-like texture. Allow the dough to cool for 20 minutes.

3. Meanwhile, in a small bowl, combine the yeast, sugar, and ⅓ cup warm water and allow it to proof for 15 minutes.

4. Add the yeast mixture to the dough and blend until combined. Add the eggs and sweet potato and blend until the dough is smooth and creamy. Scoop the dough into a large bowl, cover it with plastic wrap, and let it rise in the refrigerator overnight.

5. Remove the dough from the refrigerator and, using a rubber spatula, knead the dough into a smooth mixture by folding it over and over. Allow it to remain covered at room temperature for about 2 hours. It will double in bulk again.

6. Position an oven rack in the center of the oven and preheat to 375°F. Butter a 4½ × 8-inch loaf pan.

7. Scoop the dough into the loaf pan and smooth the surface with a spatula. Bake for 50 minutes, or until the crust is browned and the sides and bottom sound hollow when tapped.

8. Turn the bread out of the pan onto a cooling rack and allow it to cool fully before slicing.

THERE'S AN OLD, GNARLED WILD APPLE TREE in the backyard of our summer cottage. It produces early green apples, and it is a magnet for squirrels, bees, and deer. But we pick bags and bags of the spotty, twisted, and tart gems for us and the neighbors anyway. They've always gone to applesauce, but now I have a new use: gluten-free bread. Specifically, I make apple butter, which is an excellent source of pectin to bind yeasted gluten-free bread (for more on pectin see page 35).

This is a batter-type yeast bread that does not rely on pregelatinizing the starch. You'll swear you are making a quick bread with yeast, but it bakes up like regular sandwich bread. The combination of apple butter and buckwheat makes a loaf of bread with a sweet tanginess. It is a great slicing bread, plenty squishy for peanut butter and jelly sandwiches. I also recommend it for grilled cheese, where the slight hint of the apple pairs so well with sharp Cheddar.

buckwheat sandwich bread

makes one 8-inch loaf

2⅓ cups (280g) light buckwheat flour

1¾ cups (245g) tapioca starch

2 teaspoons salt

1 envelope (2¼ teaspoons) active dry yeast

1 teaspoon sugar

3 large eggs

¼ cup canola oil

2 tablespoons unflavored, unsweetened apple butter

1. In a large bowl, whisk together the buckwheat flour, tapioca starch, and salt and set aside.

2. In a small bowl, combine the yeast, sugar, and ½ cup warm water and allow it to proof for 15 minutes.

3. Using a hand mixer, mix the yeast mixture into the flour mixture, then mix in the eggs and oil. Mix the apple butter and ¾ cup water into the batter; it will be runny, like pancake batter. Cover the bowl and let the dough rest for 40 minutes.

4. Position an oven rack in the center of the oven and preheat to 350°F. Grease a 4½ × 8-inch loaf pan.

5. Scoop the batter into the loaf pan and bake for 20 minutes. Then cover the loaf with a foil tent, and bake for 40 minutes, or until the sides and bottom sound hollow when tapped. Turn bread out onto a cooling rack and allow to cool completely before slicing.

THE FIRST GLUTEN-FREE BREAD I ever baked was a rice flour–based recipe that was considered the best on a number of celiac support group websites. Like everyone else, I thought that adding xanthan gum to the dough was essential. Coming out of the oven, the loaf looked reasonably promising. I couldn't wait for the bread to cool, and then I tasted it. Disappointment . . . big disappointment. It had an off-taste and a crumbly texture just like all the commercial breads I had rejected.

After developing several dozen recipes avoiding rice flour, I finally decided to try a naturally gluten-free rice-based bread. I was interested in two things: the convenience of using a gluten-free flour blend, and a familiar taste for those who currently purchase their sandwich bread. You can either make a gluten-free blend yourself (see Note) or buy a commercial blend. Just make sure that the commercial blend does not include xanthan gum. This bread rises beautifully, slices without crumbling, and has a yeasty, rustic quality that will get you excited about white sandwich bread again.

country white sandwich bread

makes two 8-inch loaves

1½ cups (240g) gluten-free flour blend (such as King Arthur; see Note)

1½ cups (210g) tapioca starch

2 teaspoons salt

1 tablespoon active dry yeast

1 tablespoon sugar

3 large eggs

¼ cup canola oil

2 tablespoons unflavored, unsweetened apple butter

1. In a large bowl, whisk together the flour blend, tapioca starch, and salt and set aside.

2. In a small bowl, combine the yeast, sugar, and ⅓ cup warm water and allow to proof for 15 minutes.

3. Using a hand mixer, mix the yeast mixture into the flour mixture. Mix in the eggs, oil, apple butter, and ⅔ cup water until you have a thick cake-like dough. Cover the bowl and let the dough rise for 40 minutes.

4. Meanwhile, position an oven rack in the center of the oven and preheat to 350°F. Grease two 4½ × 8-inch loaf pans.

5. Spoon the dough into the loaf pans. (The dough will come to within an inch of the top of the pan.) Make sure the pans are separated by at least 2 inches to ensure even baking. Bake for 1 hour, or until the sides and bottom sound hollow when tapped. Allow the loaves to cool for 10 minutes in the pans before turning out onto a cooling rack to cool completely before slicing.

NOTE: You can make your own brown rice flour blend, as shown on King Arthur's website: 6 cups brown rice flour, 2 cups potato starch, 1 cup tapioca starch. For this recipe only, combine 187g brown rice flour, 62g potato starch, and 31g tapioca starch.

IN THE FALL OF 2012, I was selected as a finalist in America's Best Raisin Bread Contest, sponsored by the California Raisin Board. They flew me and thirty-five other finalists to the American Institute of Baking in Manhattan, Kansas, for the final competition. One of only three finalists with gluten-free entries, I knew I was out of my league as I met some of the best bakers and pastry chefs around. For me, innovation was making something gluten-free taste normal. For them, innovation was creating something with a distinct taste profile and a unique combination of ingredients and techniques.

For the competition, the California Raisin Board sent a 250-pound bounty of Thompson raisins, raisin paste, golden raisins, currants, and muscats. What drew my attention were two big jugs of thick, deep brown raisin juice concentrate, which is used in bakeries as a natural preservative, colorant, binder, antioxidant, and moisturizer. It sounded like it was designed for gluten-free bread. I now make my own raisin juice concentrate, and it produces a moist, attractive, brown loaf with great volume, no refined sugar and some of the best flavor I have tasted in gluten-free sandwich bread.

brown bread

makes one 8-inch loaf

2 cups (280g) tapioca starch

1½ cups (180g) light buckwheat flour

1 teaspoon salt

½ cup Raisin Juice Concentrate (recipe follows)

3 tablespoons salted butter

1 tablespoon active dry yeast

1 teaspoon sugar

2 large eggs

1 teaspoon unsweetened cocoa powder

1. In a food processor, combine the tapioca starch, buckwheat flour, and salt and pulse until blended.

2. In a medium saucepan, bring the raisin juice concentrate, butter, and ½ cup water to a boil, stirring constantly. Immediately pour the hot mixture into the dry mixture and process until it is moist with a sand-like texture. Allow the dough to cool for 20 minutes.

3. Meanwhile, in a small bowl, combine the yeast, sugar, and ⅓ cup warm water and allow it to proof for 15 minutes.

4. Add the yeast mixture to the dough and blend until combined. Add the eggs and cocoa and blend the dough until it is smooth and creamy. It will have a liquid, batter-like texture.

5. Scoop the dough into a large bowl, cover it with plastic wrap, and let it rise in a warm area until doubled, about 1 hour. Grease a 4½ × 8-inch loaf pan with butter.

6. Use a rubber spatula to punch down the risen dough and scoop it into the loaf pan. Cover it with well-buttered or -oiled plastic wrap and let it rest for 20 minutes.

7. Meanwhile, position an oven rack in the center of the oven and preheat to 375°F.

8. Bake the loaf for 25 minutes, or until the crust browns and becomes crusty. Then cover the loaf with a foil tent, and bake for 25 minutes, or until the sides and bottom sound hollow when tapped. Turn the bread out of the pan onto a cooling rack and allow it to cool fully before slicing.

raisin juice concentrate · makes ½ cup

2 cups (260g) raisins

4 cups boiling water

1. Coarsely chop the raisins and place in a large glass bowl. Pour the boiling water over the raisins and cover with a kitchen towel. Allow the raisin sugars to seep into the water for at least 3 hours.

2. Strain the raisin water through a fine-mesh sieve into a medium saucepan. Bring the mixture to a boil, then reduce the heat and let it boil gently until the mixture has thickened and reduced to ½ cup.

IT IS NOT TOO SURPRISING that American diets are deficient in fiber. Grain-based bread products and pizza are the primary sources of fiber in the U.S. diet according to the Centers for Disease Control (CDC). Although the average slice of white sandwich bread has less than a gram of fiber (and most of that is in the crust), there is a lot of discussion about whether a gluten-free diet provides sufficient fiber. Several gluten-free sandwich breads have a decent fiber profile, but the fiber often comes from sources like cellulose, which is surplus spruce tree wood pulp, or oat and rice bran. And while wood pulp is all natural, I would rather not eat a tree.

This sandwich bread is high-fiber and low-glycemic. It is not fluffy, but it is moist and holds together extremely well for slicing, toasting, and grilling. If you are trying to increase the amount of fiber in your diet while limiting your intake of high-glycemic flours, this is the bread for you. This is also a higher-protein bread, with the sources being eggs, coconut, and buckwheat flours.

high-fiber sandwich bread

makes one 8-inch loaf

¼ cup (30g) coconut flour

2¼ cups (270g) light buckwheat flour

⅔ cup (93g) tapioca starch

1 teaspoon salt

⅓ cup canola oil

1 tablespoon active dry yeast

1 teaspoon sugar

3 large eggs

1. In a food processor, combine the coconut flour, buckwheat flour, tapioca starch, and salt and pulse until blended together.

2. In a medium saucepan, bring the oil and 1 cup water to a boil, stirring constantly. Immediately pour the hot mixture into the flours and pulse until it is moist with a sand-like texture. Allow the dough to cool for 20 minutes.

3. Meanwhile, in a small bowl, combine the yeast, sugar, and ⅓ cup warm water and allow it to proof for 15 minutes.

4. Add the yeast mixture to the flour mixture and blend until combined. Add the eggs and blend the dough until it has a smooth, batter-like texture.

5. Cover the dough with plastic wrap, and let it rise until doubled. Grease a 4½ × 8-inch loaf pan.

6. Use a spatula to punch down the dough and scoop it into the pan. Cover with plastic wrap and let it rise for 30 minutes.

7. Position an oven rack in the center of the oven and preheat to 375°F. Bake the loaf for 55 minutes, or until the loaf sounds hollow when tapped. Turn the bread out and allow to cool fully before slicing.

ONE OF OUR MOST POPULAR PRODUCTS at Against The Grain is sesame bagels. They are way different from any other gluten-free bagels on the market because they are light, with a texture reminiscent of croissants. The ingredient that makes them unique is a hint of toasted sesame oil. Toasting the naan warms the sesame oil, filling your breakfast kitchen with the most scrumptious smell. When you want to serve gluten-free bread along with a meal, a nice toasted naan is a perfect accompaniment. You can either bake it on a baking sheet or slide the naan (on parchment paper) directly onto a pizza stone. If you are grilling, consider brushing the baked naan with a little olive oil and throwing it on the grill. Grilling the naan this way will release the sesame scent and enhance your entire meal.

This recipe is built on gluten-free rolled oats, which are toasted to gelatinize the starch. This increases the binding properties of the oats and enhances their flavor as they caramelize. When combined with sesame seeds and sesame oil, the flavor is a warm, slightly earthy taste with a hint of sweetness from the honey and apple butter. It is also a higher-fiber naan without a distinct oat taste.

toasted sesame naan

makes 2 naans

2¼ cups rolled oats

¾ cup (105g) tapioca starch

½ teaspoon salt

1 tablespoon active dry yeast

1 teaspoon sugar

½ cup milk

1 tablespoon olive oil

1 tablespoon toasted sesame oil

1 tablespoon honey

1 tablespoon unflavored, unsweetened apple butter

2 tablespoons sesame seeds

2 large eggs

1. Position an oven rack in the center of the oven and preheat to 350°F. Spread the oats evenly on a baking sheet and toast for 12 minutes. Remove from the oven and allow them to cool. Turn the oven off. Transfer the toasted oats to a food processor and process until ground into a fine flour.

2. In a large bowl, combine the oat flour, tapioca starch, and salt. Set aside.

3. In a small bowl, combine the yeast, sugar, and ½ cup warm water and allow it to proof for 15 minutes. Blend the yeast mixture into the oat flour mixture, then add the milk, olive oil, sesame oil, honey, apple butter, and 1 tablespoon of the sesame seeds. With a hand mixer, beat in the eggs. Mix the dough on high for 4 minutes. Cover the bowl with plastic wrap and allow it to rise until doubled.

4. Preheat the oven to 400°F. Line a baking sheet with parchment paper. Punch down and divide the dough in half. With a moistened spatula, smooth two flat loaves onto the baking sheet, separating the loaves by 2 inches to allow for spreading. Sprinkle the breads with the remaining tablespoon sesame seeds. Bake the naans for 15 minutes, or until nicely browned.

TO MAKE A TOPPED CHEESE PIZZA: Position an oven rack in the center of the oven and preheat to 400°F. Cover the raw shell with your favorite toppings and bake for about 15 minutes, or until the cheese is bubbling and begins to brown. (The total bake time will depend on how many toppings you put on the pizza.)

TO PARBAKE A SHELL: Preheat the oven to 375°F. Bake the shell for 10 minutes, or until the crust is beginning to brown.

GROWING UP IN A VERY RURAL AREA, I had never had an occasion to try a restaurant pizza. Of course, I had eaten what my dad *called* pizza—a Bisquick crust topped with homemade tomato sauce, mushrooms, peppers, and baked beans. The crust's recipe: For 1½ cups Bisquick, use ⅓ cup very hot water and stir only 20 times. I first suspected that my dad's pizza was out of the ordinary on my husband Tom's first visit to my childhood home, as he rolled his eyes as if to say "This is pizza?" Despite my dad's obsession with Bisquick, he was a foodie long before the word was a part of our lexicon . . . but his pizza was lost on me.

Of all the commercially available gluten-free products, pizza is one of the hardest to get right. Make this shell ahead of time and bring it with you to your favorite pizza joint. This recipe makes two balls of dough. Either parbake the crusts and freeze them for future use, or keep the extra ball of dough in the refrigerator for several days. The dough can also be used to make calzones, pizza bites, or a wrap for baked brie.

rising crust pizza dough

makes enough for two 12-inch pizzas, or 4 to 6 smaller individual pies (DF)

2 cups (280g) tapioca starch

¾ cup plus 1 tablespoon (100g) light buckwheat flour

1 teaspoon salt

¼ cup olive oil, plus 1 tablespoon for brushing shells

1½ tablespoons active dry yeast

2 teaspoons sugar

1 large egg

1. In a food processor, combine the tapioca starch, buckwheat flour, and salt and pulse until blended.

2. In a medium saucepan, bring the ¼ cup oil and 1 cup water to a boil, stirring constantly. Immediately pour the hot mixture into the dry ingredients and process until it is moist with a sand-like texture. Allow the dough to cool for 20 minutes.

3. Meanwhile, in a small bowl, combine the yeast, sugar, and ⅓ cup warm water and allow it to proof for 15 minutes.

4. Add the yeast mixture to the dough and blend until combined. Add the egg and blend until the dough is smooth and comes together. Allow it to rest for 20 minutes in a covered bowl. Lightly grease a 12-inch pizza pan.

5. Dust your hands with tapioca starch. Form the dough into a smooth ball and divide in half, then roll each half into a ball. Use your hands to gently spread out the dough on the pizza pan to the desired size. Create a rim at the edges by rolling the dough under toward the center of the shell. Brush the shell, including the rim, lightly with the remaining 1 tablespoon olive oil. Allow the crust to rest for 15 minutes.

SOMETIMES IT'S THE LITTLE THINGS that can make a major difference in your life. Take skillets, for instance. Always a fan of eggs for breakfast, I spent years scrubbing scrambled eggs out of skillets. I bought regular pans and nonstick pans, even a $70 hard-anodized pan, but nothing seemed to work.

I resigned myself to the myth of nonstick pans. Then I visited my sister, Lynn, and her husband, Joe, who had recently moved back to land after living on a sailboat for ten years. Although it was a big sailboat, and although they were foodies, they kept a minimalist kitchen. It was at breakfast the first morning where I discovered cast-iron skillets: nothing sticks in a seasoned cast-iron skillet, and you can clean it with just hot water and a brush. After all those years, I had met one of my very favorite kitchen tools.

This pizza shell puffs up a lot when parbaked, which may make you wonder how you're going to get the finished pizza out of the pan or whether you'll have to eat it right out of the pan with a fork. You have to have faith that the completed pizza will release from the skillet when done. Miraculously, it does, but make sure your cast-iron pan is well seasoned.

skillet pizza

makes one 12-inch pizza

FOR THE PIZZA SHELL:

1 cup (140g) tapioca starch

⅓ cup plus 1 tablespoon (50g) light buckwheat flour

½ teaspoon salt

2 tablespoons olive oil

2½ tablespoons active dry yeast

1 teaspoon sugar

1 egg white

FOR THE TOPPINGS:

2 tablespoons olive oil

3 garlic cloves, minced

1 can (15 ounces) diced tomatoes

4 slices bacon, cooked and cut into 1-inch pieces

10 large kalamata olives, pitted and halved

1 Italian sausage link, cooked, sliced into disks and quartered

½ jar (3 ounces) marinated artichokes, drained and chopped

1. **Make the pizza shell:** In a food processor, combine the tapioca starch, buckwheat flour, and salt and pulse until blended.

2. In a medium saucepan, bring the oil and ½ cup water to a boil, stirring constantly. Immediately pour the hot mixture into the flours and process until it is moist with a sand-like texture. Clean out the saucepan to use for the toppings. Allow the dough to cool for 20 minutes.

3. Meanwhile, in a small bowl, combine the yeast, sugar, and 2 tablespoons plus 2 teaspoons of warm water and allow it to proof for 15 minutes.

4. Add the yeast mixture to the dough and blend until combined. Add the egg white and blend until the dough is smooth and comes together. Allow it to rest for 20 minutes in a covered bowl.

5. Position an oven rack in the center of the oven and preheat to 500°F.

6. Dust your hands with tapioca starch to handle the dough. Form the dough into a smooth ball and pat it down into a 5-inch round. Place it in a well-seasoned 12-inch cast-iron skillet and work the dough to spread it evenly on the bottom of the pan and about halfway up the sides. Use your fingers to roll the sides down slightly to create a rim. Allow the crust to rest for 15 minutes.

7. **Prepare the toppings:** In a medium saucepan, heat the oil over medium heat. Add the garlic and cook just until it begins to brown. Add the diced tomatoes (and their juices) and the bacon and cook until the liquid is reduced to a spreadable paste, about 10 minutes. Set aside.

8. Slide the skillet into the oven and parbake the shell for 6 minutes.

9. Spread the tomato topping on the shell and top with the olives, sausage, and artichokes. Put the skillet back in the oven and bake for 15 minutes.

variations

barbecued chicken skillet pizza

Parbake the crust, then spread 2 tablespoons barbecue sauce over the surface. Top with 1 cup chopped grilled chicken, 1/3 cup sliced red onion, and 1 tablespoon chopped fresh cilantro, and bake for another 15 minutes to finish.

vegetarian skillet pizza

For a vegetarian version, top the parbaked crust with 1 medium onion, sliced and caramelized, 1 cup sliced fresh figs, and 1 tablespoon balsamic vinegar. Bake for an additional 15 minutes, then top with 1 cup arugula just before serving.

I HAVE A FEW OCCASIONS to visit the South each year and am always reminded of how off-limits much of Southern cuisine is to those on a gluten-free diet. On a recent trip, biscuits seemed to be on every breakfast, lunch, and dinner menu. Oddly enough, Southern-style or beaten biscuits—which are deliberately tough and more akin to what we know as hardtack—are a lot like most gluten-free biscuits. But growing up I never really liked beaten biscuits (often made at home by my dad with Bisquick). I wanted fluffy, light biscuits that crumble in your mouth and taste totally decadent with a melting pat of butter.

Of all the gluten-free formulations, I found biscuits particularly vexing. Like all other gluten-free doughs, they need to be well hydrated, but then they spread into flat hard shells. I had almost concluded that biscuits just didn't translate when I saw a reference to biscuits made with three leavening agents: yeast, baking powder, and baking soda. That was the breakthrough: Adding yeast and allowing the dough to rest and rise while the flours absorbed the liquid gave the biscuit enough structure to stand on its own. Once you have the basics, there is no end to the variations you can create.

biscuits

makes about 16 biscuits

1 tablespoon active dry yeast

1 tablespoon sugar

⅓ cup warm milk plus ¼ cup cold milk

1¼ cups (150g) light buckwheat flour

1 cup (140g) tapioca starch

1 tablespoon baking powder

¾ teaspoon baking soda

1 teaspoon salt

4 tablespoons cold salted butter, cut into pieces

4 ounces cream cheese, cut into pieces

1 tablespoon cider vinegar

1. In a small bowl, combine the yeast, sugar, and ⅓ cup warm milk and allow it to proof for 15 minutes.

2. In a food processor, pulse the buckwheat flour, tapioca starch, baking powder, baking soda, and salt. Add the butter and cream cheese and pulse just until the mixture is a coarse meal. Stir in the proofed yeast.

3. Add the remaining ¼ cup cold milk and the vinegar and pulse until the dough comes together. Transfer the dough to a large bowl, cover with plastic wrap, and allow it to rise for 20 minutes.

4. Meanwhile, position a rack in the center of the oven and preheat to 400°F. Grease two 9-inch round cake pans with salted butter.

5. Turn the dough out onto a piece of plastic wrap dusted with tapioca starch. Pat the dough down with wet hands until it is about ¾ inch thick. Use a tapioca-dusted glass to cut out biscuits 2 inches in diameter. Reroll the scraps as necessary.

6. Transfer the biscuits to the cake pans and bake for 15 minutes, or until golden brown.

HOT CROSS BUNS may be the first recipe I was ever introduced to. I still remember snuggling in my mom's lap with my brother on one side and my sister on the other, while my mom read nursery rhymes from *The Real Mother Goose* to us over and over. In a singsong voice that captivated us, she would read *Hot Cross Buns! Hot Cross Buns!* I would always ask what they were, until one day she decided that we would finally make them.

Actually, it is not so obvious what hot cross buns are—there are as many culinary interpretations of them as there are theories of what they signify. In the United Kingdom, they are traditionally eaten on Good Friday before Easter, but they are also available year-round and come in many flavors. This recipe is a pretty old-fashioned one, warmly spiced with bits of dried fruit. My favorite part is the smell of them baking, and oh yes, eating them warm, even without icing.

hot cross buns

makes 8 buns

2⅓ cups (330g) tapioca starch

1 teaspoon salt

1 teaspoon ground cinnamon

1 teaspoon ground allspice

¼ teaspoon ground cloves

¼ teaspoon freshly grated nutmeg

1 cup plus 2 teaspoons milk

½ cup canola oil

1 tablespoon granulated sugar

2 large eggs

¼ cup chopped dried pineapple

¼ cup chopped fruit-sweetened dried cranberries

½ cup golden raisins

1 tablespoon honey

½ cup powdered sugar

½ teaspoon vanilla extract

1. In a food processor, combine the tapioca starch, salt, cinnamon, allspice, cloves, and nutmeg and pulse to combine.

2. In a medium saucepan, bring 1 cup of the milk, the oil, and granulated sugar to a boil, stirring constantly. Immediately pour the hot mixture into the flour and process until it is moist with a sand-like texture. Allow the dough to cool for 20 minutes.

3. Add the eggs to the dough and process until smooth. The dough will be both sticky and runny, with the consistency of pancake batter. Scrape the dough into a bowl and fold in the dried fruits. Allow the dough to rest for 15 minutes. It will absorb more of the moisture and become thicker.

4. Meanwhile, position an oven rack in the center of the oven and preheat to 325°F. Line a baking sheet with parchment paper.

recipe continues

5. Using a spoon dipped in water, drop 8 spoonfuls of the dough onto the baking sheet. Wet your hands and smooth the top and sides of the buns as you round them.

6. Bake the buns for 55 minutes, or until the tops are lightly browned. Remove the buns from the oven and immediately brush the tops with the honey. Allow to cool completely on a cooling rack.

7. In a small bowl, combine the powdered sugar, vanilla, and remaining 2 teaspoons milk and stir until all the lumps are dissolved. Spoon the icing into a pastry bag or sealable plastic bag with a corner cut off. Pipe crosses on the tops.

variation

gingery orange hot cross buns

Substitute ¼ cup chopped crystallized ginger for the pineapple, and add 2 tablespoons of orange zest. Substitute ½ teaspoon orange extract for the vanilla extract.

WE CAN THANK HARRY POTTER for crumpets . . . at least in our house. An avid reader, Marty was in second grade when *Harry Potter and the Sorcerer's Stone* was first published in the United States. The teacher said he spent most of second grade sneaking the book off her desk and reading it over and over whenever he finished his work. In a scene right out of a fairy tale, at age twelve, Marty had the opportunity to meet J. K. Rowling in London and hear her read in Royal Albert Hall . . . and eat crumpets.

Crumpets are certainly *not* the same as English muffins, although they do show similarities. Crumpets are chewy and spongy with a surface of tiny holes created by adding baking powder to yeasted dough, whereas English muffins are more bread-like and crunchy when toasted. These crumpets combine both yeast and baking powder, and use a small amount of sour cream to increase the bubbling action of the baking powder. The baking powder is added at the last minute to provide the maximum number of holes in the surface. The resulting crumpets toast nicely, absorb lots of toppings, and can even be speared and toasted on a fork with marshmallows, just like Harry and Ron did.

crumpets

makes 6 crumpets

1 tablespoon active dry yeast

1 teaspoon sugar

1 cup (140g) tapioca starch

½ cup (60g) light buckwheat flour

2 large eggs

1 teaspoon salt

⅓ cup milk

¼ cup sour cream

2 tablespoons salted butter, melted, plus additional for brushing the skillet and rings

1 teaspoon baking powder

1. In a small bowl, whisk the yeast, sugar, and ¼ cup warm water until well blended. Allow it to proof for 15 minutes.

2. In a large bowl, combine the tapioca starch, buckwheat flour, eggs, salt, milk, sour cream, and melted butter. Add the yeast mixture. With a hand mixer, beat on high until smooth. Cover the bowl with plastic wrap and let rise until doubled, about 1 hour.

3. Preheat a well-seasoned cast-iron skillet over medium-low heat. Brush the insides of six 3-inch English muffin rings with more melted butter and lay them flat in the skillet.

4. Punch down the dough by stirring it, and whisk in the baking powder until it is uniformly blended into the batter.

5. Ladle approximately ¼ cup of the batter into one ring and test your heat. The bottom should brown nicely while the top starts to solidify with lots of tiny holes. Adjust the heat accordingly. Fill the remaining rings. When the holes appear and the top start to solidify, shake the rings until the crumpets come loose. Flip the crumpets over and cook them for 15 to 30 seconds to lightly brown the tops. If you flip them too soon, you will lose the lovely holes—but make sure you don't brown the tops too long, or you will lose the holes as well.

FROM 5KS TO MARATHONS, I've been running races for over thirty years. For me, it has always been about engaging in a healthy activity and achieving a personal best. Running my hardest early in the morning typically means finishing a race thirsty and starving, and of all the post-race offerings, orange slices and bagels are the most ubiquitous. It is always hard to pass by those bagels—piles of shiny, seeded carbs that my post-race body seems to crave.

Bagels always elicit strong opinions, but those of us on a gluten-free diet agree on one thing: Gluten-free bagels typically taste like bread with a hole in the center. Not my bagels—they are made from low-hydration dough, and the starch is pregelatinized to give the bagels their characteristically dense and chewy texture. Like traditional bagels, they are also parboiled to further gelatinize the starch on the surface. The result is a shiny, golden bagel, with a slightly crispy crust—finally, a bagel to rival the best in New York.

bagels

makes 6 bagels

FOR THE DOUGH:

2 cups (280g) tapioca starch, plus about ⅓ cup (47g) for kneading

¾ cup plus 2 tablespoons (105g) light buckwheat flour

1¾ teaspoons salt

3 tablespoons canola oil

1 tablespoon active dry yeast

1 teaspoon sugar

2 large egg whites

FOR THE WATER BATH:

2 tablespoons honey

1 teaspoon baking soda

Toppings (any or all): sesame seeds, poppy seeds, dehydrated minced onion

1. **Make the dough:** In a food processor, combine the 2 cups tapioca starch, the buckwheat flour, and salt and pulse until blended.

2. In a medium saucepan, bring the oil and 1 cup water to a boil, stirring constantly. Immediately pour the hot mixture into the dry mixture and process until it is moist with a sand-like texture. Allow the dough to cool for 20 minutes.

3. Meanwhile, in a small bowl, combine the yeast, sugar, and ⅓ cup warm water and allow it to proof for 15 minutes.

4. Add the yeast mixture and egg whites to the dough and blend thoroughly; the dough will be shaggy. Transfer the dough to a medium bowl and cover it with a damp kitchen towel. Allow the dough to rest for 15 minutes.

recipe continues

5. Using your hands, knead in about ⅓ cup tapioca starch until the dough is smooth, elastic, and just moist enough to handle without it sticking to your hands. Divide the dough into 6 equal portions and roll into balls. Place them on a piece of plastic wrap dusted with tapioca starch, cover with a damp kitchen towel, and allow the dough to rise for at least 1 hour, or until doubled in size.

6. **For the water bath:** In a large stockpot, combine 2 quarts water, the honey, and baking soda and bring to a boil.

7. Lightly dust your fingers with tapioca starch and press down on each ball using your index finger to press a hole in the center. With your other index finger, gently stretch the bagel, while enlarging the hole to 1½ to 2 inches in diameter.

8. Allow the bagels to rest on the plastic wrap while you preheat the oven to 450°F. Liberally grease a baking sheet.

9. Working two at a time, slide the bagels into the boiling water—they will float almost immediately. Allow them to boil for 1 minute, then flip them over and boil for another minute. Use a slotted spoon or flat spatula to carefully remove the bagels and transfer them to the baking sheet (see Note). While still damp from the bath, sprinkle the bagels with a topping (or multiple toppings) of your choice.

10. Bake the bagels for 25 minutes, or until they are nicely browned. Transfer the bagels to a cooling rack. They may be eaten warm or frozen for later use.

NOTE: Once formed and risen, the bagels need to be handled with care, but will hold their shape when boiled (although they may get a tad wrinkly). Gluten-free flours vary, and should your bagels fall or flatten, reduce your rising time and boil them for a shorter duration.

MY HUSBAND, TOM, AND I lived in Brooklyn, New York, for ten years. Like many young professionals starting out, we moved to the city with modest jobs that left a paltry budget for entertainment. In those first years, the city was our entertainment. Like the protagonist who moved to the city in Flannery O'Connor's *Wise Blood*, every day, we were stunned, awed, and overwhelmed. We worked all week, and Saturday we explored. It started with a copy of Gerard Wolfe's *New York: Walking Tours of Architecture and History*, given to us by a friend. Soon, it became our Saturday morning ritual to walk to some part of Brooklyn or Manhattan and just explore the area and sample the cuisine. And that is how we discovered bialys.

Everyone associates New York with bagels, and everyone in New York has an opinion about bagels, but not so many talk about bialys. A bialy is a chewy, crusty roll similar to a bagel, but it is baked rather than boiled. It doesn't have a hole, either—rather, there is a depression in the center, smeared with an onion filling. As bagels have become more and more steroidal, bialys have stayed true to their humble origins. Mimi Sheraton, the food writer and former *New York Times* food critic, wrote an entire book about bialys, tracing their origins to the

bialys

makes 8 bialys

FOR THE FILLING:

1 medium onion

1 tablespoon salted butter

Pinch of baking soda

½ teaspoon poppy seeds

FOR THE DOUGH:

2 cups (280g) tapioca starch, plus ⅓ cup (47g) for kneading

1 cup (120g) light buckwheat flour

1¾ teaspoons salt

3 tablespoons canola oil

1 tablespoon active dry yeast

1 teaspoon sugar

2 large egg whites

1. **Make the filling:** Chop the onion in the food processor until it is well minced. In a small skillet, heat the butter over medium heat. Add the onion and cook, stirring constantly. As the onion begins to soften, add the baking soda to speed up the caramelization process. Cook until the onion is soft and lightly browned. Stir in the poppy seeds. Set the filling aside.

2. **Make the dough:** Without washing the food processor bowl, combine the 2 cups tapioca starch, the buckwheat flour, and salt and pulse until they are fully mixed.

3. In a medium saucepan, bring the oil and 1 cup water to a boil, stirring constantly and vigorously. Immediately pour the hot mixture into the flours and process until it is moist with a sand-like texture. Allow the dough to cool for 20 minutes.

4. Meanwhile, in a small bowl, combine the yeast, sugar, and ⅓ cup warm water and allow it to proof for 15 minutes.

recipe continues

northeastern Polish town of Bialystok, where few survived the Holocaust. Mimi Sheraton concludes that bread is the "true soul food," and I couldn't agree more. But if you can't eat traditional bread, do you lose your soul? Not at all if you have naturally gluten-free versions. These bialys remind me of those days wandering the streets and ethnic communities of New York City. I'm sure no respectable New Yorker would deem these totally authentic, but they would undeniably have an opinion. Most likely, a big *thumbs-up.*

5. Add the yeast mixture and egg whites to the dough and pulse to blend thoroughly. It will be shaggy, not yet smooth. Transfer the dough to a medium bowl, cover the dough with plastic wrap, and allow it to rest for 15 minutes.

6. Knead in up to ⅓ cup of tapioca starch until the dough is smooth, elastic, and just moist enough to handle without it sticking to your hands.

7. Divide the dough into 8 equal portions and roll each piece into a smooth ball. Place the balls on a piece of plastic wrap dusted with tapioca starch. Press down on each ball and massage it into a 4- to 5-inch disk as if you were making an individual pizza crust. Place the disks on a well-greased baking sheet. Cover the dough and allow it to rise for at least 30 minutes.

8. Meanwhile, position an oven rack in the center of the oven and preheat to 500°F.

9. Gently create a 2- to 3-inch-wide depression in the center of each disk. Spoon the onion filling into the depression in each disk and smear it from side to side.

10. Reduce the oven temperature to 475°F and bake the bialys for about 20 minutes, or until the bottoms are lightly browned. Transfer the bialys to a cooling rack.

SOME OF MY FONDEST CHILDHOOD MEMORIES are of making breakfast over a campfire on a cool Vermont morning. My husband, Tom, grew up in the suburbs—the only time he ever camped with his family, he slept in the car with the dog. Even so, Tom willingly agreed to go camping in Yosemite Park one summer. We hadn't been there for more than an hour before we discovered the Ahwahnee Hotel, and he noticed they served eggs Benedict for breakfast. Eggs Benedict is a huge treat for Tom, so there was no roughing it around the campfire the next morning.

But for years, eggs Benedict was off-limits. No commercially available gluten-free English muffin ever really seemed like it had the right texture to Tom. Of course, I still made eggs Benedict anyway for his birthday and special occasions, but it was always on one of our rolls. That was before I developed this recipe. Oh, these English muffins! They look, taste, and feel like the real thing. You can actually split them apart with a fork, and they toast up chewy with an open crumb that traps melted butter . . . and hollandaise sauce. This recipe is definitely my breakfast toast of choice these days.

english muffins

makes 6 muffins

1²/₃ cups (234g) tapioca starch

1¼ cups (150g) light buckwheat flour

1 teaspoon salt

1 cup milk

3 tablespoons salted butter

1 tablespoon active dry yeast

1 teaspoon sugar

2 large egg whites

1. In a food processor, combine the tapioca starch, buckwheat flour, and salt and pulse until blended.

2. In a medium saucepan, bring the milk and butter to a boil, stirring constantly. Immediately pour the hot mixture into the flours and process until it is moist with a sand-like texture. Allow the dough to cool for 20 minutes.

3. Meanwhile, in a small bowl, combine the yeast, sugar, and ¹/₃ cup warm water and allow it to proof for 15 minutes.

4. Add the yeast mixture to the cooled dough and blend until combined. Remove the dough from the food processor and place in a large bowl. Cover with plastic wrap and allow the dough to rise until doubled, about 30 minutes.

5. Meanwhile, position an oven rack in the center of the oven and preheat to 350°F. Grease a baking sheet with salted butter.

6. Return the dough to the food processor and add the egg whites. Blend the dough until it is smooth. It will have a batter-like texture.

recipe continues

7. Preheat a well-seasoned cast-iron skillet or a nonstick griddle over medium-low heat. Butter the insides of six 3-inch English muffin rings and lay them flat on the cooking surface. Spoon approximately ½ cup of batter into each ring and cook on low heat for 5 minutes, or until the muffins rise and you can lift the rings so that the muffins release. The bottoms should be lightly browned. Using a slotted metal spatula, gently flip the muffins over and cook for an additional 5 minutes.

8. Place the browned muffins on the baking sheet and bake for 10 minutes, or until the centers are baked. Allow to cool fully on a cooling rack.

eggs benedict · serves 2

3 large egg yolks

3 tablespoons fresh lemon juice

3 tablespoons salted butter, melted

2 English muffins (recipe above), split and toasted

4 slices Canadian bacon

4 poached eggs

1. Make the hollandaise sauce: In the top of a double boiler set over low heat, vigorously whisk the egg yolks until they are well combined and thickened. Whisk in the lemon juice, and gradually add the melted butter until the sauce is smooth.

2. Assemble the eggs Benedict: Top each muffin half with a slice of bacon and a poached egg. Spoon the hollandaise sauce over the top.

WHEN WE WERE FIRST MARRIED, my sister-in-law Cheri gave me a gift of one of her sourdough "babies"—a jar of gloppy, wheat-based starter covered with a clear layer of liquid that looked like pond water. "Sourdough is a living thing," she told me. Her starter had been passed down to her and was a descendant of the starter sold by King Arthur Flour Company, which they describe as "a starter that's been lovingly nurtured here in New England since the 1700s." Talk about responsibility. I took it seriously and treated it as I would a pet (and it did make *great* bread). It lived in the door of my refrigerator; I fed it when it was hungry, and nurtured it for over twenty years. They say the starter takes on the characteristics of your region and climate, so this starter might as well have been a character in the movie *Baby Boom*—over the years, it moved with us from Philadelphia to New York City, to its final resting place in Vermont. Its life came to an abrupt end with my son's celiac diagnosis—overnight, it went from being a treasured part of my kitchen to poison.

It took me a long time to get up the courage to start a gluten-free sourdough. Then I learned that sourdough was the leavening agent of choice for 100% rye flour bread because rye does not contain enough gluten for baker's yeast to work

sourdough soft pretzels

makes 8 pretzels

2¼ cups (315g) tapioca starch, plus 1¼ cups (175g) for rolling pretzels

1 teaspoon salt

⅔ cup milk

½ cup canola oil

⅔ cup light buckwheat flour Sourdough Starter (page 58)

1 large egg

6 tablespoons baking soda

Pretzel salt (or extra-coarse sea salt)

1. In a food processor, combine the 2¼ cups tapioca starch and the regular salt and pulse until blended.

2. In a medium saucepan, bring the milk and oil to a boil, stirring constantly. Immediately pour the hot mixture into the flour and process until it is moist with a sand-like texture. Allow the dough to cool for 20 minutes. Clean out the saucepan.

3. Add the sourdough starter and egg to the cooled dough, and mix until smooth. The dough will have the consistency of cheesecake batter. Transfer it to a bowl and allow the dough to rest on the counter for 10 minutes. It will thicken some, yet be too sticky to handle.

4. By hand, knead up to 1¼ cups tapioca starch into the dough, just enough so that you can roll the dough by hand without it sticking—the dough should be tender and slightly dusty. Divide the dough into 8 equal pieces and roll each piece into an 18- to 20-inch rope. Form the pretzels as shown on page 92 and place on parchment paper. Generously grease a baking sheet.

recipe continues

very well. The structure of rye bread, like that of many breads made with gluten-free flours, comes mostly from the starch in the flour, so it seemed worth a try.

The tangy taste works extremely well in sourdough pretzels. Soft pretzels used to be a big deal in our household: They were the first thing my son, Marty, learned to "cook." When he was diagnosed with celiac disease, it was the food that he said he would miss most. When I first made these for him, he ate three soft pretzels, one after the other. They are chewy and salty, and just like the ones he remembers. Now, every time he comes home for a visit, he always asks: "Got any of those pretzels?"

5. Position an oven rack in the center of the oven and preheat to 375°F.

6. Bring 4 cups of water to a boil in the saucepan and dissolve the baking soda in the water; reduce the heat to a simmer. One at a time, slide a pretzel onto a slotted spatula and lower the pretzel into the baking soda bath. Boil it for 30 seconds, and then gently transfer it to the baking sheet. Sprinkle with the pretzel salt to taste.

7. Bake for 25 to 27 minutes, or until the pretzels are nicely browned.

variations

cinnamon sugar pretzels

Replace the pretzel salt with a mixture of 3 tablespoons sugar and 1 teaspoon ground cinnamon before baking.

asiago and black pepper pretzels

Add $3/4$ cup of freshly grated Asiago cheese to the dough with the egg. After boiling, sprinkle the tops with $1/4$ cup freshly grated Asiago cheese and 1 to 2 teaspoons coarsely ground black pepper.

IN THE EARLY DAYS OF
AGAINST THE GRAIN, I
stumbled upon Pão de Queijo,
or Brazilian Cheese Bread. As
with most "traditional" recipes,
there are tons of variations
on the theme, including type
and proportion of ingredients
as well as techniques. At the
point I discovered the cheese
rolls, I hadn't found any other
gluten-free bread as tasty, and
I wanted to know *why* they
puffed up the way they did
and how they developed their
tremendously chewy texture.
I had no idea the path that
inquiry would take me down.

Two main methods emerge
in the multitude of recipes:
(1) toss everything in a blender
and bake in muffin tins or
(2) create a gelatinous mixture
by preboiling the liquid and
the fat, then roll the dough
into Ping-Pong-size balls. I'm
of the preboiling camp, which
totally changes the texture and
binding properties of the flour.
But the blender method also
produces a unique and delicious
roll. The following recipe makes
light, chewy rolls perfect for
appetizers and mini sandwiches.
There is an infinite variety of
modifications you might try
with different cheeses, garlic,
and herbs.

traditional brazilian rolls (pão de queijo)

makes 24 rolls

2 cups (280g) tapioca starch

1 teaspoon salt

1 cup milk

½ cup vegetable oil

2 large eggs, lightly beaten

1½ cups freshly grated Parmesan cheese

1. Position one oven rack in the upper third of the oven and one in the lower third and preheat to 450°F. Measure the tapioca starch and salt into a large bowl.

2. In a small saucepan, bring the milk and oil to a full, rolling boil, whisking occasionally. Pour the hot mixture over the tapioca and stir until all the tapioca is moistened.

3. Knead the dough with a wooden spoon until it is cool enough to handle, then knead with your hands until the dough cools enough to hold.

4. Gradually add the beaten eggs to the dough, fully incorporating them into the dough before adding more. (If you mix the dough by hand, it will be very sticky and sort of lumpy, but the lumps will smooth out during the baking process.) Mix in the Parmesan; the dough consistency will be like soft cookie dough. Line 2 baking sheets with parchment paper.

5. Use a small ice cream scoop or a tablespoon dipped in water to drop rounded balls about the size of a golf ball on the baking sheets, 12 rolls per baking sheet, placed at least 1 inch apart.

6. Reduce the oven temperature to 375°F. Put one sheet on the upper rack and one on the lower rack and bake for 25 minutes, or until lightly browned.

SHORTLY BEFORE MY YOUNGER SON, MARTY, left to begin an MFA program in the South, we spent a few days at our cottage on the St. Lawrence River. Living in his own apartment for the first time, he was excited about cooking for himself, but he was dreading the limited gluten-free options in his small college town. What to do about gluten-free bread?

I developed this roll with minimum processing so that he would be able to bake his own. This is a versatile roll that works equally well as a dinner and sandwich roll. It is based on Traditional Brazilian Rolls (opposite), but bigger, with more substance. Bake them up in the evening, cool, and freeze them for the week.

Sitting on the front porch of our cottage, watching the water and horizon fade to the same deep blue, we toasted to his success and ate these rolls topped with thin slices of extra sharp Cheddar and smoked Gouda. I thought of the mother osprey atop the gigantic nest near the water, who so carefully tends to her offspring until they are ready to fledge. I knew Marty was ready to fly, but it was bittersweet. At least he has the comfort of home-baked gluten-free bread with him.

seeded dinner rolls

makes 6 rolls

2⅓ cups (330g) tapioca starch

1½ teaspoons salt

1 cup milk

½ cup canola oil

1 teaspoon toasted sesame oil

2 large eggs

1 tablespoon sesame seeds

1 tablespoon chia seeds

1 tablespoon golden flaxseeds

1. In a food processor, combine the tapioca starch and salt and pulse until blended.

2. In a medium saucepan, bring the milk, canola oil, and sesame oil to a boil, stirring constantly. Immediately pour the hot mixture into the flour and process until it is moist with a sand-like texture. Allow the dough to cool for 20 minutes.

3. Add the eggs, one at a time, and process until smooth. Blend in the sesame seeds, chia seeds, and flaxseeds. The dough will be both sticky and runny, with the consistency of pancake batter. Scoop the dough into a bowl and allow the dough to rest for 20 minutes. It will absorb more of the moisture and thicken.

4. Position an oven rack in the center of the oven and preheat to 350°F. Grease a 9 × 13-inch glass baking dish and line with parchment paper.

5. Wet a tablespoon with cold water and spoon the dough in 6 balls spaced equally in the baking dish. Use the wet spoon to shape, smooth, and round the rolls.

6. Bake for 1 hour, or until the tops are lightly browned. Let the rolls cool in the baking dish for 10 minutes, then transfer them to a cooling rack to cool. (The cooling process is almost as important as the baking process since the tapioca structure continues to develop as the rolls cool.)

AS A FAMILY WITH GLUTEN INTOLERANCE and celiac disease, we eat what we make. So, even before we determine whether a product would be profitable, we ask ourselves, "Would *we* buy this?" If the answer is "Not really," or even "Maybe," the idea is scrapped. It was through this process that we developed pumpernickel rolls, and they quickly became a favorite among our family and staff. When we made them, we looked forward to indulging in a thick Reuben Sandwich (page 380).

Frozen food aisles are the most expensive real estate in the supermarket, and staying on those shelves is a very Darwinian process. When we introduced our pizzas several years ago, we couldn't make them fast enough to keep up with demand. Customers loved the pizzas, and it wasn't long before the pizzas killed off the slower-selling pumpernickel rolls. Loyal customers have been mourning them ever since. For all of you pumpernickel fans out there these are for you. They are not exactly the same as Against The Grain's version, but they are a great substitution that can easily be made at home. They are crusty with an open crumb and a moist interior.

pumpernickel rolls

makes 6 rolls

2⅓ cups (330g) tapioca starch

2 tablespoons unsweetened cocoa powder

1 tablespoon caraway seeds

1 teaspoon salt

½ cup milk

½ cup canola oil

2 tablespoons molasses

2 large eggs

1. In a food processor, combine the tapioca starch, cocoa, caraway seeds, and salt and pulse until blended.

2. In a medium saucepan, bring the milk, canola oil, molasses, and ¼ cup water to a boil, stirring constantly. Immediately pour the hot mixture into the flour and process until it is moist with a sand-like texture. Allow the dough to cool for 20 minutes.

3. Add the eggs, one at a time, and process until smooth. The dough will be both wet and sticky. Scoop the dough into a bowl and allow the dough to rest for 20 minutes. It will absorb more of the moisture and thicken.

4. Position an oven rack in the center of the oven and preheat to 350°F. Grease a 9 × 13-inch glass baking dish and line with parchment paper.

5. Wet a tablespoon with cold water and spoon the dough in 6 balls spaced equally in the baking dish. Use the wet spoon to shape, smooth, and round the rolls.

6. Bake for 1 hour, or until the tops are lightly browned. Let the rolls cool in the baking dish for 10 minutes, then transfer them to a cooling rack to cool. (The cooling process is almost as important as the baking process since the tapioca structure continues to develop as the rolls cool.)

WHEN YOU OWN A BREAD FACTORY, you eat a lot of pizza. I'd hate to think about how many pizzas I've eaten since Against The Grain's inception. However, sometimes you want a pizza that is not really a pizza, but gives you the same comfort feeling. That's where focaccia bread comes in.

Back in my gluten days, I loved to use extra pizza dough, puffy with yeast, to make a small focaccia loaf. I dimpled the top with my fingers and drizzled garlic-infused olive oil over the surface, creating little golden puddles. Rather than the main attraction of a meal, focaccia is a perfect side to soup or a salad. And since the caramelized onions are baked on top, this keeps them from drying out and losing some of their characteristic sweetness and aroma. Like many roasted vegetables, caramelized onions are both sweet and savory. There is some debate about which onions are the sweetest—I vote for Georgia Vidalias, but any sweet onion will make an excellent topping for this focaccia. Here the caramelization is hastened by adding a tiny amount of baking soda (1/8 teaspoon). The baking soda decreases the acidity of the onions and allows them to brown faster without losing as much moisture.

caramelized onion focaccia

makes two 9-inch focaccia

FOR THE FOCACCIA:

2 cups (280g) tapioca starch

1 cup (120g) light buckwheat flour

1 teaspoon salt

1 cup milk

3 tablespoons olive oil

1 tablespoon active dry yeast

1 teaspoon sugar

1 large egg

FOR THE CARAMELIZED ONIONS:

2 tablespoons olive oil

1 medium sweet onion, thinly sliced

1/2 teaspoon salt

1/8 teaspoon baking soda

2 teaspoons chopped fresh rosemary

1. **Make the focaccia dough:** In a food processor, combine the tapioca starch, buckwheat flour, and salt and pulse until blended.

2. In a medium saucepan, bring the milk and oil to a boil, stirring constantly. Immediately pour the hot mixture into the dry mixture and process until it is moist with a sand-like texture. Allow the dough to cool for 20 minutes.

3. Meanwhile, in a small bowl, combine the yeast, sugar, and 1/3 cup warm water and allow it to proof for 15 minutes.

4. Add the yeast mixture and egg to the dough and blend until it is smooth. Scoop the dough into a large bowl, cover it with plastic wrap, and let it rise in a warm area until doubled, typically about 1 hour.

recipe continues

5. While the dough rises, make the caramelized onions: In a 12-inch skillet, heat the oil over medium heat. Add the sliced onions, salt, and baking soda and cook until just browned. Set the skillet aside.

6. Position an oven rack in the center of the oven and preheat to 400°F.

7. Grease two 9-inch round cake pans and line each with a round of parchment paper. Punch down the dough with a rubber spatula and divide it in half. With wet hands, shape each dough half into a mound, and place each one in a cake pan. Press the dough evenly into the pan. Wet your fingers and press them lightly into the tops of the mounds to create depressions. Top each mound with the caramelized onions (including any of the onion cooking oil), spreading them over the top and into the depressions. Sprinkle the chopped rosemary over the top. Allow the dough to rise uncovered for 45 minutes, or until it is puffy. It will not rise a lot with the oil and the weight of the onions.

8. Bake the focaccia for 30 minutes, or until browned and fragrant. Transfer the focaccia from the pans to a cooling rack to cool completely.

MY LOVE AFFAIR WITH BREAD began in New Orleans. I grew up on the modern conveniences of white sandwich bread, and Sunday dinner fare was pop-and-serve crescent rolls. I landed in New Orleans as a college freshman and felt like I was an exchange student in a foreign country.

When I ventured out into the French Quarter, I found the Central Grocery, an Old World Italian grocery store. I discovered its world-famous muffuletta sandwich, set on a round, relatively flat Italian loaf, and it awakened a palate I didn't know existed—for real bread. Some people remember their college years fondly for the academic challenges or just the thrill of coming-of-age. Among the things that I remember most fondly was the heritage and unique cuisine of New Orleans, particularly the bread.

For years, I tried to make gluten-free versions of French and muffuletta bread. New Orleans bread has a thin, crisp crust that crinkles when it cools, and a soft, airy interior. The distinct balance of crust and crumb is hard to match, and many speculate that baking it below sea level creates just the right temperature and humidity conditions. Although it has a crust reminiscent of peasant bread or *pane rustica*, the crumb is light and filled with air bubbles. This isn't quite New Orleans muffuletta bread, but it is well worth the effort.

rustic boule

makes 3 to 4 boules

2½ cups (350g) tapioca starch

½ cup (60g) light buckwheat flour

1½ teaspoons salt

1 cup milk

½ cup canola oil

1 tablespoon yeast

1 teaspoon sugar

2 large eggs

2 teaspoons baking powder

2 teaspoons cider vinegar

1. Position an oven rack in the center of the oven and preheat to 325°F. Grease four round 4½-inch mini springform pans or soufflé dishes (or three 6-inch pans).

2. In a food processor, blend the tapioca starch, buckwheat flour, and salt.

3. In a medium saucepan, bring the milk and oil to a boil, stirring constantly. Immediately pour the hot mixture into the dry mixture and process until it is moist with a sand-like texture. Allow the dough to cool for 20 minutes.

4. Meanwhile, in a small bowl, combine the yeast, sugar, and ⅓ cup warm water and allow it to proof for 15 minutes.

5. Add the yeast mixture to the dough and process until it is thick and creamy. Add the eggs and blend, then add the baking powder and vinegar.

6. Scoop the dough equally into the prepared pans. Bake for 60 minutes, or until the boules are lightly browned and sound hollow when tapped. Transfer to a cooling rack and immediately remove from the pans. Allow the boules to cool fully before slicing.

ONE OF THE CAREERS I HAD pre–Against The Grain was as a real estate agent selling properties near Mt. Snow in West Dover, Vermont. It was a pretty crazy time, just as the Internet was becoming a real estate agent's most useful tool. I knew the world was changing when I sold a 10-acre parcel I'd never seen to someone whom I had never met. There was a lot of prospecting, and waiting, and e-mailing, and occasionally viewing new properties on the market.

But one of the only reasons I did that job for several years was lunch: Every day the broker and I would make the short walk across Route 100 to a small bakery that sold ciabatta bread, a bit bigger than a roll but smaller than a loaf. It was rustic with a crisp, but chewy crust that you had to tear into, and with a spongy crumb with just the right amount of holes. We asked the baker how he made it, and he told us it was complicated and took 2 days. I now know why, after trying to make a gluten-free version. This is a wet dough that produces the rustic, open crumb and chewy texture. It is a bit harder to work with, but it produces a unique roll unlike any other gluten-free bread. And the baker was right, it takes 2 days to produce.

ciabatta bread

makes four 5-inch loaves

2 cups (280g) tapioca starch

1 cup (120g) light buckwheat flour, plus ½ cup (60g) for kneading

1 teaspoon salt

1 cup milk

3 tablespoons canola oil

2 teaspoons active dry yeast

1 teaspoon sugar

1. In a food processor, combine the tapioca starch, 1 cup buckwheat flour, and the salt and pulse until blended.

2. In a medium saucepan, bring the milk and oil to a boil, stirring constantly. Immediately pour the hot mixture into the dry mixture and process until it is moist with a sand-like texture. Allow the dough to cool for 20 minutes.

3. Meanwhile, in a small bowl, combine the yeast, sugar, and ⅓ cup warm water and allow it to proof for 15 minutes.

4. Add the yeast mixture to the dough and process until it is smooth and creamy. It will have a very liquid, batter-like texture. Scoop the dough into a large bowl, cover it with plastic wrap, and refrigerate overnight.

5. Remove the dough from the refrigerator and use a wet rubber spatula to scrape it out of the bowl. Wet your hands slightly and use your hands to form the dough into a compact ball. Sprinkle it with the remaining ½ cup buckwheat flour and knead all of the flour into the dough until it is smooth.

6. Divide the dough into 2 balls, then divide those to make a total of 4 balls. Place them at least 2 inches apart on a well-greased baking sheet. Cover the dough with well-buttered or -oiled plastic wrap and let it rise until each loaf is doubled in size. (This may take 2 to 3 hours, as the dough has to warm up to room temperature before rising. As the dough rises, the high ratio of liquid to flour will make the ciabatta flatten and spread into 5-inch-diameter rounded loaves.)

7. Position an oven rack in the center of the oven and preheat to 400°F. Remove the plastic wrap and bake the loaves for 35 to 40 minutes, or until crusty. (Like wheat-based ciabatta, the loaves tend to brown less than traditional loaves.)

8. Transfer the loaves to a cooling rack and allow them to cool thoroughly before serving. During the cooling process, the interior texture will transform from slightly gummy to a chewy, open crumb.

variation

savory herb and artichoke ciabatta bread

After step 5, add a 6-ounce jar of artichokes, drained and chopped, 2 teaspoons chopped fresh marjoram, and 1 tablespoon chopped fresh rosemary. Then proceed with dividing the dough into balls before rising.

A LOT HAS BEEN WRITTEN about the positive benefits of a family dinner on the well-being of adolescents. When I was growing up in the fifties and sixties, Sunday dinner was an elaborate affair, a time when my dad could test out some new gourmet recipe or technique. But one thing was a constant: a bowl of pickles, celery, carrot sticks, and olives. Perhaps on behalf of my sister, who has always had an insatiable appetite for olives, we had an unstated rule that each person could have only three olives. Once when a dinner guest reached for the olive bowl, one of my siblings blurted out, "You know you can only have three olives." Taken aback, he promptly withdrew his hand and we all had a good laugh. There's nothing like rationing to make something ordinary seem really special. To this day, I love all types of olives in salads, on pizzas, in lasagna, and just about anywhere else I can slip them in.

In this flatbread, kalamata olives star as both the garnish and for the comforting flavor they impart to the bread. This bread is meant as a side to soup or salad, but it could just as easily be dressed up as a rustic pizza or focaccia with the addition of marinated artichokes, roasted red peppers, or slices of fresh mozzarella.

olive flatbread

makes 1 large flatbread

1¼ cups (150g) light buckwheat flour

½ cup (50g) oat flour

1 cup (140g) tapioca starch

1 teaspoon minced garlic

1 teaspoon salt

¼ cup olive oil, plus more for drizzling

1 tablespoon active dry yeast

1 tablespoon honey

2 large eggs

½ cup large kalamata olives, pitted and halved

1 tablespoon chopped fresh rosemary

1. Position an oven rack in the center of the oven and preheat to 375°F. Line a baking sheet with parchment paper (or grease an oval baking dish).

2. In a food processor, combine the buckwheat flour, oat flour, tapioca starch, garlic, and salt and pulse until blended.

3. In a medium saucepan, bring the olive oil and ¾ cup water to a boil, stirring constantly. Immediately pour the hot mixture into the flours and process until it is moist with a sand-like texture. Allow the dough to cool for 20 minutes.

4. Meanwhile, in a small bowl, combine the yeast, honey, and ¼ cup warm water and allow it to proof for 15 minutes. Add the yeast mixture to the cooled dough and blend until combined. Add the eggs and blend until smooth and creamy.

5. Spread the dough evenly, ½ to ¾ inch thick, on the baking sheet (or spread the dough in the baking dish). Arrange the olives in an attractive pattern on top of the dough, pressing each olive lightly into the dough. Scatter the rosemary over the dough and lightly drizzle more olive oil over the top.

6. Bake the flatbread for 35 minutes, or until it is lightly browned. Transfer to a cooling rack.

quick breads,
breakfast foods,
and muffins

BANANA BREAD IS A COMFORT FOOD. Today, more than ever, people are seeking familiar foods and flavors. Ask the experts who follow trends, and they will tell you that the principal flavors that evoke nostalgia are banana, coconut, and chocolate. This banana bread has all three, and they positively sing when made into banana bread. When I developed this recipe, I brought it to work and served it to our staff. I wasn't prepared for having to swat away hands that were grabbing for seconds before everyone could get a taste. The cutting board was empty within seconds, and several people remarked that they didn't even like banana bread, but wanted more.

I understand their sentiment. I don't really view banana bread as comfort food, but it was when I strayed from the traditional banana bread recipe—bananas, sugar, flour, butter, and eggs—that I fell in love with it. This recipe doesn't scream "bananas." Rather, the strong flavors of coconut and banana work together to create an entirely different flavor profile. The chocolate chips only highlight that flavor. This is a healthy banana bread, naturally sweetened by the bananas and coconut with very little added sugar.

chocolate chip banana bread

makes one 8-inch loaf

3 ripe medium bananas

1/2 teaspoon salt

1/2 cup sugar

1/4 cup canola oil

3 large eggs

1/4 cup full-fat coconut milk

1/2 cup (56g) coconut flour

1/2 cup (70g) tapioca starch

1/2 teaspoon ground cinnamon

1/2 teaspoon ground cardamom

1 teaspoon baking powder

1/2 teaspoon baking soda

1 teaspoon vanilla extract

3/4 cup dairy-free mini chocolate chips (such as Enjoy Life)

1. Position a rack in the center of the oven and preheat to 350°F. Grease a 4 1/2 × 8-inch loaf pan.

2. In a small bowl, mash the bananas and salt with a fork. Set aside.

3. In a large bowl, combine the sugar, oil, and eggs. Beat with a hand mixer for 3 minutes. Add the mashed banana and coconut milk.

4. In a medium bowl, blend the coconut flour, tapioca starch, and spices and gradually add them to the egg mixture. Beat with a hand mixer for 2 more minutes, making sure to scrape down the sides. Allow the batter to rest for 5 minutes to let the coconut flour absorb the liquid.

5. Add the baking powder, baking soda, and vanilla to the batter, mixing them thoroughly. Fold in the chocolate chips.

6. Spoon the batter into the loaf pan. The batter will come to about 1 inch below the rim. Bake for 60 to 70 minutes, or until the top is firm and the crust is browned.

PEOPLE WHO KNOW ME LAUGH when I tell them I danced ballet for seven years, since grace has never been associated with my name. For my last year of classes at age 13, my sister and I were cast as soloists in the *Pied Piper of Hamelin*. One evening we stayed late practicing at our ballet teacher's house, and since it was late, she invited us to eat dinner with her and her family. The entire meal was a huge hunk of warm gingerbread topped with cream of mushroom soup. It was probably the strangest dinner I had ever eaten. It sounded yucky, but being a polite (and ravenous) young girl, I smiled and ate it. Much to my surprise, it was delicious.

I never forgot that home-made gingerbread. But honestly, it tastes a lot better topped with Triple Sec–flavored whipped cream instead of mushroom soup. This gingerbread was inspired by Ina Garten's Old-Fashioned Gingerbread recipe, but given a tropical twist with coconut flour and raisins soaked in orange juice. This makes for a moist, rich, intensely gingery gingerbread.

orange gingerbread

makes one 10-inch Bundt cake

½ cup orange juice

½ cup golden raisins

1 cup (112g) coconut flour

½ cup (70g) tapioca starch

½ cup powdered sugar

1 teaspoon baking powder

½ teaspoon baking soda

2 teaspoons ground ginger

1 teaspoon ground cinnamon

½ teaspoon ground cloves

¾ cup dark molasses

½ cup sour cream

¼ cup canola oil

2 teaspoons grated orange zest, plus 1 teaspoon for serving

3 large eggs

½ teaspoon salt

Triple Sec Whipped Cream (recipe follows)

1. Position an oven rack in the center of the oven and preheat to 350°F. Grease a 10-inch Bundt or tube pan.

2. In a small saucepan, combine the orange juice and golden raisins, bring to a boil, and turn off the heat. Set aside to let the raisins absorb the liquid.

3. In a medium bowl, whisk together the coconut flour, tapioca starch, powdered sugar, baking powder, baking soda, and spices until fully blended.

4. In a large bowl, combine the molasses, sour cream, oil, the 2 teaspoons orange zest, eggs, and salt. With a hand mixer, beat the mixture until it is fully blended and foamy.

5. Add the dry mixture to the wet mixture and beat until fully moistened. Pour off any excess liquid from the raisins before folding them into the batter. Allow the batter to sit for 10 minutes to let the coconut flour absorb the liquid. The batter will thicken considerably.

recipe continues

6. Pour the batter into the Bundt pan and tap the pan lightly on the counter to make sure that the batter is evenly distributed in the bottom of the pan.

7. Bake for 40 minutes, or until the top springs back when pressed. Allow the gingerbread to cool in the pan for 10 minutes before inverting it onto a cake plate. Allow it to cool fully for neat and clean slices before cutting. Serve with a generous dollop of Triple Sec Whipped Cream and sprinkle with 1 teaspoon orange zest.

triple sec whipped cream · makes 1 cup

1 cup heavy (whipping) cream

2½ teaspoons sugar

1 tablespoon Triple Sec liqueur

In a medium bowl, with a hand mixer, whip the cream until it is thickened and stiff peaks are about to form. Add the sugar and Triple Sec. Beat until stiff peaks form. Do not overbeat, or it will lose some of its loft.

I FAVOR WORKING WITH SEEDS over nuts—although I love the taste nuts deliver, we run a nut-free facility, so I have naturally gravitated toward baking with seeds. I've been amazed by their properties and I often use pumpkin seeds instead of walnuts in baked goods. When I first developed this recipe, I left the nuts out, but I felt it needed a little more texture and crunch. About that time, we were playing around at work with roasting pepitas (hulled pumpkin seeds), and one of our workers, Harry, mentioned that his brother made authentic Jamaican jerk, a spicy concoction of scallions, habanero pepper, allspice, thyme, nutmeg, and sugar. Then it occurred to me that sweet and spicy pepitas would be the perfect complement to the pumpkin bread. Before I knew it, I had sweet and spicy pepitas, which Harry had prepared by soaking them in a Jamaican jerk and sugar solution before roasting them.

This is a perfect fall recipe to make from scratch with a small pie pumpkin, and you can either buy spicy pepitas or make your own. The addition of coconut flour adds a natural sweetener and makes a very moist, low-fat loaf with plenty of fiber and flavor.

pumpkin bread with sweet and spicy pepitas

makes one 8-inch loaf

½ cup (60g) light buckwheat flour

½ cup (70g) tapioca starch

½ cup (56g) coconut flour

½ teaspoon salt

½ teaspoon ground cinnamon

½ teaspoon ground allspice

¼ teaspoon freshly grated nutmeg

½ teaspoon ground ginger

¼ teaspoon ground cloves

½ cup packed brown sugar

½ cup honey

½ cup canola oil

2 large eggs

1 15-oz can canned unsweetened pumpkin puree (or home-roasted and pureed fresh pumpkin)

1 teaspoon baking soda

1 cup spicy roasted pepitas (hulled pumpkin seeds), coarsely chopped

1. Position an oven rack in the center of the oven and preheat to 350°F. Generously grease a 4½ × 8-inch loaf pan.

2. In a large bowl, whisk together the buckwheat flour, tapioca starch, coconut flour, salt, and spices and set aside.

3. In another large bowl, combine the brown sugar, honey, oil, and eggs. Using a hand mixer, beat until frothy. Add the pumpkin puree and ¼ cup water and beat until well blended.

4. Add the flour mixture to the wet ingredients and beat until all the dry ingredients are fully incorporated. As the coconut flour absorbs moisture, the batter will thicken. Add the baking soda and beat for another minute. Fold in the pepitas.

5. Spoon the batter into the pan and bake for 1 hour 15 minutes, or until a toothpick in the center comes out clean.

ZUCCHINIS, FOR SOME REASON, flourish in Vermont, while we struggle to have our tomatoes ripen before the first fall frost. Tender, freshly picked zucchini is definitely a summer treat. Thankfully I'm no longer intimidated by the summer's bounty because I've discovered that zucchini makes fabulous bread and freezes well. What a joy to have a little piece of the Vermont summer in the dead of winter.

The inspiration for this bread came from a bumper crop of carrots in addition to zucchini. The addition of carrots allows you to bump up the nutritional and fiber profile of the bread with a whopping 420 grams of veggies—that makes one-quarter of the weight of each loaf purely fresh vegetables. And unlike many other zucchini breads that are often half sugar, the carrots add natural sweetness without being overly sweet. The honey and sour cream hold in the moisture, and the raisins and crystallized ginger add a great burst of sweetness in every bite. This recipe makes 2 loaves: one for eating and one for freezing or sharing with a neighbor.

zucchini carrot bread

---

makes two 8-inch loaves

1½ cups (210g) tapioca starch

1¾ cups (210g) light buckwheat flour

1 teaspoon ground cinnamon

1 teaspoon ground ginger

½ teaspoon freshly grated nutmeg

¼ teaspoon ground cloves

1 cup packed brown sugar

1½ teaspoons baking soda

4 large eggs

1 cup sour cream

⅓ cup canola oil

¼ cup honey

1 teaspoon vanilla extract

2½ cups grated zucchini, drained and dried

1 cup finely grated carrots

½ cup raisins

½ cup chopped crystallized ginger

1. Position an oven rack in the center of the oven and preheat to 350°F. Grease two 4½ × 8-inch loaf pans and line with parchment paper.

2. In a large bowl, blend the tapioca starch, buckwheat flour, spices, brown sugar, and baking soda.

3. Add the eggs, sour cream, oil, honey, and vanilla. With a hand mixer, beat the mixture well until it is light and foamy. Add the grated zucchini and carrots, then the raisins and crystallized ginger. Blend well. Spoon the batter into the loaf pans.

4. Bake for 55 minutes to 1 hour, or until the tops of the loaves spring back when touched and a toothpick inserted in the center of the top comes out clean. Let the loaves cool in the pans for 15 minutes before attempting to remove them from the pans. Transfer to a cooling rack. Let the loaves cool thoroughly before slicing.

ONCE I STARTED making various types of gluten-free bread, others that I hadn't thought of in years came to mind. Brioche was one of those that I viewed as a challenge. Gluten is a huge component of the bread, and developing the right amount of elasticity makes the difference between a delicate, buttery bread and a dense blob. Brioche is a very wet dough that produces something between a bread and a pastry, and it is all about the tender, buttery texture. Was it possible to create a gluten-free version? I love a challenge, and this one *was* a challenge.

Honestly, in none of the steps did my brioche seem anything like what wheat bakers described until I refrigerated the dough overnight, a step I followed after reading that chilling a rich dough is the secret to being able to manipulate it. It was still sticky, but with wet hands I could divide it into individual brioche pans . . . barely. Bravely, I soldiered on. But, oh my gosh, did it emerge from the oven with a heavenly scent and a tender, buttery crumb. Whereas wheat-based brioche recipes are all about technique, this one seems more about faith.

brioche

makes 8 individual brioches

1 cup (120g) light buckwheat flour

3/4 cup (105g) tapioca starch

2 tablespoons milk

2 large eggs

1 teaspoon salt

2 tablespoons sugar

1 tablespoon active dry yeast

8 tablespoons cold salted butter, cut into cubes

1. In a food processor, combine the buckwheat flour, tapioca starch, milk, eggs, salt, sugar, yeast, and 2 tablespoons water. Process the dough until it is well blended.

2. A little at a time, add the cold butter. Process the mixture as little as possible until it is smooth and has the consistency of cake icing. Transfer the dough to a large bowl, cover it with plastic wrap, and allow it to rise for 1 hour. Punch it down using a dampened rubber spatula, cover it, and refrigerate it overnight.

3. Grease 8 individual 3-inch brioche molds with salted butter. (Buttered ramekins or flan pans may be used instead of brioche molds.) Remove the dough from the refrigerator and divide it into 8 equal balls and place each ball in a brioche mold.

4. Place the filled molds in a baking pan with 2-inch sides. Cover the pan with buttered plastic wrap and let rise for about 1 hour, or until the dough almost entirely fills the mold.

5. Meanwhile, position an oven rack in the center of the oven and preheat to 375°F.

6. Bake the brioche for 20 minutes, or until the tops are golden brown. Transfer to a cooling rack.

WHAT WE KNOW OF AS BISCUITS TODAY have some very interesting origins as hardtack, an extremely dry, often quadruple-baked biscuit. I once accompanied kids on a field trip to a museum where the docent made authentic hardtack for the kids to try. The whole room was filled with kids squirming and giggling as they tried the chalky mass. Historically, hardtack was kept extremely dry to keep it from spoiling on long voyages at sea. Ironically, hardtack softens as it ages, while gluten-free biscuits often are already, or become, hardtack. But not these biscuits.

These biscuits have more in common with rolls than they do hardtack. They are leavened with a combination of yeast and chemical leavening agents (both baking soda and baking powder), which makes them both fluffy with an open crumb and biscuit-like at the same time. The sour cream tenderizes the biscuits, and its acidity cools the effect of the jalapeños. The cheese adds protein that strengthens the structure, while moisturizing the biscuits and giving them a satisfying mouthfeel. These biscuits are great served warm alongside a meal or used to sandwich thin slices of ham and cheese.

jalapeño and cheese biscuits

makes 16 biscuits

1 tablespoon active dry yeast

1 tablespoon sugar

⅓ cup warm milk plus ¼ cup cold milk

1¼ cups (150g) light buckwheat flour

1 cup (140g) tapioca starch

1 tablespoon baking powder

¾ teaspoon baking soda

4 tablespoons cold salted butter, cut into pieces

4 ounces cream cheese, cut into pieces

1 tablespoon cider vinegar

1 cup shredded Parmesan cheese

½ cup shredded sharp Cheddar cheese

¼ cup canned diced green chilies or 2 tablespoons chopped fresh jalapeños

1. In a small bowl, combine the yeast, sugar, and ⅓ cup warm milk and allow it to proof for 15 minutes.

2. In a food processor, combine the buckwheat flour, tapioca starch, baking powder, and baking soda and pulse the mixture until well blended. Add the butter and cream cheese and pulse just until the mixture is a coarse meal. Add the yeast mixture and pulse to combine.

3. Add the remaining ¼ cup cold milk, the vinegar, cheeses, and chilies or jalapeños. Pulse until the dough comes together. Transfer the dough to a large bowl, cover with plastic wrap, and allow it to rest for 20 minutes.

4. Meanwhile, position an oven rack in the center of the oven and preheat to 400°F. Grease two 9-inch round cake pans with salted butter.

5. Turn the dough out onto a piece of plastic wrap dusted with tapioca starch. Pat the dough down with wet hands until it is about 3/4 inch thick. Use a juice glass dusted with tapioca starch to cut out biscuits 2 inches in diameter. Reroll the scraps as necessary. Transfer the biscuits to the cake pans so that they will touch as they rise and expand.

6. Bake the biscuits for 15 minutes, or until lightly browned. Transfer to a cooling rack or serve warm.

variation

Try adding 2 teaspoons of smoked chipotle powder instead of the green chilies, and substitute Gruyère cheese for the Cheddar cheese.

THE REST OF THE COUNTRY associates maple syrup with Vermont. We associate maple syrup with mud season, when Vermont's unpaved roads turn into muddy quagmires, not unlike some gluten-free doughs. Almost sixty percent of Vermont's roads remain unpaved, so negotiating mud season is a big deal around here. I sort of enjoy slogging along the road and experiencing firsthand the earth waking up. Maple buckets are affixed to trees along our road, and when the syrup flows, the constant dripping pings into buckets. Gnarled burls, now 15 to 20 feet in the air, mark where taps once hung and remind us that this activity has been going on for over a hundred years.

And of course, no spring is complete without stopping by a local sugarhouse while they are boiling syrup. You leave the sugarhouse with the sweet, smoky smell of the condensation in your clothes, and a jug of fresh maple syrup under your arm. In Vermont, maple syrup isn't just for pancakes, it is for baking, glazing, marinating, and sweetening everything from coffee to cocktails. These biscuits are a perfect breakfast food or accompaniment to a big warm bowl of chili on a damp spring evening.

maple toasted oat biscuits

---

makes 16 biscuits

FOR THE MAPLE CRUMBLE TOPPING:

¼ cup maple syrup

¼ cup packed brown sugar

2 tablespoons tapioca starch

2 tablespoons salted butter, melted

FOR THE BISCUITS:

1 tablespoon active dry yeast

1 tablespoon maple syrup

⅓ cup warm milk plus ¼ cup cold milk

1½ cups (150g) toasted oat flour (see Note)

1 cup (140g) tapioca starch

1 tablespoon baking powder

1 teaspoon baking soda

1 teaspoon salt

4 tablespoons cold salted butter, cut into pieces

4 ounces cream cheese, cut into pieces

1 tablespoon cider vinegar

1. **Make the maple crumble topping:** In a small bowl, combine the maple syrup, brown sugar, tapioca starch, and melted butter and work it until the mixture is well blended. Set aside.

2. **Make the biscuits:** In a small bowl, combine the yeast, maple syrup, and the ⅓ cup warm milk and allow it to proof for 15 minutes.

3. In a food processor, combine the toasted oat flour, tapioca starch, baking powder, baking soda, and salt and pulse until combined. Add the butter and cream cheese and pulse just until the mixture is a coarse meal. Add the yeast mixture and pulse to combine.

4. Add the remaining ¼ cup cold milk and the vinegar, and pulse until the dough comes together. Transfer the dough to a large bowl, cover with plastic wrap, and allow it to rest for 20 minutes.

5. Meanwhile, position an oven rack in the center of the oven and preheat to 400°F. Grease two 9-inch round cake pans with salted butter.

6. Turn the dough out onto a piece of plastic wrap dusted with tapioca starch. Pat the dough down with wet hands until it is about ¾ inch thick. Use a juice glass dusted with tapioca starch to cut out biscuits 2 inches in diameter. Reroll the scraps as necessary.

7. Transfer the biscuits to the cake pans so that they will touch as they rise and expand. Sprinkle/spread the tops of the biscuits with the maple crumble topping.

8. Bake the biscuits for 15 minutes, or until lightly browned. Transfer to a cooling rack or serve warm.

NOTE: Toasted oat flour is even more flavorful than plain oat flour. Start with rolled oats, toast them for 12 minutes at 375°F on a baking sheet, and grind them into flour.

HONESTLY, THE FIRST TIME I ever baked scones was as a gluten-free recipe. I had tried again and again to perfect a light and moist biscuit: They became a mouthful of crumbles, spread into flat cookies, or were better suited as croquet balls. The problem was how to support tender dough—not easy without gluten to shore it up. Then I discovered that the shape of a big flattened ball of dough cut into 6 or 8 wedges was ideally suited to gluten-free baking. Typically with wheat-based recipes, the disk would be rolled to a thickness of 1 inch or so, but to compensate for the lack of gluten, these scones are rolled out into a thickness of 1½ inches. The wedges, separated from each other by ½ inch, are close enough to support each other as they rise in the oven. So long before I got biscuits "right," I was making savory scones.

There are many varieties of scones, but most recipes rely on chemical leavening agents like baking powder and baking soda as well as butter and cream. Much like making a pie crust, the trick is to not overmix the dough. It should be loose enough so that it remains tender as it bakes, but sufficiently moistened so it doesn't crumble when you look at it. Scones are also baked at a

bacon-parmesan scones

---

makes 6 to 8 scones

---

1 cup (140g) tapioca starch

1¼ cups (150g) light buckwheat flour

2 teaspoons baking powder

½ teaspoon baking soda

8 tablespoons cold salted butter, cut into pieces

5 slices cooked crisp bacon, cut into 1-inch pieces

¾ cup shredded (not grated) Parmesan cheese

1 cup sour cream

1 large egg

1 tablespoon honey, warmed (optional)

1. In a food processor, combine the tapioca starch, buckwheat flour, baking powder, and baking soda and pulse until they are well blended. Add the butter and pulse a few times to just cut it into the flour.

2. Add the bacon and Parmesan and pulse several times to distribute it in the dough. Add the sour cream and egg, pulsing it just until there are large, semi-wet crumbs.

3. Position an oven rack in the center of the oven and preheat to 425°F. Line a baking sheet with parchment paper and dust it with tapioca starch.

4. Gather the dough with your hands and dump it out into a pile on the baking sheet. Lightly work and pat the dough into a 1½-inch-thick disk, flattening the top and smoothing the edges. Lightly dust the dough with tapioca starch, if necessary, to handle the dough without it sticking.

5. With a large knife, cut the disk into 6 or 8 wedges and gently transfer them to a 12-inch cast iron skillet. (If you so desire,

brush the tops lightly with the warmed honey to create a darker crust.)

6. Bake the scones for 20 minutes, or until lightly browned. For crusty scones, cool them in the skillet. For a tender crust, transfer the scones to a cooling rack and cover them with a clean kitchen towel to let the heat and moisture soften the crust. Allow the scones to cool enough for the dough to set, but serve warm.

higher temperature than most gluten-free baked goods so the dough sets quickly, forms a crust, and seals in a moist interior crumb. These savory scones are perfect for breakfast or as a side to a salad, soup, or stew. The bacon and Parmesan are paired to create a strong, salty flavor that blends well with the doughy interior.

WE FIRST INTRODUCED OUR PRODUCTS directly to consumers through gluten-free expos, celiac support groups, and celiac food fairs. In the early years, it seemed as though either Tom or I was on the road at least once a week, lugging huge coolers packed with frozen bread and pizzas through airports. It was a Johnny Appleseed approach—we put all of our marketing dollars into meeting consumers face-to-face. One of the first requests we got for marketing materials was for bumper stickers. We had several types made, and for one of them we picked up the quote (from Oscar Wilde) that had been on the production floor since the beginning: *When the gods wish to punish us, they answer our prayers.* Some people scratch their heads when they read it. Others, once they have found our products, get it because they now realize they will always have tasty bread and pizza to tempt them.

These doughnuts are definitely a *When the gods wish to punish us* recipe. I thought about calling them "scary" doughnuts because they are frighteningly easy to make, and even easier to eat one . . . or three. The doughnuts were inspired by Spudnuts® doughnuts, which were sold at a chain founded in the 1940s by two brothers. At its peak, there were 350 doughnut shops that made doughnuts based on dehydrated potatoes

tater doughnuts with silky chocolate glaze

makes 8 doughnuts

FOR THE DOUGHNUTS:

1 cup milk

8 tablespoons salted butter

1 cup (192g) potato starch

¼ cup granulated sugar

1 teaspoon baking powder

½ teaspoon freshly grated nutmeg

½ teaspoon salt

1 teaspoon vanilla extract

3 large eggs

3 cups solid shortening, for frying

FOR THE CHOCOLATE GLAZE:

1½ cups powdered sugar

2 tablespoons unsweetened cocoa powder

¼ teaspoon salt

3 tablespoons milk

1 tablespoon canola oil

2 tablespoons rainbow nonpareil sprinkles (optional)

1. **Make the doughnuts:** In a medium saucepan, bring the milk and butter to a boil.

2. In a small bowl, stir together the potato starch, granulated sugar, baking powder, nutmeg, salt, and vanilla and pour the mixture into the saucepan. Keep stirring the dough until it pulls away from the sides of the pan, 1 to 2 minutes. Remove it from the heat.

3. Transfer the dough to a large bowl and beat it with a hand mixer until cool to the touch. Add the eggs, one at a time, scraping down the sides of the bowl as you go. It will be clumpy

recipe continues

and milk solids (their recipe included some wheat as well). Any baked good based on a nonwheat source always gets my attention. It had never occurred to me to make a potato doughnut, and I was astonished at how well potato starch works in this recipe. Note: It is hard to believe that puffy, tender doughnuts can easily be made from a single grain-free starch, but one taste of these melt-in-your-mouth doughnuts will have you making them way too often.

and bumpy and look like solidified scrambled eggs, which is what it should look like.

4. In a deep fryer, heat the shortening to 375°F.

5. Divide the dough into 8 pieces. Wet your hands and roll each piece into a ball just about the size of a billiard ball. Flatten the ball down in the palm of your hand like a burger until it is 2½ to 3 inches wide—not too thin. Poke the center with your forefinger, then use your wet thumb to hollow out the center. At this point, it will look like a big, thick pineapple ring.

6. Drop the doughnuts, one or two at a time into the fryer. The doughnuts will first sink, then float, at which time, flip them over with tongs. Turn the doughnuts every 2 minutes or so for about 10 minutes total cooking time. Use tongs to remove them from the fryer and place them on a plate lined with paper towels to drain.

7. **Make the glaze:** In a bowl, combine all the glaze ingredients and whisk together until smooth. (Warming it slightly in a microwave for 15 seconds will make it even easier to apply.)

8. When the doughnuts are mostly cool, dip the doughnut tops in the glaze and allow them to partially dry before adding the sprinkles (if using).

I GREW UP IN THE SOUTH where doughnuts rule, Krispy Kreme Doughnuts in particular. Founded in North Carolina in the late thirties, Krispy Kreme developed a truly unique product and actually trademarked "original glazed" as a part of their logo. They by no means make the only good glazed doughnut: You haven't yet tasted these, which also happen to be naturally gluten-free. The concept behind these doughnuts came from my lukewarm feeling about gluten-free cake doughnuts. They've always been tasty enough, but in a cupcake- or muffin-like way. I wanted something more melt-in-your-mouth and squishy—a doughnut so good that you had a hard time eating only one. The search for ingredients and process led me to yeasted doughnuts. I know I have a winner when my family asks me over and over again to make just one more batch.

glazed yeast doughnuts

makes 8 doughnuts

FOR THE DOUGHNUTS:

2 cups (280g) tapioca starch, plus ¾ cup (105g) for kneading

¾ cup (90g) light buckwheat flour

½ cup powdered sugar

1 teaspoon salt

1 cup milk

3 tablespoons salted butter

1 tablespoon active dry yeast

1 teaspoon granulated sugar

1 large egg

3 cups solid shortening, for frying

FOR THE GLAZE:

2 tablespoons salted butter

2 cups powdered sugar

2 teaspoons vanilla extract

1. **Make the doughnuts:** In a food processor, combine the 2 cups tapioca starch, the buckwheat flour, powdered sugar, and salt and pulse until blended.

2. In a medium saucepan, bring the milk and butter to a boil, stirring constantly. Immediately pour the hot mixture into the flours and process until it is moist with a sand-like texture. Allow the dough to cool for 20 minutes.

3. Meanwhile, in a small bowl, combine the yeast, granulated sugar, and ⅓ cup warm water and allow it to proof for 15 minutes.

4. Add the yeast mixture to the cooled dough. Blend until the dough is combined, then add the egg. Pulse the dough until it is smooth and creamy. It will have a thick, batter-like texture.

5. Scoop the dough into a large bowl, cover it with plastic wrap, and refrigerate overnight. It will rise and double in bulk.

recipe continues

6. Remove the dough from the refrigerator and knead it in the bowl with a rubber spatula until the dough is smooth. It will be on the runny side. By hand, knead in up to about 3/4 cup of tapioca starch, a little at a time—just until you can handle the dough and cut out doughnut shapes.

7. In a deep fryer, heat the shortening until it reaches 375°F.

8. Turn the dough out onto a piece of plastic wrap dusted with tapioca starch. Pat it into a 1/2-inch thickness. Dust a doughnut cutter by dipping it in tapioca starch (or use a glass and your thumb to create a hole). Cut out 2 1/2-inch doughnuts. (You can fry the doughnut holes if you like!)

9. One or two at a time, fry the doughnuts until they are lightly browned, turning each doughnut with tongs after it floats. Transfer the doughnuts to paper towels to drain.

10. **Make the glaze:** In a small bowl, whisk the butter, powdered sugar, vanilla, and 1/4 cup hot water together until the butter melts and the glaze is smooth.

11. While the doughnuts are still warm, dip the doughnut tops in the glaze and set aside to dry.

NO TRIP TO NEW ORLEANS is complete without a trip to Café du Monde in the French Quarter. When I went to school in New Orleans, trips to Café du Monde in the middle of the night were an exam-week ritual. Where else could you go at 3 a.m. for chicory coffee and a plate of puffy fried doughnuts smothered in powdered sugar to tank up for your exam the next morning?

There is a lot of debate about what constitutes an authentic beignet. Beignets are essentially square pieces of fried dough. Some believe true beignets use yeast as the leavening agent. Others (like me) say beignets aren't "real" beignets unless they rise from the steam created by the dough. Traditional choux pastry contains butter, water, wheat flour, and eggs, making for a high-moisture dough that creates steam and puffs the pastry. This beignet recipe is a variation on choux pastry, and it is leavened beautifully by steam. The additional tapioca starch required to roll out the dough is added after the dough has been refrigerated overnight. I'm not sure we'll be seeing gluten-free beignets in New Orleans any time soon, but in the meantime, these beignets have the look, taste, texture, and smell of the real thing.

beignets

makes 9 beignets

2⅓ cups (330g) tapioca starch, plus ½ cup (70g) for kneading

1 teaspoon salt

1 cup milk

½ cup canola oil

2 large eggs

3 cups vegetable oil or shortening

½ cup powdered sugar, plus ½ to 1 cup for dusting

1. In a food processor, combine the 2⅓ cups tapioca starch and the salt and pulse until blended.

2. In a medium saucepan, bring the milk and canola oil to a boil, stirring constantly. Immediately pour the hot mixture into the flours and process until it is moist with a sand-like texture. Allow the dough to cool for 20 minutes.

3. Add the eggs to the cooled dough and blend until the dough is smooth and creamy. It will have a liquid, batter-like texture.

4. Scoop the dough into a large bowl, cover it with plastic wrap, and refrigerate for at least 8 hours or overnight. It will rise and thicken into the consistency of pudding.

5. In a deep fryer or deep saucepan, heat the oil until it reaches 375°F. Using a rubber spatula, punch down the dough in the bowl and work in ½ cup powdered sugar and the remaining ½ cup tapioca starch. It should be quite tender, but easy enough to pat out and cut into squares.

6. Dust a piece of plastic wrap with tapioca starch and turn one-third of the dough onto the wrap on a counter. Lightly pat the dough into a ⅓- to ½-inch-thick sheet. Using a dough scraper or a knife, cut the dough into 2½-inch squares. Repeat the process for the remaining dough.

7. Transfer one square at a time into the fryer using a flexible metal spatula, frying up to 3 at a time. They will initially drop to the bottom, but after about 30 seconds will float to the surface. After 30 more seconds lightly flip the beignets over. They will begin to balloon up like a pillow, so be careful not to puncture the sides. Continue turning the beignets every 30 seconds until they are lightly browned—about 4 minutes in total. Make sure the temperature of the oil comes back up before frying the next batch.

8. Use tongs to remove the cooked beignets, and transfer them to a plate lined with paper towels. Allow them to cool for about a minute, then coat them with powdered sugar by shaking them in a paper bag containing powdered sugar. Beignets are best served fresh and warm.

NOTE: Traditional New Orleans Creole beignets are always served three to a plate. If you want the authentic experience, make sure you serve them in threes—serving any fewer is like serving a hot dog without a bun.

I LEARNED TO MAKE THE FLUFFIEST PANCAKES from my brother Martin. It wasn't that he had a secret recipe, he just knew where to look for the best one, in the *Joy of Cooking*. The secret to his fluffy pancakes was right there: *Beat the egg whites until stiff, but not dry, and fold them lightly into the blended batter.* Even though our household is exclusively gluten-free, to this day I often refer to the *Joy of Cooking*, and my book always falls open to that same recipe.

Gluten-free pancakes are one baked good that has distinct advantages over its wheat-based counterpart. The formation of gluten in wheat can quickly turn a wheat-based pancake into a rubbery Frisbee if the batter is overmixed, so most recipes call for just moistening the ingredients and ignoring any lumps in order to keep the pancakes as tender as possible. Structure is not an issue with a puddle of gluten-free batter, so no additional binders are necessary. My advice is to make the batter a little thicker than normal to start with and then thin it slightly with water to get your ideal consistency. These pancakes are the perfect starting point for adding fresh blueberries, bananas, chocolate chips, or any other fruits and spices to dress them up.

fluffy buckwheat pancakes

makes 10 to 12 medium pancakes

3 large eggs

¼ cup sour cream

3 tablespoons canola oil

1 cup (120g) light buckwheat flour

1 cup (140g) tapioca starch

3 tablespoons sugar

2 teaspoons baking powder

1 teaspoon salt

1½ cups milk

1. Separate the eggs, placing the egg whites in a medium bowl (it is important to make sure you do not get any egg yolk in the whites, or it will reduce their volume when whipped). Place the yolks in a large bowl.

2. Use a hand mixer to beat the egg whites until they are stiff and form firm peaks. Set the bowl aside.

3. Add the sour cream and oil to the egg yolks and beat with the hand mixer until well blended. Add the buckwheat flour, tapioca starch, sugar, baking powder, and salt, and beat the mixture until it is fully blended and no lumps remain.

4. Gradually add the milk. You may want to hold back ¼ cup so that you can adjust the consistency. Beat the mixture until the milk is fully incorporated into the batter.

5. Gently fold in the egg whites until they are fully blended, taking care to retain as much of their loft as possible. You may find that the egg whites have separated a little at the bottom, but that's okay—just add the liquid whites to the batter.

6. Heat an oiled griddle or cast-iron skillet over medium heat. Try one test pancake to check the ideal temperature and the pancake consistency. If you have held back some milk, you can adjust the batter to your preference. If the batter is too thin, add light buckwheat flour in tablespoon increments. If the batter is too thick (and you have added all the milk), add water in tablespoon increments.

7. Ladle ¼ cup batter onto the hot surface, one pancake at a time. Turn the pancake when bubbles begin to form on the top, about 6 minutes. Flip the pancakes only once and cook them just until the underside is lightly browned, about 3 minutes. The cook time for the second side of the pancakes will be about half the time it took to cook the first side.

8. If you are making many pancakes, keep them warm and separated with a clean folded kitchen towel. Once cooled, the pancakes may be separated with wax paper and frozen in a resealable freezer bag.

WE HAVE A TREMENDOUSLY BOUNTIFUL vegetable garden every summer, but we seem to be fruit-challenged. Not only are our apple trees pretty paltry bearers, but our blueberry bushes rarely bear more than a handful of berries. Lucky for us, we have a friend awash in blueberries and a local organic pick-your-own blueberry orchard. I associate the Fourth of July with blueberries, and we just can't seem to get enough of them. We eat them plain, we eat them in desserts and salads, and we eat them in pancakes, crepes, and baked goods.

The following crepe recipe is based on a popular, two-ingredient flourless pancake recipe that contains just banana and eggs. This crepe adaptation uses less egg to make it more crepe-like and less omelet-like (the original recipe calls for 2 large eggs). Sour cream is used in place of the second egg and pairs well with the blueberries and bananas. A hint of cinnamon and vanilla accentuates the natural banana and blueberry flavors. Fried in a thin film of coconut oil, this is a very moist crepe that can be served either hot as a breakfast crepe or cold and rolled around a thin layer of cream cheese.

flourless blueberry banana crepes

makes about 8 thin crepes

1 large ripe banana

1 large egg

2 tablespoons sour cream

1 teaspoon vanilla extract

½ teaspoon ground cinnamon

½ cup fresh blueberries

1 tablespoon coconut oil

1. In a medium bowl, mash the banana with a fork. Whisk in the egg and sour cream. Add the vanilla and cinnamon. Place the blueberries in a small bowl and set aside.

2. Heat a griddle or cast-iron skillet over low heat. Melt the coconut oil on the hot surface and spoon about 2 tablespoons of batter onto the griddle. Sprinkle with some blueberries. Try to keep the crepes under 4 to 5 inches in diameter, otherwise they will be unwieldy when flipping them.

3. Check the bottom of the crepe after about a minute. If it is close to being flipped, it should not stick. Flip the crepe over when it feels solid enough to handle. Cook the crepe until both sides are browned and some of the moisture has dissipated. The underside has a tendency to brown very quickly, and it takes patience waiting to turn the crepes. Serve the crepes warm.

NOTE: Try serving this crepe folded with whipped cream and topped with caramel sauce. Make your own single-serving caramel sauce by melting 1 tablespoon salted butter, 1 tablespoon brown sugar, and 1 teaspoon vanilla extract in the microwave. Stir until entirely smooth. It will thicken some as it cools.

WE DON'T GET THAT MANY VISITORS here in Vermont. Perhaps it is the fact that the closest airport is two hours away or that the warm season lasts only a few months. But when we first moved to Vermont and the kids were little, my mother came to visit. After spending a day or so, she said she'd like to buy us a waffle maker. I readily agreed and we made waffles the following morning with lots of pure Vermont butter and maple syrup. It turned out that my picky-eater kids really liked waffles so we made special breakfasts for them from time to time. The next time I visited my mother in South Carolina, she said she needed a waffle maker, so off we went to buy one. By now, I had figured out that my mom was gaga about my waffles. So were the kids, so it must have been genetic.

This past year, at age ninety-one, my mother was diagnosed with borderline diabetes. When I went to visit, there was the waffle maker staring at me. I agreed to make her waffles, but this time I needed a low-glycemic flour. I had just discovered light buckwheat, so I whipped up a batch—and it produces very flavorful and satisfying waffles, light and crispy yet filling. These waffles are one of the few gluten-free baked goods that work using a single flour. As far as diabetes goes, some research suggests that a diet rich in buckwheat

buckwheat waffles

makes 16 waffles

3 large eggs

⅓ cup canola oil

2 cups (240g) light buckwheat flour

1 tablespoon sugar

2 teaspoons baking powder

1 teaspoon salt

1½ cups milk

1. Separate the eggs, placing the egg whites in a medium bowl (it is important to make sure you do not get any egg yolk in the whites, or it will reduce their volume when whipped). Place the yolks in a large bowl.

2. Use a hand mixer to beat the egg whites until they are stiff and form firm peaks. Set the bowl aside.

3. Add the oil to the egg yolks and beat with the hand mixer until well blended. Add the buckwheat flour, sugar, baking powder, and salt, and beat the mixture until it is fully blended and no lumps remain.

4. Gradually beat in the milk until fully incorporated into the batter. Gently fold in the egg whites until they are fully blended, taking care to retain as much of their loft as possible. You may find that the egg whites have separated a little at the bottom. This is okay—just add the liquid whites to the batter.

5. Preheat and grease your waffle maker according to the manufacturer's instructions.

6. Ladle about ½ cup of the batter into the center of the waffle maker. Follow the waffle maker directions and cook the waffles until steam no longer comes out of the waffle maker.

7. Serve warm. To freeze any remaining waffles, cool them completely and separate each waffle with a sheet of wax paper. Store in a sealable freezer bag. The waffles reheat easily in a regular toaster.

may lower blood glucose levels. For my mom's waffles, I substituted 2 teaspoons of Truvia® for the 1 tablespoon sugar, which you can also do if you are on a sugar-restricted diet.

CONVENIENCE RULES IN THE
BREAKFAST-FOOD CATEGORY,
and there is nothing like a
breakfast food that can be
toasted, handheld, and eaten
on the go. Over the years there
have been some pretty odd and
failed attempts at on-the-go
toaster items, including eggs,
French fries, and bacon. Toaster
pastries, though, have been
an enormous hit with a cult
following. Kellogg's alone sells
over 2 billion Pop-Tarts a year
in nearly 30 flavors.

You can't make a shelf-stable
gluten-free toaster pastry at
home, but you can make a
healthier toaster pastry that is
just as tasty and satisfies that
convenience food craving. This
recipe produces toaster pastries
that look very much like the
commercial ones, as long as you
poke the vent holes in the same
pattern. The sides hold together
without leaking strawberry
preserves all over your toaster,
and the baked dough has just
the right amount of tenderness
and flexibility. Let's face it,
toaster pastries are more about
the concept than the actual
food, but these would be
superb just as a filled pastry—
untoasted, they are just as
good. They may be the perfect
gluten-free car snack for long
travels with kids. And how can
you argue with 8 ingredients
rather than 46 and no artificial
food coloring?

strawberry toaster pastries

makes 8 pastries

1 cup (120g) light buckwheat flour

1 cup (140g) tapioca starch, plus more for rolling out the dough

4 tablespoons salted butter

½ cup packed brown sugar

1 large egg white

2 tablespoons unflavored, unsweetened apple butter

1 teaspoon vanilla extract

½ cup pure strawberry preserves (my favorite is Sidehill Farm strawberry jam)

1. In a medium bowl, combine the buckwheat flour and ¾ cup plus 2 tablespoons of the tapioca starch and stir to combine.

2. In a food processor, cream the butter and brown sugar. Add the egg white, apple butter, and vanilla and pulse to combine. Add the flour mixture and blend until the dough comes together in a ball. Wrap in plastic wrap and refrigerate for 2 hours.

3. In a small bowl, combine the strawberry preserves and the remaining 2 tablespoons tapioca starch and combine with a fork until it creates a well-blended paste. You may have to add a tiny extra amount of tapioca starch, depending on the thickness of your preserves. The consistency of the paste should be such that it does not puddle when spooned on the pastry crust.

4. Position an oven rack in the center of the oven and preheat to 350°F. Line a baking sheet with parchment paper.

5. Divide the dough into 8 pieces and roll into logs. Lightly dust some plastic wrap with additional tapioca starch and roll each log in it. Using a rolling pin, roll out each log into a rectangle 3$\frac{1}{2}$ to 4 inches wide and 9 to 10 inches long. Trim the rectangle with a bench scraper or a knife, squaring the sides and the ends.

6. On the upper half of the rectangle, spread 1 to 2 teaspoons of the strawberry filling, leaving a $\frac{1}{2}$-inch border around the top and sides. Using the plastic wrap to support the dough, fold the bottom half up over the filling. Using your forefinger, gently press the dough together around the edges to seal the pastry, including the bottom fold. Blunt the corners so that the points of the corners don't bake unevenly.

7. Using the tines of a fork, dock the top of the pastry in 4 to 6 places so that steam can escape during baking. Using a flexible metal spatula to support the pastry, transfer it to the baking sheet.

8. Bake the pastries for 20 minutes, or just until they begin to brown. Allow the toaster pastries to cool completely on the baking sheet for 45 minutes. Store in an airtight container or freeze until you toast them.

I GREW UP BEFORE BIG BOX
SUPERMARKETS were the
norm, and before grocery
stores were open 24 hours.
Sunday was our shopping day:
After church we would drive
30 minutes to Bohn's store,
where my parents did the
shopping and the kids stayed
out of trouble. Desserts in
my family were always for
special occasions, yet we were
all allowed to pick out one
packaged dessert at the store
on Sunday morning. At first
I gravitated toward visually
enticing things like Hostess
Sno Balls, but even then I
recognized that some things
looked a lot better than they
tasted. My favorite treat ended
up being a prepackaged cherry
turnover.

Like the city kid who doesn't
know where milk really comes
from, I had no idea that fresh
cherries were related to the pie
kind or to maraschino cherries,
for that matter. Actually, it is
sort of amazing how heat, sugar,
and tapioca can transform a
fresh fruit into something that
seems entirely different. To this
day, I like cherry pie filling, but
if I can, I try to make the cherry
filling from fresh cherries. If
they are not available, canned
red tart cherries packed in
water work as well if you
sweeten and thicken them on
your own.

cherry turnovers

makes 9 turnovers

FOR THE DOUGH:

Sweetcrust Pastry (page 314)

1 teaspoon almond extract

FOR THE CHERRY FILLING:

3 cups pitted cherries

⅓ cup granulated sugar

1 to 2 tablespoons tapioca
starch, depending on juiciness of
cherries

2 tablespoons lemon juice

FOR THE GLAZE:

2 tablespoons milk

½ cup powdered sugar

1. **Make the dough:** Prepare the pastry crust, adding the almond extract to the dough when you add the milk, and refrigerate until ready to use.

2. **Make the filling:** Coarsely chop the cherries, just enough to release the juices. In a medium saucepan, combine the cherries and granulated sugar. Cook over medium heat for 5 minutes, stirring constantly. Once the cherries come to a boil, reduce the heat and simmer for 5 more minutes.

3. In a small bowl, stir several tablespoons of the cherry juice into 1 tablespoon of the tapioca starch, then add it back to the saucepan. (Add more tapioca if the cherries are exceptionally juicy.) Continue stirring until the cherries thicken. Remove the cherries from the heat and stir in the lemon juice. Allow the cherries to cool before filling the turnovers.

4. Position an oven rack in the center of the oven and preheat to 375°F. Line a baking sheet with parchment paper.

recipe continues

quick breads, breakfast foods, and muffins   141

5. Divide the dough into thirds, and work with one-third at a time, leaving the remainder in the refrigerator. On a piece of plastic wrap dusted with tapioca starch, roll out the dough into a rectangle approximately 12 × 4 inches. Using a dough scraper or decorative pie cutter, cut the rectangle crosswise into thirds: You will have three 4 × 4-inch squares. Spoon 1 to 1½ tablespoons of cherry filling into the center of each square. Fold the dough over into a triangle and press the edges together lightly with your fingers until they are sealed. Cut three small slits in the top to vent steam as the cherry filling cooks.

6. Place the turnovers on the baking sheet and bake for 18 to 20 minutes, or until lightly browned. Transfer the turnovers to a wire rack and let cool.

7. **Make the glaze:** In a small bowl, combine the milk and powdered sugar until it is perfectly smooth.

8. Drizzle the glaze over the turnovers when they are mostly cool.

IF YOU ARE CRAZY ABOUT COCONUT like me, you will love this recipe. It is a wonderfully nutritious natural sweetener and binder in both gluten-free baked goods and nonbaked goods. Although you can buy coconut butter commercially, you can make your own far more economically.

Coconut butter is dried unsweetened coconut ground into a spread. There is no end to the ways you can use coconut butter in recipes. It can be cooked into bars, added to sauces for flavor and thickness, or combined with raw ingredients into nutrition-dense bars and confections. I love filling a tart shell with nothing more than a half dozen or so fresh strawberries pureed with ½ cup coconut butter. Or another favorite is to stuff sweet red peppers with a savory spread of coconut butter, fresh cilantro, and mint. Although coconut butter is shelf-stable, if you have added any fresh ingredients, make sure to store it in the refrigerator.

coconut butter

makes 1 pint

6 cups unsweetened shredded coconut

1. In a food processor, process the coconut until the coconut is liquefied, about 10 minutes. (Make sure to give your food processor a rest if it begins to get warm.) The coconut will go through many stages: from coconut dust to clumps to a thick, cookie dough–like texture, to a spreadable liquid. Stop the processor periodically and scrape down the sides with a rubber spatula.

2. Pour and scrape the finished coconut butter into a covered pint jar. It can be stored at room temperature.

IT WAS PRETTY TOUGH for me to go back to work when my son Alex was born, but we were extremely lucky to find a young nanny from Nebraska named Julie. Julie's creativity was contagious, and over the years she worked for us, our kids had the most enriched days. One day I stumbled home to find Alex and Julie in the kitchen, Alex sitting up on the counter next to her, screeching in delight. There was flour everywhere. Alex was covered head to toe, as was the counter . . . and Julie. Taken aback, I calmly asked: "Whatcha doing?"

"Making Monster Cookies!" Julie answered.

Well, we had monster cookies for dinner that night, and they seemed like the size of dinner plates. They are probably a lot larger in my memory, but that was before every convenience store had huge cookies propped up next to the cash register. These are breakfast monster cookies, but consider them really a bowl of oatmeal spiced with butter and sugar in an on-the-go form. They are sweet enough to pass for real monster cookies, but so healthy that you won't feel like you're eating dessert for breakfast. The coolest thing about them is that you make them in individual servings, and they only take 1½ minutes to "bake" in the microwave—less time than it takes to prepare oatmeal.

monster microwave oatmeal raisin breakfast cookie

makes one 5-inch breakfast cookie

1 tablespoon salted butter

1 tablespoon brown sugar

1 tablespoon unflavored, unsweetened apple butter

¼ teaspoon baking powder

¼ teaspoon salt

¼ teaspoon ground cinnamon

1 tablespoon oat flour

1 tablespoon tapioca starch

2 tablespoons rolled oats

2 tablespoons chopped raisins

1. In a small bowl, use a fork to cream the butter, brown sugar, and apple butter. Add the baking powder, salt, and cinnamon. Mix in the oat flour and tapioca starch, then the oats, and finally the raisins.

2. Cut out a 7 × 7-inch square of parchment paper and place it on a microwave-safe dinner plate. Dampen your hands and form the dough into a ball—it will be a tad smaller than a tennis ball. Place it in the center of the parchment paper and flatten it until it is approximately 4 inches in diameter and ½ inch thick with smooth edges.

3. Microwave the cookie on high for 1 minute. You will see it puff all over. Check it. Microwave for another 30 seconds. If your microwave doesn't have a turntable, turn the plate 90 degrees before microwaving it a second time.

4. Transfer the cookie on the parchment paper—very carefully, as the hot cookie will be fragile and very crumbly—to a cooling rack and let it cool thoroughly before eating. (Go ahead and eat it warm if soft and crumbly doesn't bother you.)

AIRPORTS HAVE TO BE the greatest gluten-free wastelands of all. Sure, there are some exceptions, but standard gluten-free fare is bruised bananas, nuts, yogurt, and a tired salad, if you are lucky. Add to that the need to have corn-free and soy-free food, and searching for food reminds me of the frantic squirrel outside my window, digging, finding nothing, and moving on. I developed this breakfast bar just for circumstances like these, and no one in our family travels without a half dozen of these bars. They are small enough to pack in your carry-on; robust enough to stuff in a bike pannier crammed full of outerwear, cameras, cell phones, and drinks; and even edible after an afternoon in a car in the California desert sun.

Inspired by Ina Garten's popular Homemade Granola Bars, these granola bars are sweet and spicy. Honey and molasses keep them moist and chewy, unlike most dry and crunchy commercial versions. For a vegan version, you can easily substitute 3 tablespoons of coconut oil for the butter and maple syrup for the honey (although the maple syrup makes them less chewy since it doesn't share the same binding properties as honey).

granola breakfast bars

makes 16 granola bars

2 cups rolled oats

½ cup hulled pumpkin seeds, chopped

1 cup unsweetened shredded coconut

½ cup (50g) oat flour

½ cup crystallized ginger

½ cup fruit-sweetened dried cranberries

½ cup pitted dates

4 tablespoons salted butter

½ cup honey

2 tablespoons molasses

⅓ cup packed brown sugar

1 teaspoon vanilla extract

1. Position an oven rack in the center of the oven and preheat to 350°F. Mix the oats, pumpkin seeds, and coconut and spread on a baking sheet. Bake the mixture for about 12 minutes, until lightly browned, stirring it halfway through. Allow the mixture to cool, then pour into a large bowl. Leave the oven on but reduce the temperature to 300°F.

2. Butter a 9 × 13-inch glass baking dish and line it with parchment paper, allowing the parchment paper to overhang the longer sides of the dish.

3. Measure the oat flour into a food processor. One at a time, add the ginger, cranberries, and dates and pulse each fruit until it is chopped. Add this mixture to the toasted mixture and blend.

4. In a medium saucepan, combine the butter, honey, molasses, brown sugar, and vanilla and bring the mixture to a full rolling boil, stirring constantly. Still stirring, let the mixture boil for 2 minutes. Take it off the heat and pour it over the toasted oatmeal and fruit mixture. Stir until all of the ingredients are well moistened.

recipe continues

5. Spoon the mixture into the baking dish. Using a dampened rubber spatula or wet fingers, press the mixture evenly into the pan, paying particular attention to pack the edges tightly.

6. Bake the granola bars for 25 minutes, or until they are just beginning to brown. Transfer the baking dish to a cooling rack and let cool for 1 hour.

7. Gently lift the solid bar by the parchment paper "handles" and place it on a cutting board to cool for at least 2 more hours. The bar sets and solidifies during the cooling process. Cutting it ahead of time may result in broken and fragile bars.

8. Once the bar is fully cooled, cut it into 16 pieces using a sharp knife or pizza cutter. Wrap them individually in plastic wrap; store in an airtight container for several months.

NOTE: With minor modifications, these granola bars may be made both dairy- and grain-free. Coconut butter, which enhances the flavor of the shredded coconut, can be substituted for the butter. Quinoa flakes may be substituted for the rolled oats, and light buckwheat flour works well in lieu of the oat flour.

THE SUMMER OF 1976, my husband, Tom, and I finally grew up. Tom flew out to meet me where I was doing research at the University of Montana, and we decided it was now or never: hitchhiking across America. Two scruffy graduate students, heavy with backpacks stuffed with camping gear, we stuck out our thumbs. Now I wonder *What were we thinking?*—but we were young, idealistic, and still had reason to trust others. We were giddy with excitement when we stuck out our thumbs and a vehicle screeched to a stop. Our adventure grew stranger as the days wore on. A hearse driven by a very eerie couple of carnival workers picked us up around midnight in Washington State. Did we have any drugs, and did we want to join them at a party? *No and no, just take us to the next rest stop.*

More than anything, though, we remember being hungry, tired of vending-machine food, and exhausted from staying up all night to keep drivers awake. That, it turned out, was often the motivation for giving us a lift. This was nearly fifteen years before the pioneering CLIF Bar was invented, and what we could have really used was a backpack full of these yummy, nutritious, and filling protein bars.

pineapple-cranberry protein bars

makes 16 bars

¼ cup (42g) chia seeds

1 can (15 ounces) Great Northern beans, drained and rinsed

½ cup coconut butter, store-bought or homemade (page 143)

½ cup sunflower seed butter (such as SunButter Organic)

¼ cup honey

¾ cup dried figs, with stems removed

½ cup pitted dates

1 cup (80g) whey powder

¼ cup orange juice

Grated zest and juice of 1 lemon

1½ cups (180g) oat flour (or substitute 144g rolled oats for a chewier bar)

½ cup fruit-sweetened dried cranberries

½ cup chopped dried pineapple

1. Position an oven rack in the center of the oven and preheat to 350°F. Grease a 9 × 13-inch baking dish.

2. In a small bowl, combine the chia seeds and ½ cup water and allow the slurry to absorb and thicken for 15 minutes.

3. In a food processor, process the beans, coconut butter, sunflower butter, chia slurry, honey, figs, and dates until smooth. Add the whey powder, orange juice, and lemon juice and process until well blended. Scoop the dough into a large bowl and work in the oat flour by hand until it is thoroughly blended. Work in the cranberries, dried pineapple, and lemon zest.

4. Spoon the dough into the baking dish. With wet hands, smooth the dough in the pan, pushing the dough into the corners.

5. Bake the dough for 30 minutes, or until set. Allow the bars to cool fully before cutting.

WE'VE BEEN TRYING TO GROW
APPLES in Vermont for over
five years, and yet our apple
trees have yielded less than
a dozen apples. It is kind of
embarrassing in a state that
ranks among the top twenty
producers of apples. But to be
fair, they have to endure a lot.
The first year, deer trimmed
one of the trees just after
budding, and another year, an
ice storm wreaked havoc on
the adolescent limbs. Last year,
green caterpillars showed up
for brunch and destroyed over
half of one tree in the space of
a day.

We love apples, and apples
in the fall are a big deal around
here. There are heirloom apple
tastings, thousands of home-
baked apple pies are sold to
leaf-peepers, and fresh cider
is pressed along the side of
the road. There is nothing like
eating a crisp, just-picked apple,
but I also love them baked into
cakes, breads, and muffins. This
recipe is the ultimate apple
muffin, with fresh apple cider,
applesauce, and unsweetened
apple butter. It is a tangy,
not-too-sweet muffin, with a
pleasing texture from all the
pectin, which comes from
the peels and cores. When the
apple crop is long gone or the
apples have passed their peak,
this is a recipe that recalls
pleasant memories of a fall with
an abundance of apples.

raisin–apple butter muffins

makes 18 muffins

1 cup (100g) toasted oat flour

1 cup (120g) light buckwheat flour

1 cup (140g) tapioca starch

1 teaspoon baking powder

½ teaspoon baking soda

1 teaspoon salt

½ cup sugar

3 large eggs

½ cup canola oil

½ cup unflavored, unsweetened apple butter

½ cup unsweetened applesauce

1 cup apple cider

¾ cup raisins

1. Position an oven rack in the center of the oven and preheat to 350°F. Grease 18 cups of 2 standard muffin tins or line with paper liners.

2. In a large bowl, whisk together the oat flour, buckwheat flour, tapioca starch, baking powder, baking soda, and salt until thoroughly blended.

3. In another large bowl, whisk together the sugar, eggs, oil, apple butter, applesauce, and apple cider.

4. Fold the flour mixture into the wet mixture, using as few strokes as possible but moistening all the flour. Fold in the raisins.

5. Ladle the batter into the muffin cups, filling them about two-thirds full. Bake for 28 minutes, or until the tops spring back when pressed. Transfer to a cooling rack.

ON THE EAST BANK OF THE CONNECTICUT RIVER, just opposite Brattleboro, Vermont, is Mt. Wantastiquet. It is a moderate hike to the summit along a carriage trail built in 1891 that provides outstanding views of the Connecticut River Valley. My son Alex and I love hiking the trail, but our favorite part is beating everyone to the first wild blueberries growing on the summit. Our most recent berry-picking adventure was a scene right out of Robert McCloskey's *Blueberries for Sal*, except that our blueberry-picking solitude was interrupted not by a bear, but by a Jack Russell terrier and a guy talking on his cell phone. Welcome to the "connected" world.

If we are really lucky, the first wild blueberries of the season coincide with the wild raspberries. I developed this recipe to showcase the wild berries—though you can also make them with fresh or frozen berries. I have found tiny blueberries to be ideal for foods like muffins and pancakes because they are less juicy. This recipe also uses coconut milk, which lends both a richness and a natural sweetness, and pairs extremely well with the tartness of the berries. The resulting muffins are nicely domed with a deep golden color from the interaction of the light buckwheat flour with the baking powder.

berry good muffins

makes 18 muffins

1¼ cups (150g) light buckwheat flour

¾ cup (105g) tapioca starch

1 teaspoon salt

1 teaspoon baking powder

¾ cup granulated sugar

¾ cup powdered sugar

3 large eggs

½ cup canola oil

⅔ cup full-fat coconut milk

1 teaspoon vanilla extract

¾ cup raspberries

¾ cup blueberries

1. Position an oven rack in the center of the oven and preheat to 350°F. Grease 18 cups of 2 standard muffin tins or line with paper liners.

2. In a large bowl, whisk together the buckwheat flour, tapioca starch, salt, and baking powder until thoroughly blended.

3. In another large bowl, whisk together both sugars, the eggs, oil, coconut milk, and vanilla.

4. Fold the flour mixture into the wet mixture, using as few strokes as possible but moistening all the flour. Fold in the berries.

5. Ladle the batter into the muffin cups, filling them about two-thirds full. Bake for 35 minutes, or until the tops are lightly browned and spring back when pressed. Transfer to a cooling rack.

EVERY MORNING when I worked on Wall Street, I would stop in the same coffee shop, where there was a line snaking out the door. Like all the rest of the hole-in-the-wall coffee shops on every block, it had trays of big cakey muffins the size of softballs. People would buy these for breakfast; some would plop them on their cubicle desk and pick at them until lunch. Were they really eating breakfast food or were they eating cake?

Frosted or not? More sugar, less sugar? Creamed or just mixed? Dense or light-crumbed? These are distinctions between cakes and muffins that the culinary set has debated for years. To me, muffins are denser and are the easiest gluten-free baked good to make. A light, moist cake that rises higher than a Frisbee is a feat of engineering. A cupcake is just light moist cake scrunched in a muffin pan. I declare these to be muffins, not cupcakes masquerading as muffins. They have the perfect muffin texture, a crumb with springiness that kind of tears as you bite into it. They also are not overly sweet, with much of the sweetness coming from the coconut milk and coconut flour.

lemon poppy seed muffins

makes 9 muffins

½ cup sugar

¼ cup canola oil

½ cup full-fat coconut milk

3 large eggs

½ cup (56g) coconut flour

½ cup (70g) tapioca starch

1 teaspoon baking powder

½ teaspoon baking soda

1 tablespoon poppy seeds

Grated zest of 1 lemon

1 teaspoon lemon extract

1. Position an oven rack in the center of the oven and preheat to 350°F. Line 9 cups of a standard muffin tin with paper liners.

2. In a large bowl, combine the sugar, oil, coconut milk, and eggs. Beat the mixture with a hand mixer for approximately 4 minutes. (You want to incorporate as much air as possible.)

3. In a separate bowl, combine the coconut flour and tapioca starch and gradually add them to the egg mixture. Beat the batter for several more minutes, making sure to scrape down the sides. Add the baking powder, baking soda, poppy seeds, lemon zest, and lemon extract, mixing them thoroughly into the batter.

4. Spoon the batter into the muffin cups, filling them about two-thirds full. Bake for 25 minutes, or until the tops spring back when pressed. Transfer to a cooling rack.

BIKE RIDING WHEN TRAVELING allows you to see and experience many things you might not otherwise. The most breathtaking bike trip I've ever done was on Prince Edward Island, with its reddish-orange cliffs overlooking the deep blue water. Although the reality of farming that land is monumental, the shimmery fields of oats made it seem totally magical. Honestly, I had never experienced oat fields up close, and it was hard to make the connection between the undulating fields marching to the sea and a bowl of oatmeal.

Like many, I love the taste (and health benefits) of oatmeal, but not the texture. When gluten-free oats became widely available, I developed many recipes to capitalize on their taste, and frankly, the gluey texture turned out to work wonders. One of the many things I discovered about oats was that they blended beautifully with light buckwheat flour, from both a taste and textural point of view. These honey-oat muffins have no refined sugar, and they contain plenty of fiber. They are great as a breakfast item or a snack, but pair equally well with soup, stew, or salad.

honey-oat muffins

makes 12 muffins

1 cup (100g) toasted oat flour

½ cup (60g) light buckwheat flour

½ cup (70g) tapioca starch

1 teaspoon baking powder

½ teaspoon baking soda

1½ teaspoons salt

1 cup rolled oats, plus more for sprinkling (optional)

1 cup full-fat coconut milk

½ cup unsweetened applesauce

3 large eggs

½ cup canola oil

¼ cup honey

1. Position an oven rack in the center of the oven and preheat to 350°F. Grease 12 cups of a standard muffin tin or line with paper liners.

2. In a medium bowl, combine the oat flour, buckwheat flour, tapioca starch, baking powder, baking soda, and salt. Whisk until thoroughly blended.

3. In a large bowl, whisk together the rolled oats, coconut milk, applesauce, eggs, oil, and honey. Let the mixture sit for 5 minutes to allow the oats to absorb moisture.

4. Fold the flour mixture into the wet mixture, using as few strokes as possible but moistening all the flour. Spoon the batter into the muffin cups. Sprinkle a few rolled oats on the top of each muffin, if desired.

5. Bake the muffins for 28 minutes, or until the tops spring back when pressed. Transfer to a cooling rack.

BANANAS MAY BE THE PERFECT FOOD for nutrition and convenience, but I can't think of any other food that induces such a sense of guilt as it ripens. After doing the math for how many bananas I think we will eat before they get too ripe, I select for the optimal level of ripeness. Most of the time, I get it right, but sometimes a bunch of brown-spotted, fragrant bananas is sitting in the bowl on the kitchen counter staring at me. The guilt sets in, and I begin thinking about what I could make with the overripe bananas.

One of my favorite things to make with overripe bananas is Banana, Nut Butter, and Jelly Muffins. I can make up a batch, freeze them, and have individual-size, nutritious snacks to put in the week's lunches. These muffins are a good lower-carb, low-glycemic treat. Although the recipe calls for sunflower seed butter, the muffins are equally good with peanut or other nut butters. This recipe also employs a technique borrowed from cake baking, that of creaming the butter and sugar, which makes for a tender muffin that also rises to form a nice crown.

banana, nut butter, and jelly muffins

makes 12 muffins

1 cup sunflower seed butter (such as SunButter Organic; see Note)

¼ cup sugar

3 large eggs

⅔ cup mashed ripe bananas

1 teaspoon vanilla extract

½ cup (60g) light buckwheat flour

1½ teaspoons baking powder

2 tablespoons seedless raspberry jelly

1 tablespoon tapioca starch

1. Position an oven rack in the center of the oven and preheat to 350°F. Line 12 cups of a standard muffin tin with paper liners.

2. In a large bowl, combine the sunflower butter and sugar. Using a hand mixer, cream on high until the butter is light and the sugar well incorporated. Beat in the eggs, mashed banana, and vanilla until the batter is thick and creamy, 2 to 3 minutes. Beat in the buckwheat flour and baking powder and beat for 2 minutes more.

3. In a small bowl, combine the jelly and tapioca starch and hand-blend until there are no lumps and the jelly is slightly thickened and smooth.

4. Spoon half of the batter into the bottoms of the muffin cups. Drop a ½-teaspoon dollop of the jelly mixture on top of the batter. Finish filling the muffin cups to about three-quarters full. (Alternative: Using all the batter, fill the muffin cups three-quarters full, then drop the dollop of jelly on top. It makes a bit of a mess when it bakes, but it looks really cool when the dome of the muffin is covered with thinned jelly.)

5. Bake the muffins for 20 minutes, or until the tops spring back when pressed. Let the muffins cool in the pan for 5 minutes, or until you can handle them, then transfer to a cooling rack. Carefully remove the paper liners as soon as the muffins are cool enough to handle; they will be a bit sticky from the jelly. Allow the muffins to cool fully (and let the warm preserves thicken) before serving.

NOTE: The temperature of the sunflower seed butter is crucial in this process. If you take the butter directly from the refrigerator, it is too hard to mix without spewing butter and sugar all over your kitchen. If it is too soft and the fat melts, bubbles will either not form or collapse. The solution for butter temperature? Leave the butter at room temperature for about 10 minutes, so it's barely soft enough to incorporate the sugar. If it feels a little too melted, put it in the refrigerator for 10 minutes to cool down, then beat a little more and proceed.

DURING THE SUMMER, we grow all of our own vegetables. A row of carrots is always among them. Late last summer, our little 12-foot row yielded over 30 pounds of carrots (as an aside, don't listen when people tell you to thin the rows; we didn't, and our carrots were massive). We go through lots of carrot recipes—roasted, steamed with rosemary, mixed in with summer squash, and even a carrot lasagna. Chester, our golden retriever, eats his share of them, and my son Alex takes the really gnarly ones to his horseback riding lessons.

One of my favorite things to do with carrots is make carrot cakes and carrot muffins. The natural sweetness of carrots, combined with the delicate, moist crumb that cooked carrot creates, makes carrots excellent for gluten-free adaptations. This is a vegan recipe that uses a chia slurry in place of eggs—the slurry adds moisture and springiness to the muffins, and binds the ingredients together. High in protein and fiber, chia seeds also give the muffins a nutritional boost. The recipe contains far less fat than most carrot cakes, with the fat coming from the canola oil. The twist in this recipe is the use of crystallized ginger and orange juice, which results in the bursts of ginger against a carrot-orange backdrop.

vegan carrot muffins

makes 24 muffins

1 tablespoon chia seeds

½ cup granulated sugar

½ cup powdered sugar

½ teaspoon ground cinnamon

⅛ teaspoon freshly grated nutmeg

½ teaspoon salt

½ cup canola oil

½ cup unsweetened applesauce

1⅓ cups finely shredded carrots

1 cup (140g) tapioca starch

1 cup (120g) light buckwheat flour

1 teaspoon baking soda

½ cup orange juice

½ cup finely chopped crystallized ginger

1. In a small bowl, whisk together the chia seeds and 6 tablespoons warm water. Allow the slurry to absorb water for at least 30 minutes. (This will make more slurry than the recipe calls for. The remainder may be kept in the refrigerator for 2 weeks and used in other baking projects, in cooked cereals, or in smoothies.)

2. Position an oven rack in the center of the oven and preheat to 350°F. Line 24 cups of 2 standard muffin tins with paper liners.

3. In a large bowl, combine both sugars, the spices, salt, and oil. Using a hand mixer, beat it on high until the oil and sugars are well blended, about 2 minutes. Add ¼ cup of the chia slurry and beat well for 2 minutes. Add the applesauce and carrots to the mixture, beating well to incorporate air into the batter.

4. Add the tapioca starch, buckwheat flour, and baking soda and beat the batter until well blended. The batter will be thick. Slowly pour the orange juice into the batter and beat on high for 2 minutes. Fold in the crystallized ginger.

5. Spoon the batter into the muffin cups, filling them to just below the top. The muffins will rise and dome, but they will not overflow the tins.

6. Bake the muffins for 25 minutes, or until the tops spring back when lightly pressed. Allow the muffins to cool fully in the pan for them to set.

variation

cranberry orange muffins

Substitute chopped fruit-sweetened dried cranberries for the crystallized ginger, and add in 2 tablespoons grated orange zest.

I HAVE BEEN A RUNNER more of my life than not. Before switching to a gluten-free diet, I found myself less and less able to run more than two or three times a week. Every time I ran, it would take my knees and elbow joints several days to recover. I figured it was just the natural process of aging, but after three months on a gluten-free diet, the joint pain disappeared. I was both stunned and a convert. It is not to say that a gluten-free diet has made me totally free from all aches and pains. If I overdo it, I pay for it, and the combination of lots of rain and low barometric pressure can leave me feeling like a rusty hinge. It was during one of these rainy periods that I thought: What if I made a muffin with naturally anti-inflammatory foods?

Zyflamend, a natural anti-inflammatory herbal supplement, was my inspiration for combining fresh rosemary, turmeric, ginger, and green tea in a breakfast treat to warm my bones one chilly November morning. I added lemon zest and fruit-sweetened cranberries for contrast, and the result was a beautifully sunny, yellow muffin that is at once buttery, spicy, tart, and warm—a muffin that stimulates all your senses. And yes, the turmeric in the muffins definitely leaves you with a warming glow that has you reaching for more.

sunrise warming muffins

makes 12 muffins

1 cup (120g) light buckwheat flour

3/4 cup (105g) tapioca starch

1/2 cup sugar, plus 1 tablespoon for sprinkling (optional)

2 teaspoons turmeric

1 teaspoon baking powder

1/2 teaspoon baking soda

6 tablespoons cold salted butter, cut into tablespoons

1 tablespoon chopped fresh rosemary

1/3 cup finely chopped crystallized ginger

Grated zest of 1 lemon (1 tablespoon plus 1 teaspoon)

1/4 cup brewed green tea, cooled

1 cup sour cream

1/2 cup chopped fruit-sweetened dried cranberries

1. In a food processor, combine the buckwheat flour, tapioca starch, sugar, turmeric, baking powder, baking soda, and butter. Pulse until the butter is incorporated and the flour is a sandy texture.

2. Add the rosemary, crystallized ginger, and lemon zest. Pulse the dough to just mix in the ingredients.

3. Add the green tea and sour cream and mix well. Transfer the dough to a large bowl and fold in the chopped cranberries. Cover and refrigerate for at least 30 minutes.

4. Position a rack in the center of the oven and preheat to 400°F. Line 12 cups of a standard muffin tin with paper liners.

5. Spoon the dough into the muffin cups, filling them about two-thirds full. If you want a crackly crust, sprinkle the tops with the 1 tablespoon sugar. Bake for 22 to 25 minutes, or until the center springs back when pressed. Transfer to a cooling rack.

savories

WHEN I MEET CUSTOMERS, the question I get the most often is: *How do I make a pie crust? How do I make the same kind of pie I have made for years?* I once faced the question from a local celiac support group, so I gladly took their e-mail addresses to send them a recipe. One older woman apparently didn't do e-mail, so I walked her through making the crust over the phone. A few months later, I was shopping at the grocery store and a woman comes up to me with a huge smile on her face. It was the pie crust lady, and she was so excited that she had made her best pie ever.

A really good, gluten-free pie crust is not hard to make. My major breakthrough was learning to work with plastic wrap. Before I had always used wax paper or parchment paper, neither of which is very flexible when wrinkled . . . and it is hard to tuck a flat crust into a round pie plate without encountering wrinkles. Plastic wrap eliminates that problem. It tucks, folds, and releases easily with a light touch. In this recipe, the strength of the dough comes from the egg white. The resulting pie shell is strong enough to be baked in a tart pan with a removable bottom and served as a stand-alone quiche or tart. The egg white is also another source of protein for optimal browning. It works wonderfully for sweet pies as well as savory quiches and pot pies.

shortcrust pastry (pâte brisée)

makes enough for a single 10-inch pie crust

¾ cup (105g) tapioca starch

1 cup (120g) light buckwheat flour

1 teaspoon salt

8 tablespoons cold salted butter, cut into 10 to 12 pieces

1 large egg white

1. In a food processor, combine the tapioca starch, buckwheat flour, and salt and pulse to combine. Add the butter and pulse until the chunks of butter are no larger than peas.

2. Add the egg white and pulse to combine. Add up to 3 tablespoons cold water, 1 tablespoon at a time. The dough will start to come together, but it will still be loose and crumbly. Transfer the dough to a bowl and knead lightly to combine the dough into a ball. Wrap the dough ball in plastic wrap, and refrigerate for 20 minutes.

3. Roll out the dough between two pieces of plastic wrap. Peel back the top layer of the plastic, place a 9-inch pie plate upside down in the center of it, and invert the pie plate and pastry together so the pastry ends up over the pan. Gently press the pastry into the sides of the pan, flattening the bottom and pressing it against the inner walls, and remove the remaining plastic wrap. Trim the overhang and gently flute the rim by pinching the crust between your forefinger and thumb, and pressing with your other forefinger.

MY SON MARTY was the last of our family to graduate from college, and family members came from around the country for this celebratory occasion. We were a group with diverse dietary needs: gluten-free, soy-free, corn-free, low-glycemic, and vegetarian. I developed this quiche in honor of Marty, whose senior fellowship topic was a project on the pastoral tradition in contemporary poetry. The heroes of these new and ancient poems are shepherds, real and metaphoric, who sing of their love, their flocks, and their surroundings. It just so happens that Vermont Shepherd Cheese (from Putney, Vermont) is his very favorite cheese. Although Vermont Shepherd Cheese makes this quiche sing just like dueling shepherds, you can substitute a cheese of your choice. This particular cheese was a 50/50 blend of raw sheep's milk and raw cow's milk. I baked this quiche in a tart pan with a removable bottom. It makes a beautiful, stand-alone, golden brown crust with just the right amount of tender butteriness. This is a rich, creamy quiche that is both sturdy and melts in your mouth at the same time.

vermont shepherd quiche

makes one 10-inch quiche

Shortcrust Pastry (opposite)

2 tablespoons olive oil

2 large leeks, white and light green parts, thinly sliced

5 ounces any 50/50 raw sheep's milk and raw cow's milk cheese, cut into 1/2-inch cubes

2 1/2 ounces any Alpine cheese (such as raclette), cut into 1/2-inch cubes

4 large eggs

1 1/2 cups half-and-half

1 teaspoon finely chopped fresh oregano

1 teaspoon finely chopped fresh thyme

1/4 teaspoon freshly grated nutmeg

Freshly ground black pepper

1. Make the pastry crust and roll out as directed. Use it to line a 10-inch tart pan with a removable bottom. Place on a baking sheet and set aside.

2. Position an oven rack in the center of the oven and preheat to 450°F.

3. In a medium skillet, heat the oil over medium-low heat. Add the leeks and cook until they soften, about 5 minutes.

4. Line the bottom of the quiche shell with the cubed cheese. Layer the sautéed leeks on top.

5. In a bowl, lightly beat the eggs. Add the half-and-half, oregano, thyme, nutmeg, and pepper to taste and whisk until the mixture is thick and foamy. Pour the mixture over the leeks.

6. Bake for 10 minutes. Reduce the temperature to 375°F and bake the quiche for 40 minutes, or until the center is set. Transfer the quiche to a cooling rack, allow it to cool for 15 minutes, and unmold it from the pan before serving.

CARROTS ARE SUPPOSED TO BE one of the easiest garden vegetables to grow. Tell that to our garden. The rainbow chard has always leafed out in splendor, the broccoli matures and rewards us all summer with side shoots, and the green beans are so prolific they are hard to keep up with. But carrots, we typically haven't had much luck . . . until the past few years. Perhaps it has been a string of hotter summers, or the quality of the seeds, but we've been swamped with carrots ever since. The variety of carrots we plant takes 65 to 70 days to mature, and by the end of August we can have as many as 30 pounds of carrots from a single packet of seeds.

The good thing about carrots is that they store well so we can eat them all winter, but it is always nice to make interesting dishes with freshly harvested vegetables. The tart combines the spiciness of the carrot sauce with a ricotta and cheese mixture reminiscent of cheese ravioli. It is a perfect dish for a luncheon or dinner when paired with a garden salad and garlic bread.

sherried carrot and kale tart

makes one 10-inch tart

Shortcrust Pastry (page 162)

FOR THE CARROT SAUCE:

2½ tablespoons salted butter

1 medium onion, chopped

3 large carrots, chopped (about 230g)

½ cup cooking sherry

1 teaspoon freshly ground black pepper

FOR THE RICOTTA FILLING:

1 container (15 ounces) full-fat ricotta cheese

1 cup shredded Parmesan cheese

2 cups finely chopped raw kale (you can also substitute fresh or frozen spinach)

1 large egg

1 to 2 tablespoons chopped fresh parsley

1. **Make the pastry crust** and roll out as directed. Use it to line a 10-inch tart pan with a removable bottom. Place on a baking sheet and set aside.

2. Position an oven rack in the center of the oven and preheat to 375°F.

3. Prebake the tart shell for 15 minutes. Remove the shell from the oven and set aside. Leave the oven on.

4. **Meanwhile, make the carrot sauce:** In a large skillet, melt the butter over medium heat. Add the onion and cook until it is translucent, about 3 minutes. Add the carrots, sherry, pepper, and ¾ cup water. Bring the mixture to a boil, then cover the skillet and let it simmer for 20 to 25 minutes, or until the carrots are tender. Transfer the carrot mixture to a food processor and puree until smooth. Set aside.

5. Make the ricotta filling: In a bowl, whisk together the ricotta, Parmesan, kale, and egg until they are well blended.

6. Spread the ricotta filling in the bottom of the tart shell and top with the carrot sauce. Insert a butter knife in the tart and gently swirl the ricotta mixture with the carrot sauce until you get a marbled effect.

7. Bake for 45 to 50 minutes, or until the center is set. Allow to cool for 10 minutes before cutting. Sprinkle with chopped parsley to serve.

AS A PLACE TO WORK, Against The Grain is known as a haven for foodie liberal arts majors. We talk foodie topics all the time, but the chatter reaches a fevered pitch in late April and early May. That's when wild leeks, also known as ramps, emerge as an emerald green splotch after the snow recedes. This past spring, a staff member and locavore caterer brought a bag of them to work, and two other staff members found an undisturbed two-acre parcel in the woods. We can't escape reading about ramps in the food media, but we're pretty smug—southern Vermont is ramp ground zero.

Ramps are sort of a pungent cross between spring onions and wild garlic—you eat the leaves and bulbs, either cooked or raw. They are prevalent in the Appalachian Mountains and grow in deciduous forests from Canada to Tennessee and North Carolina, and as far west as Missouri and Minnesota. Here I use one of the popular Appalachian recipes for ramps fried with bacon, potatoes, and scrambled eggs as the inspiration. Thinly sliced new potatoes are tossed in ramp pesto, layered with prosciutto, baked in a buttery tart shell, and garnished with bright pimientos. The tart smells and tastes as good as it looks. If ramps are not available or in season, you can substitute store-bought basil pesto.

potato and prosciutto tart with wild leek pesto

makes 6 mini-tarts

FOR THE PESTO:

1/2 cup sunflower seeds

About 5 medium ramps, bulbs and leaves chopped

1/4 cup olive oil

Juice of 1 lemon

Salt and freshly ground black pepper

1/2 cup freshly grated Parmesan cheese

FOR THE TART:

Shortcrust Pastry (page 162)

5 small new potatoes, thinly sliced

2 tablespoons olive oil

1/4 pound thinly sliced prosciutto

1/2 cup freshly grated Cheddar cheese

1 tablespoon sliced pimientos

1. **Make the pesto:** In a food processor, process the sunflower seeds until reduced to a fine meal. Add the ramps, oil, lemon juice, and salt and pepper to taste. Blend until the ramps are broken down and the pesto is uniformly mixed. Add the Parmesan and blend until it is mixed in.

2. **Make the tart:** Prepare the pastry crust, divide into 6 equal pieces, and roll out as directed. Line 6 mini-tart pans with removable bottoms with the dough; place the tart pans on a baking sheet.

3. Position an oven rack in the center of the oven and preheat to 450°F.

recipe continues

4. Place the sliced potatoes in a medium bowl. In a small bowl, blend the oil with the ramp pesto. Drizzle the pesto over the potatoes and toss to mix.

5. Arrange a layer of potatoes in the bottom of each tart shell. Top with a layer of prosciutto, then Cheddar. Repeat this layering, and top the tarts with a layer of the potatoes. You will have three layers of potatoes. Dot the top with sliced pimientos.

6. Bake for 10 minutes. Reduce the oven temperature to 375°F and bake the tarts for an additional 30 minutes, or until the pesto is fragrant and starting to bubble and the potatoes start to get crispy. Remove the tarts from the baking sheet and place on a cooling rack to set for 10 minutes before unmolding and serving.

variation

For a tangy tasting tart, substitute chopped fresh asparagus for the Cheddar cheese, and sprinkle ½ cup of crumbled goat cheese over the top with the pimientos.

I'VE ALWAYS ASSOCIATED CREPES with my late mother-in-law. On my first trip to Houston to meet my future in-laws, Tom's mother took me out to a restaurant popular with the ladies-who-lunch crowd—The Magic Pan in Houston's Galleria. In every restaurant, a crepe chef in full view would make crepes on a carousel of upside-down pans that passed through a circle of flames. Instead of filling crepe pans with batter, the hot pan was dipped in the batter. It was mesmerizing to watch, and it made perfect crepes.

Buckwheat is an ideal flour for gluten-free crepes. Indeed, it is the main ingredient in Acadian ployes, sort of a cross between a pancake and crepe, popular in northern Maine and Canada. It is important to not overbeat crepe batter to minimize the air bubbles, and it is best to chill the batter at least 2 hours or even overnight. Filled with a rich Mornay sauce and fresh asparagus, this is an easy-to-prepare gourmet meal.

savory crepes stuffed with asparagus

makes 12 crepes

FOR THE CREPE BATTER:

½ cup (60g) light buckwheat flour

½ cup potato starch

Dash of salt

3 large eggs

½ cup canola oil

1½ cups milk

FOR THE MORNAY SAUCE:

4 tablespoons salted butter

¼ cup chopped sweet onions

1 tablespoon light buckwheat flour

1 cup heavy (whipping) cream

2 ounces shredded Swiss cheese

2 ounces ounces freshly grated Parmesan cheese

½ cup finely chopped fresh parsley

Salt and freshly ground black pepper

Butter or oil, for cooking the crepes

4 bunches fresh asparagus, steamed

½ cup freshly chopped chives (optional)

1. **Make the crepe batter:** In a bowl, whisk together the buckwheat flour, potato starch, and salt. Add the eggs and oil to make a thick paste. Gradually add the milk and whisk until smooth. Cover the bowl with plastic wrap and refrigerate the batter for at least 2 hours (overnight is even better).

2. **Make the sauce:** In a medium saucepan, melt the butter over low heat. Add the onions and sauté until they are soft and transparent. Add the buckwheat flour and allow it to cook as a paste for about 5 minutes, or just until it begins to brown. Blend in the cream thoroughly and cook until the sauce

recipe continues

thickens, but don't let it boil. Stir in the cheeses until they are melted, then add the parsley and salt and pepper to taste. Keep the sauce warm until ready to assemble the crepes.

3. **Make the crepes:** Allow the batter to come to room temperature. (The batter should have the consistency of thick cream. Thin it with a teaspoon of water at a time, if necessary.) Using a 12-inch seasoned or nonstick pan over medium heat, brush the pan with butter or oil as necessary. Pour about ¼ cup of batter into the pan. Tip the pan to coat the bottom with a thin layer. Flip the crepe when the edges start to brown, and cook briefly to brown the other side. The crepe should still be flexible. Place the crepes between folds of clean kitchen towels to keep them warm until serving.

4. To serve, place 4 spears of asparagus in the center of a crepe. Spoon 1 tablespoon of sauce along the asparagus. Fold up both sides, top with another tablespoon of sauce, and sprinkle with the chives (if using) to serve.

THE BEST RAVIOLI I ever tasted was at a restaurant outside of Zurich on a business trip. My hosts had taken us to an out-of-the-way restaurant, of which I remember two things: the unforgettable homemade ravioli, and the fact that there was a horse-riding ring in the center of the restaurant. Two small, homemade cheese ravioli were served on an unadorned white plate, with just a tiny puddle of Alfredo sauce. I could have ended the meal right there.

In general, dry gluten-free pasta is pretty decent, and there are a number of brands to choose from. But fresh gluten-free pasta is a rarity, and frozen gluten-free ravioli are both rare and expensive. The expense is not surprising when you look at the process it takes to make a homemade version, but it is *so* worth it. Gluten-free ravioli dough has to bind together, be stretchy and pliable enough to handle, and has to withstand a rolling boil without leaking or exploding. This dough has just four ingredients and uses the natural stretchiness of mozzarella to give it all the elasticity and chew it needs. Fill the ravioli with this creamy summer squash–cheese filling or any other filling of your choice. Top it with a tomato vodka or Alfredo sauce, or simply toss it with olive oil and chunks of grilled summer squash and onions.

lemon thyme– summer squash ravioli

makes 8 to 10 ravioli

FOR THE FILLING:

1½ tablespoons salted butter

1 small onion, chopped

3 baby yellow summer squash, chopped

½ teaspoon freshly ground black pepper

2 teaspoons fresh lemon thyme leaves

2 tablespoons lemon juice

½ teaspoon salt

4 ounces cream cheese

1 large egg yolk

FOR THE DOUGH:

1 cup (140g) tapioca starch

3 tablespoons cold salted butter, cut into cubes

4 ounces shredded mozzarella cheese

1 large egg

1. **Make the filling:** In a medium skillet, melt the butter over medium heat. Add the onion, squash, pepper, and lemon thyme and cook for about 3 minutes, or until the vegetables are softened. Add the lemon juice and salt and cook for an additional 5 minutes, or until all the liquid has evaporated. Place the mixture in a covered bowl in the refrigerator to cool for 30 minutes.

2. Transfer the sautéed vegetables to a food processor and blend with the cream cheese and egg yolk until it is smooth and creamy. Return the mixture to the refrigerator while you prepare the ravioli dough.

3. Make the dough: In a food processor, combine the tapioca starch, butter, mozzarella, and whole egg and process the dough until the mixture looks like small curds.

4. Transfer the mixture to a bowl and press it together with your hands to form a smooth ball. Roll the dough between two pieces of parchment paper to the desired thickness—$1/16$ to $1/8$ inch works well. Using a dough scraper or pizza cutter, cut the dough into eight to ten 2 × 5-inch rectangles. Place 1 heaping teaspoon of filling on the bottom half of each rectangle and fold the top half of the rectangle down to cover the filling. Lightly press around all edges with your fingers—the dough will stick together without wetting the sides or using an egg wash. Use the dough scraper or a knife to neaten the edges. Use the dough scraper or a spatula to pick up each ravioli and transfer it to a plate. Cover the ravioli with plastic wrap to keep them from drying out while you roll out and stuff the remaining ravioli.

5. To cook the ravioli, bring a pot of water to a boil. Drop the ravioli, several at a time, into the boiling water. The ravioli are done when they float and the filling is hot—depending on the size and thickness of the ravioli, this may take 2 to 3 minutes. (You can also cover the ravioli with plastic wrap and refrigerate or freeze until ready to cook.)

CHESTER, OUR GOLDEN RETRIEVER, is our office receptionist: He barks when someone is at the door and chases away salesmen. He's great with people but only has one dog friend in the world, Clover, a dark golden retriever. Chester and I walk with Clover and her "mom," Tammy, during our summer getaways at the St. Lawrence River. One morning, while I was working on this ravioli, Tammy told me that someone had just given her a whole bunch of fresh garlic. Later that afternoon she delivered a bunch to my cottage, and roasted garlic became the centerpiece of this ravioli.

This pasta relies on both tapioca starch and potato starch to create a gel that can withstand rolling and boiling. The addition of the mashed potato adds both structure and tenderness to the finished ravioli. The egg white adds protein to the mix and serves as the binder that holds the dough together. I have always been fascinated with vegan cheese, but have never tasted any commercially prepared vegan cheeses that were substitutes for the real thing. Then I discovered cashew cheese: Soaked raw cashews make the creamiest base for all kinds of vegan cheese spreads. Add some freshly roasted garlic and it makes a creamy, savory filling for the ravioli. No one will have any idea that it is gluten-free.

ravioli with creamy roasted garlic filling

makes 10 ravioli

FOR THE FILLING:

7½ ounces raw cashews

1 head garlic

2 teaspoons olive oil

¼ cup lemon juice

1 teaspoon salt

FOR THE DOUGH:

½ cup (70g) tapioca starch

½ cup (96g) potato starch

¼ cup cooked mashed potato

3 tablespoons palm oil or other solid shortening

1 large egg white

2 teaspoons honey

1 teaspoon cider vinegar

1 teaspoon salt

1. **Make the filling:** Measure the cashews into a medium bowl and pour 3 cups water over them. Cover the bowl with plastic wrap and set it on the counter overnight.

2. Preheat the oven to 375°F. Remove the outer layers of skin from the head of garlic, leaving the bulb and cloves intact. With a sharp knife, cut about 1 inch off the top of the garlic bulb to expose all of the cloves. Place the head of garlic in the middle of a 7 × 7-inch (or larger) piece of foil. Brush the olive oil over the exposed cloves. Wrap the bulb tightly in the foil, place on a baking sheet, and bake for 40 to 45 minutes, or until it is soft and fragrant.

3. Rinse and drain the cashews and transfer them to a food processor. Blend until they are smooth and creamy. Pop the roasted garlic out of its skin by squeezing on the side of the cloves and add it to the cashew cream. Add the lemon juice and salt and process the filling until it is smooth. Return the

filling to the bowl and refrigerate until ready to make the ravioli. (The filling may be prepared a day ahead.) This recipe may make more filling than you need. Serve the remainder as cashew "cheese."

4. **Make the dough:** In a food processor, pulse to combine the tapioca starch, potato starch, mashed potato, palm oil, and egg white. Add the honey, vinegar, and salt and process the dough until the mixture looks like small curds.

5. Transfer the mixture to a bowl and press it together with your hands to form a smooth ball. Roll out the dough between two pieces of parchment paper to the desired thickness—$1/16$ to $1/8$ inch works well. Using a dough scraper or pizza cutter, cut the dough into ten 2 × 5-inch rectangles. Place 1 teaspoon of filling on the bottom half of the strip and fold the top half of the strip down to cover the filling. Lightly press around all edges with your fingers—the dough will stick together without wetting the sides or using an egg wash. Use the dough scraper or a knife to neaten the edges. Use the dough scraper or a spatula to pick up each ravioli and transfer it to a plate. Cover the ravioli with plastic wrap to keep them from drying out while you roll out and stuff the remaining ravioli.

6. To cook the ravioli, bring a pot of water to a boil. Drop the ravioli, several at a time, into the boiling water. The ravioli are done when they float and the filling is hot—depending on the size and thickness of the ravioli, this may take 2 to 3 minutes. (You can also cover the ravioli with plastic wrap and refrigerate or freeze them until ready to cook.)

NOTE: Making the filling is a 2-day process if you want to achieve the creamiest possible filling. You also can roast the garlic ahead of time and keep it in the refrigerator until you are ready to assemble the filling.

THE NIGHT BEFORE my son Marty's college graduation, my family booked three hotel rooms in central New York. With a family of diverse dietary challenges, my sister, Lynn, planned a literal moveable feast (apologies to Hemingway). In one room we had wine and appetizers, we moved on for the main course, and in the last room, we had dessert and gifts. The challenge was to make a fresh-tasting feast that required assembling rather than cooking. That evening, we gave new meaning to "lobster rolls" by using rice paper rounds, which are "cooked" using nothing more than a bowl of hot water. While one of us dunked and softened the stretchy rice rounds, the other stuffed the wraps with the lobster filling, sprinkled them with fresh arugula leaves, and folded them tightly. It was a truly moveable feast.

This recipe might just as well be subtitled "Gourmet Travel Food." It was inspired by Ina Garten's Lobster Cobb Salad Rolls and was adapted to be both gluten-free and hotel room–friendly. Typically, I don't use prepackaged ingredients, but in this case rice paper wraps (also known as spring roll wraps) can't be beat.

lobster rolls

serves 8 (2 rolls per person)

2 pounds cooked lobster meat, cut into ¾-inch cubes

½ pound bacon, cooked and crumbled

6 ounces Gorgonzola cheese, crumbled

2 avocados, cut into ½- to ¾-inch cubes

Juice of 2 lemons

¼ cup olive oil

2 tablespoons Dijon mustard

1 teaspoon salt

½ teaspoon freshly ground black pepper

2 packages rice paper wraps (8 rounds per package)

3 cups fresh baby arugula

1. In a large salad bowl, toss together the lobster, bacon, Gorgonzola, and avocados.

2. In a screw-top jar, combine the lemon juice, olive oil, mustard, salt, and pepper and shake until the dressing comes together. Pour the dressing over the lobster mixture and toss until the salad is well mixed.

3. To prepare the rice paper wraps, fill a shallow bowl with hot water. One at a time, using two hands, dip the wrappers into the hot water until they are just moistened. Place them on a clean kitchen (or hotel) towel to finish softening.

4. Onto each rice paper wrap, spoon a strip of lobster salad about 3 inches long down the center, and cover with a small handful of arugula. Roll the rice wrapper like a burrito, folding both ends in and then rolling the wrap around the filling. The rice wrapper when moistened will naturally stick together.

NEW YORK CITY is full of pizza snobs. We are reminded of this often by customers from the city who tell us that we "nailed" gluten-free pizza. They reminisce about the oversized slices of pizza available all over the city that you fold in half and let orange oil drip all over your paper plate—and according to them we've created an appealing substitute. When we worked on Wall Street, my building was a few blocks from one of those hole-in-the-wall pizza joints. I didn't go there for the pizza, though. It was their puffy, crescent-shaped spinach and cheese calzones that I was after.

At Against The Grain, pizza is all about the crust, and that is definitely the case with calzones. A calzone is typically made with pizza crust, but the crust is folded over into a semicircular shape. Where calzones differ from pizzas, though, is the opportunity to stuff the calzone with a variety of fillings that are contained by the crust. Some calzones are fried, but most, like these, are baked. When I bite into the crusty exterior and the cheesy filling oozes out, it reminds me of the calzones that we ate as we threaded our way back through the lunchtime crowd to our cubicles high above Wall Street.

calzones

makes 6 calzones

FOR THE DOUGH:

2 cups (280g) tapioca starch, plus up to ½ cup (70g) kneaded in for rolling

¾ cup (90g) light buckwheat flour

1 teaspoon salt

1 cup milk

¼ cup canola oil

1 tablespoon active dry yeast

1 teaspoon sugar

1 large egg

FOR THE FILLING:

1 cup full-fat ricotta cheese

1 cup shredded mozzarella cheese

1 large egg

⅓ cup grated Parmesan cheese

½ cup chopped cooked kale or spinach, with water squeezed out

¼ teaspoon freshly grated nutmeg

1. **Make the dough:** In a food processor, combine 2 cups tapioca starch, the buckwheat flour, and salt and pulse until blended.

2. In a medium saucepan, bring the milk and oil to a boil, stirring constantly. Immediately pour the hot mixture into the flours and process until it is moist with a sand-like texture. Allow the dough to cool for 20 minutes.

3. Meanwhile, in a small bowl, combine the yeast, sugar, and ⅓ cup warm water and allow it to proof for 15 minutes.

4. Add the proofed yeast to the flour mixture and blend until combined. Add the egg and blend the dough until it is smooth and comes together. Cover and allow it to rest for 20 minutes.

5. While the dough is still in the bowl, use a rubber spatula to knead in up to ½ cup tapioca starch so that it can be handled, but is still tender and not stiff. Turn the dough out onto a piece of plastic wrap dusted with tapioca starch.

6. Divide the dough into 6 equal portions and roll into balls. Cover them with oiled plastic wrap and allow to rise while you prepare the filling.

7. Position an oven rack in the center of the oven and preheat to 400°F. Line a baking sheet with parchment paper.

8. **Make the filling:** In a bowl, by hand, stir together the ricotta, mozzarella, egg, Parmesan, kale or spinach, and nutmeg until the filling is well blended.

9. Working on the plastic wrap, dust your hands with tapioca starch and pat each ball into a 5-inch-diameter round, one at a time. Spoon one-sixth of the filling on the lower half of the circle. Using the plastic wrap to support the dough, fold the top over to form a half-moon, and lightly pinch the seams together. The dough will stretch slightly as you fold it. Lift the calzone using the plastic wrap like a sling, and invert it onto the baking sheet. With a sharp knife, score the top with 3 or 4 steam vents. Repeat with the remaining dough and filling.

10. Bake for 25 minutes, or until browned at the edges and the filling oozes out of the slits. Transfer to a cooling rack or serve warm.

THE FIRST MEAL I ever made for my husband, Tom, was the summer before our senior year in college, when I stayed in New Orleans to take a summer school course. We had gone shopping at Schwegmann Brothers Giant Supermarket, an only-in-New-Orleans institution where shopping was an event. There, in the middle of the red sea of meat, we found a little cast-iron hibachi grill, and I declared that I was going to make burgers. "If we're going to have burgers," Tom said, "we really ought to have mashed potatoes." That day, we made probably the best mashed potatoes I've ever eaten, and mashed potatoes have remained one of Tom's very favorite dishes.

When I first learned about Tattie Scones, a traditional Scottish potato scone, I figured they meant Tom could have mashed potatoes for breakfast. They are tasty accompaniments to eggs and are sort of a cross between the crustiness of hash browns on the outside and the creaminess of mashed potatoes on the inside. In this recipe I use eggs as a binder, and the buckwheat and chives give them a crispy texture and savory taste. They are also pretty simple to throw together in the morning, particularly if you have leftover potatoes.

tattie scones with chives

makes 8 scones

1 pound new potatoes, cooked and mashed with skins on (about 4 medium potatoes)

2 tablespoons salted butter, softened, plus 1 tablespoon melted for brushing tops

1 large egg

1/2 teaspoon salt

2/3 cup (80g) light buckwheat flour

1/3 cup (45g) tapioca starch, plus a little extra for rolling out, if needed

1 teaspoon baking powder

1 tablespoon chopped fresh chives

1. Position an oven rack in the center of the oven and preheat to 400°F. Line a baking sheet with parchment paper.

2. In a medium bowl, with a hand mixer, beat the mashed potatoes with the softened butter and egg. Add the salt, buckwheat flour, tapioca starch, and baking powder and mix on high until stiff and fully blended. Fold in the chives by hand.

3. Wet your hands and form the dough into 2 balls. The dough will be sticky but hold its shape. Dust the dough with a little tapioca starch, if necessary. Flatten each ball on the baking sheet to a round about 1/2 inch thick. Use your damp fingers to smooth the edges. Cut each round into quarters. Do not separate the quarters, but gently slide them about 1/4 inch apart using a dough scraper. Brush the tops with the melted butter.

4. Bake the scones for 25 minutes, or until golden brown. (You can also "bake" the scones on the stovetop in a buttered cast-iron skillet over medium heat. Brown, then flip and brown the other side, for a total of 5 to 7 minutes per side.)

MY LATE MOTHER-IN-LAW elevated entertaining to a high art, and she lived long enough to achieve her goal of hosting a fiftieth anniversary sit-down dinner in her home for 100 people. We flew to Houston for the event, and it was dinner party mastery at its best: a piano player in the living room, guests circulating through the rooms to various hors d'oeuvres tables, and couples sitting down to a hot, unhurried meal. She had a number of entertaining rules, but simplicity was the overriding factor. One rule was to strive for simple elegance—dishes that didn't require fussing over.

She recommended this particular dish to me for entertaining. It is easy to prepare and doesn't involve standing over the stove: You whip it up just before guests arrive, and pop it in the oven. While guests are circulating during cocktails, it bakes to perfection, infusing the kitchen with a delicious smell. The original recipe, from the *1968 Houston Junior League Cook Book,* called for Bisquick, Cheddar cheese, and canned green chilies. Here, I have substituted a self-rising gluten-free mix, fresh jalapeños, and sharp Cheddar. Served with a side salad and Cheesy Breadsticks (page 190), this dish satisfies vegetarians, carnivores, and gluten-free guests alike.

snappy jalapeño cheese bake

serves 8

2 medium fresh jalapeño peppers, seeds removed and finely diced

1 pound sharp Cheddar cheese (such as Cabot Seriously Sharp), freshly shredded

¾ cup (90g) light buckwheat flour

½ cup (70g) tapioca starch

¼ cup (48g) potato starch

½ teaspoon baking soda

6 large eggs

1 quart milk

1. Position an oven rack in the center of the oven and preheat to 350°F. Grease a 9 × 13-inch baking dish.

2. Sprinkle the jalapeños in the bottom of the baking dish. Cover the jalapeños with the shredded cheese.

3. In a large bowl, beat together the buckwheat flour, tapioca starch, potato starch, baking soda, eggs, and milk until they are somewhat thickened and well blended. Pour the mixture over the cheese. It will be liquid enough that it will spread to the sides of the dish.

4. Bake in the middle of the oven for 1 hour, or until the center is set and lightly browned. Allow to cool 10 minutes before slicing into servings.

EVEN THOUGH WE HAVE LIVED IN VERMONT for twenty years, I am still in awe of how the watery sap from maple trees can become a thick, amber sweetener. During one of our first springs, we tapped a half-dozen trees in our yard. Tending those taps was a devotion, a bit like tending a sick baby, but we learned firsthand that it takes 43 gallons of sap (and back-breaking effort) to produce only 1 gallon of syrup.

These are about the simplest crackers in the world, and are the marriage of two ingredients with amazing properties: flaxseeds and maple syrup. Flaxseeds are well known for their health benefits, including their high omega-3 heart-healthy fats and lots of fiber. They are also hydrocolloids, which means that they (the outer seed layer, in this case) form a gel when combined with water, which, when dried, *is* the structure for these crackers. These crackers are most easily made with a food dehydrator, but it is also possible to make them in the oven—I've included directions for both here. These are sweet, crunchy, healthy crackers that will delight adults and kids.

maple flaxseed crackers

makes 2 baking sheets of irregular-shaped crackers

1 cup golden flaxseeds

2 tablespoons maple syrup

½ teaspoon ground cinnamon

1. In a medium bowl, combine the flaxseeds and 2½ cups water. Allow the seeds to soak for at least 1 hour. The seeds will form a gel and the mixture will be gelatinous and thick.

2. Add the maple syrup and cinnamon and stir well.

3. **Make the crackers in a dehydrator:** Spread the crackers on the fruit roll or nonstick sheets of your dehydrator (you can also use parchment paper). Make them as thin as possible, although they will spread some on their own. Every dehydrator differs, but I set mine on the maximum temperature and allow the crackers to dry overnight. You can hasten drying by turning them after 4 to 5 hours. The crackers will first be kind of chewy, then gradually more brittle and crunchy. How long to dry them is a matter of preference. When done, break the crackers into irregular pieces and store them in an airtight container. They will last for months.

Make the crackers in an oven: Preheat the oven to 200°F and line 2 baking sheets with foil. Spread the flaxseed mixture on the baking sheets and bake the crackers for 3 hours, or until the tops of the crackers dry out. Remove the sheets from the oven and peel the crackers from the foil. Flip the crackers over and return them to the oven for another 2 to 3 hours. At this point the crackers should be brittle. Turn the oven off and allow the crackers to cool in the oven. Break them into pieces when completely cooled.

LONG BEFORE we were eating a gluten-free diet, I stumbled upon a sesame and honey wafer at a cheese shop in eastern Canada. I thought they were very clever and bought several for hiking and biking. At the time I never would have imagined that I would be relying on sesame in gluten-free baking, and the memory of those wafers was the inspiration for these crackers. These crackers rely on two ingredients that I think suffer from somewhat of an identity crisis: figs and sesame seeds.

I'm not sure how old I was before I realized what a fig looked like. My understanding of the fruit was a thin layer wedged inside a slightly crumbly cookie shell. Who ever knew that figs are high in potassium and dietary fiber, and a source of calcium? I've always liked the sweetness and chewiness of dried figs, as well as the crunchy seeds. Everyone is familiar with sesame in savory foods like tahini and sesame oil, but few realize it has similar properties to flour. In this recipe, the figs provide the glue and sesame is the structure. The natural sweetness of the figs, combined with the maple syrup and coconut, offsets the slightly bitter taste of concentrated sesame seeds. This dough also makes an excellent base for a cheesecake or a savory fig and goat cheese tart.

sweet sesame-maple-fig crackers

makes thirty-six 2-inch round crackers

8 ounces dried figs (about 25 figs), with stems removed

¼ cup maple syrup

2½ cups unsweetened shredded coconut

2 cups sesame seeds

1. In a food processor, combine the figs, maple syrup, coconut, and 1¼ cups water. Blend the mixture until all the liquid has been incorporated into the figs and coconut. Transfer the mixture to a medium bowl and work in the sesame seeds by hand. It should be a rollable dough.

2. Working with a third of the dough at a time, roll it out on a piece of parchment paper to a thickness of about ⅛ inch (you can make them thicker if you like, but the drying time will be longer). Dampen your hands and the rolling pin slightly if the dough is sticking. Cut out 2-inch rounds or whatever size and shape you'd like. Repeat with the remaining dough.

3. **Make the crackers in a dehydrator:** Transfer the crackers to the fruit roll or nonstick sheets of your dehydrator (you can also use parchment paper). Every dehydrator differs, but I set mine on the maximum temperature and allow the crackers to dry overnight. You can hasten drying by turning them after 4 to 5 hours. The crackers will first be kind of chewy, then gradually more brittle and crunchy. How long to dry them is a matter of preference. When done, allow them to cool and store them in an airtight container. They will last for months.

Make the crackers in an oven: Preheat the oven to 200°F and line 2 baking sheets with foil. Transfer the crackers to the baking sheets and bake them for 3 hours, or until the tops of the crackers dry out. Remove the sheets from the oven and peel the crackers from the foil. Flip the crackers over and return them to the oven for another 2 to 3 hours. At this point the crackers should be brittle. Turn the oven off and allow the crackers to cool in the oven.

variation

A similar cracker can be made by substituting dates for the figs and honey for the maple syrup. Finely ground pecans or almonds may be substituted for the sesame seeds.

THE FIRST TIME I perfected these savory, cracker-like appetizers, I cut them out in stars. When they came out of the oven, they were light and flaky little golden stars, with a puff pastry–like texture. It was exhilarating to see a gluten-free formulation look, well . . . normal. My very favorite Dr. Seuss story, *The Sneetches*, came to mind: It's about star-bellied creatures who are singled out for their differences.

Although gluten-free has become mainstream, it is difficult to have to advocate for yourself and your dietary needs. It can also be difficult watching your friends chow down on something so basic as peanut butter cheese crackers. These cheese puffs can't be found in vending machines . . . but dab a little peanut butter between two of these, and you've got basically the same thing. When making these puffs, it is important to make the thickness as consistent as possible to ensure the puffs crisp and brown evenly. The "puff" comes from the water in the butter and the added water that is incorporated into the dough. It seems counterintuitive, but water that is converted to steam as the puff bakes makes it crispy.

cheddar puffs

makes 30 to 40 crackers

1 cup grated Cheddar cheese

1 cup shredded Parmesan cheese

¾ cup (90g) light buckwheat flour

½ cup (70g) tapioca starch

4 tablespoons cold salted butter, cut into small pieces

½ teaspoon paprika

1. In a food processor, combine the Cheddar, Parmesan, buckwheat flour, tapioca starch, butter, and paprika and pulse until the cheese and butter have been incorporated into the flour and the texture is sand-like.

2. Slowly add ¼ cup water to the mixture and pulse until the dough begins to come together as larger curds. (You should be able to shape the dough between your fingers.) Knead the dough into one big ball and divide it into quarters. Set aside one-quarter of the dough and refrigerate the rest.

3. Position an oven rack in the center of the oven and preheat to 375°F. Line a baking sheet with parchment paper.

4. Working with one-quarter of the dough at a time, pat it down on a piece of parchment paper on the counter. Using a rolling pin guide, roll the dough out evenly to a thickness of ⅛ to 3/16 inch. Either cut the dough into small squares using a pizza cutter or cut the dough into shapes using canapé cutters. Repeat with the remaining dough.

5. Transfer the puffs to the baking sheet and bake for 10 minutes, or until the edges begin to brown. Serve warm as an appetizer or room temperature with a dab of peanut butter or Cheddar cheese spread. Store in an airtight container for several days. To recrisp them, if necessary, place on a baking sheet in a 350°F oven for 3 to 5 minutes.

WHEN WE FIRST MOVED TO VERMONT, we enrolled the kids in the Meetinghouse School, a Waldorf-like preschool. Having just arrived from New York City, I was your typical insecure country mom. When my turn arrived to provide the weekly snacks, I got it into my mind that I was going to make crackers from scratch. Mind you, I had never made crackers before from scratch. The cracker recipe looked so simple and yummy, it didn't occur to me to have a backup plan in case my baking went awry. Crackers, I learned, are anything but simple: The night before, I faithfully followed the recipe, and came out with the snarliest, worst-looking crackers imaginable. With nothing else to share, I brought the crackers into school with my tail between my legs. Much to my surprise, when I went back to pick up the boys, I was met by a tangle of preschoolers, all raving about my crackers. That was my first understanding that homely homemade baked goods with quality ingredients trump anything from the grocery store.

cheddar cheese crackers

makes 24 to 30 crackers

1 cup (120g) light buckwheat flour

¾ cup (105g) tapioca starch

1 teaspoon baking powder

1 tablespoon sugar

1 teaspoon salt

4 tablespoons cold salted butter, cut into cubes

6 ounces shredded Cheddar cheese

1 large egg white

1. In a food processor, combine the buckwheat flour, tapioca starch, baking powder, sugar, and salt and pulse until well blended. Add the butter and cheese and pulse until the mixture is just crumbly, but don't overblend. Add the egg white and pulse to combine.

2. Add 3 tablespoons water and process the dough just until it begins to come together. Transfer it to a large bowl and form 2 balls. Cover and place the dough in the refrigerator for 1 hour.

3. Position an oven rack in the lower third of the oven and preheat to 400°F. Line a baking sheet with parchment paper.

4. Working with one ball of dough at a time, remove a ball from the refrigerator and roll out the dough between two pieces of parchment paper as thin as you can get it without it sticking (about 1/16 inch). Using a sharp knife or a pizza cutter, cut out the crackers in whatever shape you'd like. Transfer the individual crackers to the baking sheet. Using the tines of a fork, poke docking holes into the crackers (to allow steam to escape). Repeat with the remaining dough.

5. Bake the crackers for 13 to 15 minutes, or until they begin to brown around the edges. (Differences in the moisture content of the cheese could alter the baking time by several minutes.) Check your crackers frequently toward the end. You want crispy crackers, but you don't want them too browned.

6. Transfer the baked crackers to a cooling rack to cool completely. Store in an airtight container for up to 5 days. If the crackers lose their crispness after a few days, recrisp them in a 350°F oven for 5 minutes.

Gluten-free crackers are not that hard to make, but getting them to puff up with the right degree of crispiness is the challenge. In this recipe, crispiness is achieved through the oil in the butter and cheese. The puffiness comes from steam created by the water, as well as the water content of the butter and the cheese, which can be almost 40%. The egg white serves as both a binder and a drying agent.

EVERYONE REMEMBERS his or her first dinner party: Mine was not long after we were married and had moved into our first apartment in Philadelphia. I made a lovely spinach noodle casserole, a salad, and some breadsticks fashioned from a prepackaged dough. After hors d'oeuvres, we moved from the living room to our dining room table (a repurposed picnic table with tippy benches). My guests were quite taken with the golden breadsticks, but halfway into the meal, my colleague's husband asked, "What are these, anyway, green beans?" referring to my spinach noodle casserole. Tom almost fell backwards off the bench laughing. I stressed myself out to make a gourmet meal, and this guy couldn't tell the difference between spinach noodles and green beans . . . but he ate practically the entire batch of crummy breadsticks.

That was my early lesson on the importance of what food looks like, not just how it tastes. People like familiar, attractive, and comforting foods. These breadsticks are just that—twisty, golden . . . and they don't *look* gluten-free. They are also made of a few simple, quality ingredients that will impress your guests at your next dinner party, even if you are dining at a picnic table.

cheesy breadsticks

makes thirty 12-inch breadsticks

1 cup plus 1 teaspoon (150g) tapioca starch

4 ounces sharp Cheddar cheese, freshly grated

2 ounces freshly shredded Parmesan cheese

4 tablespoons salted butter, cut up and chilled

1 large egg

1. Position an oven rack in the center of the oven and preheat to 400°F. Line a baking sheet with parchment paper.

2. In a food processor, combine the tapioca starch, Cheddar, Parmesan, butter, and egg and blend until the dough just begins to come together.

3. Pinch out tablespoon chunks (30g) of dough and roll them out on the counter into 12-inch ropes of even thickness. Carefully transfer each rope to the baking sheet. Using your forefinger, press on the rope every inch or so to create a twisted rope effect. You can place them fairly close to each other since they don't puff up much during baking.

4. Bake the breadsticks for 10 minutes, or until they are lightly browned on the bottom. Cool completely on a cooling rack.

WHEN MY SON MARTY graduated from high school, my sister, Lynn, hosted a family RV/campground party at Ft. Dummer State Park in Brattleboro. The bright and casually elegant picnic table was laid with a variety of mouthwatering antipastos, freshly steamed lobster, and mountains of corn on the cob. For dessert, my sister had brought Marty a surprise— gluten-free graham crackers "imported" for s'mores. Poor kid, he had forgotten what graham crackers tasted like . . . alone, he finished at least half of the package. Although the crackers were the best gluten-free version we had ever tasted, they were still more like a platform than a cracker.

Realistic graham crackers have remained some of the most elusive comfort foods of the gluten-free world. Any gluten-free graham cracker recipe I tried always seemed like cookies. However, the minute I tasted my first baked good made with light buckwheat flour, I was struck by its slightly grainy texture, light crispness, and an almost sweet aftertaste.

graham crackers

makes twenty-four 3-inch square graham crackers

1 cup (140g) tapioca starch

1¼ cups (150g) light buckwheat flour

¼ cup (48g) potato starch

⅓ cup packed brown sugar

1 teaspoon baking powder

½ teaspoon salt

¼ teaspoon ground cinnamon

8 tablespoons cold salted butter, cut into 8 slices

¼ cup milk

2 tablespoons honey

1 tablespoon dark molasses

1 teaspoon vanilla extract

3 tablespoons granulated sugar mixed with 1 teaspoon ground cinnamon (optional)

1. In a food processor, combine the tapioca starch, buckwheat flour, potato starch, brown sugar, baking powder, salt, and cinnamon and pulse to combine. Add the butter and pulse until the dough is mealy.

2. In a bowl, whisk together the milk, honey, molasses, and vanilla. Pour the milk mixture into the processor and combine until the dough holds together. Divide the dough in half and form into 2 logs 8 inches long. Cover the dough and refrigerate for 1 hour. Keep one log refrigerated while you work with the other.

3. Position an oven rack in the center of the oven and preheat to 350°F.

4. On a piece of parchment paper, roll a log of dough out into a sheet ⅛ inch thick. Score or cut the dough into twelve 3-inch squares using a pizza cutter. Don't worry about the scraps along the side—just bake them and reserve them for graham cracker crumbs. Poke holes in the dough for expansion. (For cinnamon crackers, sprinkle the granulated sugar–cinnamon mixture evenly over the dough.)

5. Slide the entire piece of parchment paper onto an ungreased baking sheet and bake for 15 minutes, or until the sides are lightly browned. Allow the crackers to cool for several minutes on the baking sheet and rescore the lines while the crackers are still warm to minimize breakage. Repeat with the remaining dough.

NOTE: One of the keys to making these crackers crisp is rolling them out to a uniform ⅛-inch thickness. The best way to do that is to use rolling pin guides. Commercially available guide rings work well, or you can make your own ⅛-inch-thick strips to place alongside the dough. The wooden paint stirrers you get at paint stores for free are exactly ⅛ inch thick and work as well as anything.

It screamed *GRAHAM CRACKERS* to me. They bake up with just the right texture, a pleasant but not too sweet taste, and a hint of cinnamon. In this recipe, butter lends to the crispiness, but it needs to be well chilled to harden the fat in the dough. Molasses gives the cracker its characteristic color and lends to the "graham" flavor.

WHEN WE LIVED IN NEW YORK CITY, croissants were a huge treat on Sunday morning served with dabs of blackberry jam and the *New York Times*. It all seems kind of retro now, between our digital paper subscription and the lack of gluten-free croissants. Croissants are one of our most requested products from customers, mostly because it's so hard to pass a tray of freshly baked croissants and know they are off-limits. Gluten-free dough is not typically stretchy, and it is the stretchiness of croissant dough that makes it expand and flake when the water in the dough creates steam during baking. The butter gives the croissant its rich taste and functions to separate its many layers.

Traditional croissants are made with yeasted, laminated dough. The lack of gluten makes it nearly impossible to create stretchy sheets of dough with or without any gums or stabilizers. Instead, I developed a puffy pastry that has the taste and texture of a croissant: a modification of my choux pastry piped out in the form of a croissant, made and baked in less than an hour. The tapioca gel created by adding tapioca starch to boiled milk and water is quite stretchy, and the taste and texture bear a distinct resemblance to traditional croissants. Guess what we've now added to our Sunday morning breakfasts?

puff pastry croissants

makes 6 croissants

½ cup milk

4 tablespoons salted butter

½ teaspoon salt

1 cup (140g) tapioca starch

2 large eggs

1. Position an oven rack in the lower third of the oven and preheat to 425°F. Line a baking sheet with parchment paper.

2. In a saucepan, bring the milk, butter, salt, and 2 tablespoons water to a boil over medium heat, stirring constantly. Immediately stir in the tapioca starch. Continue stirring and cooking for about 1 minute, until you have a gelatinous mass. Allow the dough to cool for 10 minutes.

3. Using a hand mixer, beat in one egg at a time until fully incorporated. At first, it will seem like scrambled eggs; continue beating the dough until the dough becomes pasty before adding the second egg. (You may have to scrape down the sides and beaters multiple times.) The dough is ready when it thickens and stretches back when tugged—any small lumps will bake out.

4. Gather the dough together and spoon it into a sealable plastic bag. Snip off about ½ inch of one corner of the bag to use for piping.

5. Build a crescent-shaped croissant by piping the dough starting with a tapered "leg." Zigzagging back and forth, pipe the croissant wider toward the center and then taper it down for the other "leg."

6. Bake the croissants for 15 minutes. Reduce the oven temperature to 350°F and bake for 15 minutes, or until they are light golden brown. Transfer to a cooling rack.

LIKE EVERYONE ELSE, we began our gluten-free journey worrying about what we were going to do about sandwiches. Our boys went to small, rural schools, and lunch was a brown-bag affair. We started out with romaine lettuce wraps, but by the time the wraps got to lunchtime, they resembled damp washcloths. We tried corn tortillas for a while, but they dried out or became kind of flabby. Then we tried commercially available gluten-free tortillas. They seemed to break in venetian blind strips at every fold.

These homemade tortillas are now a staple in our house—they are stretchy, chewy, and flexible without cracking or drying out. The secret to their flexibility is that they are not flattened dough balls. Rather, they begin as a batter and are more pancake-like until they are baked. The tortillas are made one at a time in an electric tortilla press, and inserted between the folds of a clean kitchen towel to retain their moisture and flexibility until all 8 have been made. We use these tortillas for leftover barbecued chicken or pork, but they are also excellent with a big spoonful of Great Northern or black beans as the base.

flour tortillas

makes 8 tortillas

1¾ cups (245g) tapioca starch

1 teaspoon salt

¾ cup milk

¼ cup canola oil

3 large eggs

1. In a food processor, combine the tapioca starch and salt.

2. In a medium saucepan, bring the milk and oil to a full boil, stirring constantly to keep the milk and oil in solution. Pour the hot mixture into the food processor and pulse until the mixture is fully moistened and grainy. Allow the mixture to rest and cool for 15 minutes.

3. Add the eggs, one at a time, and pulse the batter until it is fully blended. The batter will have the consistency of thick pancake batter. Pour the batter into a medium bowl and set it next to your tortilla press as it preheats according to the manufacturer's instructions.

4. Pour approximately ¼ cup of batter onto the center of the press. Press down lightly with the lid, then release it. Within seconds the bottom will be cooked enough that you can spin the tortilla with your fingers 90 degrees and press down again. Repeat this process until the tortilla extends to the edge of the tortilla press bed and is the desired thickness. Open the press, let the bottom cook for a few seconds, and flip the tortilla over using a spatula. You can flip it over as many times as you like, but make sure that you don't overcook the tortilla or it will get too crispy. A done tortilla should be light and stretchy and have barely any browned marks on it. Making perfect tortillas takes a bit of practice, but even wrinkled ones work and taste just fine. If you find that the batter is too thick as you work,

thin it with 1 tablespoon of water at a time until you attain the desired consistency.

5. Place the cooked tortillas between the folds of clean kitchen towels to retain their warmth and flexibility as you prepare the remainder of the tortillas. Keep them in the towels until you serve them; otherwise, they will dry out.

NOTE: If you have any tortillas left over, they can be frozen between sheets of wax paper in a sealable plastic bag. Heating up a frozen tortilla is a simple matter of microwaving it on a plate for 10 seconds or leaving it in the sealable bag on the counter until it reaches room temperature.

HOMEMADE GLUTEN-FREE TORTILLAS are well worth the effort. I often rely on tapioca starch to create a starch-based gel and use eggs for their natural binding properties. Such is the case in the recipe for regular Flour Tortillas (page 196). This recipe, on the other hand, is based on flax meal as an egg replacer. Flax, which forms an egg white–like gel when soaked in water, is the binder, but it also adds an overpowering taste if not used sparingly.

Not one to shy away from challenges, I developed this recipe to showcase the optimum balance of starch and flaxseed to create a flavorful, bendable, and robust tortilla. Flax forms a viscous gel in a ratio of about 1:3 flaxseed to water. The spinach adds color, and its flavor neutralizes the distinctive taste of flaxseeds. You will need an electric tortilla press to make this recipe, but you can make the tortillas as big as your machine will allow. Fill with a combination of garlic-sautéed portobello mushrooms and fennel with shredded lettuce for a light vegan treat.

vegan spinach tortillas

makes 8 tortillas

1 tablespoon flax meal

1½ cups (210g) tapioca starch

⅓ cup (40g) light buckwheat flour

1 teaspoon active dry yeast (included for flavor; optional)

1½ teaspoons salt

¼ cup canola oil

1 tablespoon cider vinegar

¼ cup chopped spinach, fresh or frozen (with excess moisture pressed out)

1. In a small bowl, make the flaxseed slurry by combining the flax meal with 3 tablespoons water.

2. In a food processor, combine the tapioca starch, buckwheat flour, yeast (if using), and salt and pulse to combine.

3. In a medium saucepan, bring the oil and ⅔ cup water to a full boil over medium heat, stirring constantly to keep the water and oil emulsified. Pour the hot mixture into the food processor, add the vinegar, and pulse until the mixture is fully moistened and grainy. Allow the mixture to rest and cool for 15 minutes.

4. Add the flax slurry, the spinach, and ¼ cup water to the food processor. Pulse the dough until it comes together as a ball. It will be stretchy and a bit sticky, but easy to make into 8 individual balls.

5. Preheat a tortilla press according to the manufacturer's instructions. Place one ball onto the center of the press. Press down lightly with the lid, then release it. Within seconds the bottom will be cooked enough that you can spin the tortilla with your fingers 90 degrees and press down again. Repeat this process until the tortilla extends to the edge of the tortilla press bed and is the desired thickness. Open the press, let the bottom cook for a few seconds, and flip the tortilla over using a spatula. You can flip it over as many times as you like, but make sure that you don't overcook the tortilla or it will get too crispy. A done tortilla should be light and stretchy and have barely any browned marks on it.

6. Place the cooked tortillas between the folds of clean kitchen towels to retain their warmth and flexibility as you prepare the remainder of the tortillas. Keep them in the towels until you serve them; otherwise, they will dry out.

ONE OF THE MOST CHALLENGING ASPECTS of gluten-free baking is that you must always be thinking about structure. The high hydration levels required for gluten-free bread mean that tasks like making layered puff pastry are compromised at best, since gluten-free dough has a tendency to collapse under its own weight. Then there is *pâte à choux*, a puffy pastry dough that traditionally contains flour, water, butter, and eggs. Pâte à choux, or choux pastry, is the basis for éclairs, savory cream puffs, profiteroles, and gougères. As a gluten-free dough, it has its own internal structure and it can be shaped into rings and even swans. This dough is formulated somewhat differently from wheat-based dough: canola oil, which spreads less than butter, allows the pastry to rise more, and using milk rather than water adds protein while providing a traditional buttery taste. When piped onto parchment paper, the dough is rather gelatinous, but it keeps its shape as it rises and bakes. Fill this pastry with savory ingredients or add 2 to 3 teaspoons of sugar to the dough and fill with Pastry Cream (page 341). In less than an hour, you can have a striking appetizer or dessert that no one will know is gluten-free.

pâte à choux

makes enough pastry for a 9-inch gougère or 8 cream puffs

½ cup milk

¼ cup canola oil

½ teaspoon salt

1¼ cups (175g) tapioca starch

2 large eggs

2 to 3 teaspoons sugar (optional for dessert pastry)

1. Position an oven rack in the lower third of the oven and preheat to 425°F. Line a baking sheet with parchment paper.

2. In a saucepan, bring the milk, canola oil, salt, and 2 tablespoons water to a boil over medium heat, stirring constantly. Immediately stir in the tapioca starch. Continue stirring and cooking for about 1 minute until you have a gelatinous mass. Allow the dough to cool for 10 minutes.

3. Using a hand mixer, beat in one egg until the egg is fully incorporated. Continue beating the dough until the dough becomes pasty before adding the second egg. (You may have to scrape down the sides and beaters multiple times.) The dough is ready when it is too thick to mix and stretches back when tugged—it may still have small lumps in it, but they will bake out.

4. Gather the dough together and spoon it into a sealable plastic bag. Snip off about ½ inch of one corner of the bag to use for piping. Pipe the dough in whatever shape you like onto the baking sheet—elongated éclairs, rounded cream puffs or smaller profiteroles, or a connected ring of puffs.

5. Bake the pastry for 15 minutes. Reduce the temperature to 350°F and bake for 20 minutes more. Open the oven and allow the pastry to cool in the oven for 15 minutes to help it dry out.

NOTE: The trick to good choux pastry is a combination of temperature and moisture, so make sure your oven is baking to its true temperature.

YOU MIGHT FIND it surprising to find a pet treat recipe included in this collection, but our golden retriever, Chester, has been my front-line recipe tester throughout this book. Of course, he didn't taste recipes with ingredients off-limits to dogs, but he did get to chase several bread bloopers that were more akin to edible Frisbees.

Why feed your pet highly processed treats when you can make your own without grains, binders, or fillers? These are vegan biscuits—flaxseeds are the natural binders—that are cut out and dried. Store them in an airtight container and you will always have them on hand for man's best friend . . . or a horse. These pet treats are most easily made with a food dehydrator, but it is also possible to make them in the oven—I've included directions for both.

c-biscuit pet treats for dogs and horses

makes thirty 2-inch treats DF

2 tablespoons flaxseeds

1 cup (140g) tapioca starch

1¼ cups (150g) light buckwheat flour

2 cups chopped carrots

2 tablespoons palm or solid shortening

1 tablespoon chopped fresh rosemary

2 tablespoons molasses

1. In a small bowl, combine the flaxseeds and 6 tablespoons water and set aside to form a gel.

2. In a food processor, combine the tapioca starch, buckwheat flour, carrots, shortening, rosemary, molasses, and flax gel. Process until the dough comes together as a ball. Roll out the dough to a ½-inch thickness and cut into shapes.

3. Make the treats in a dehydrator: Transfer the treats directly to the rack of your dehydrator. Every dehydrator differs, but I set mine on the maximum temperature and allow the treats to dry overnight until all the moisture has evaporated. You can hasten drying by turning them after 4 to 5 hours. When done, cool and store them in an airtight container.

Make the treats in an oven: Preheat the oven to 200°F and line a baking sheet with foil. Transfer the treats to the baking sheet and bake them for 3 hours, or until the tops of the treats dry out. Remove the sheet from the oven and peel the treats from the foil. Flip the treats over and return them to the oven for another 2 to 3 hours, or until the treats are completely dry. Turn the oven off and allow the treats to cool in the oven.

NOTE: To make these treats tasty for cats, add a 5-ounce can of tuna in oil and decrease the palm shortening to 1 tablespoon—dogs will like them too.

cookies *and* bars

WHEN WE MOVED TO PHILADELPHIA for graduate school, we lived five blocks north of the Italian Market, the oldest outdoor market in the country. It was a colorful place, from the vendors who wouldn't let you touch the beautiful displays of fruits and vegetables, to one who sold us a big bag of pecans without any meat in the shells. And then there were the Italian bakeries and delis. What a feast for the senses they were—the hanging cheeses and salamis, the buttery Italian cookies, and the cannoli! We didn't often have the money to splurge on anything but basic meals, but when we did we always went for either cannoli or the Italian tricolor rainbow cookies. Who could resist such beautiful almond-scented delicacies?

These cookies are the first tricolor cookies I have had in years. Because these cookies are based principally on almond paste, they are ideally suited to a gluten-free adaptation. I'm not a big fan of using food coloring, but I could barely contain my excitement when I took all three colorful layers out of the oven. The smell brought me right back to the Italian Market bakeries, teeming with customers on a Saturday morning. These cookies have light sponge layers, spread with seedless raspberry or apricot jam, and covered in a dark chocolate shell.

italian tricolor rainbow cookies

makes 3 dozen cookies

3 large eggs, separated

¾ cup sugar

12 tablespoons salted butter

7 ounces almond paste, store-bought or homemade (page 336)

1 teaspoon almond extract

½ cup (96g) potato starch

½ cup (70g) tapioca starch

¼ teaspoon salt

1 jar (10 ounces) seedless raspberry or apricot jam

1 cup dark chocolate chips

¼ cup coconut oil

Food coloring (red and green)

1. Position an oven rack in the center of the oven and preheat to 350°F. Grease the sides and bottoms of three 8 × 8-inch pans with butter. (Disposable aluminum pans work well, or you can use one pan, bake a layer, cool it, bake another pan, and so on.) After buttering the sides of the pans, line each pan with parchment paper, allowing a flap to extend over two sides.

2. In a bowl, with a hand mixer, beat the egg whites on high until medium peaks are formed. Set aside.

3. In a separate bowl, cream the sugar and butter. Add the almond paste, almond extract, and egg yolks and beat on high until they are well mixed. The batter will be quite stiff.

4. Fold in the potato starch, tapioca starch, and salt by hand until incorporated. Fold in the egg whites, taking care to keep the batter as light as possible with minimal stirring. Weigh the batter, if possible, to divide it equally among 3 separate bowls.

recipe continues

5. Add 8 to 15 drops of red food coloring to one bowl and 8 to 15 drops of green to another; leave the third without additional coloring. Spoon each batter into a separate pan and smooth the surface using a butter knife or spatula.

6. Bake the three layers for approximately 20 minutes, or until the cakes are slightly springy in the centers and the sides start to pull away from the edges of the pans. Allow the cakes to cool in the pans for approximately 5 minutes. Then lift the cakes out using the parchment paper flaps and transfer to a cooling rack (leaving the parchment in place). Allow the cakes to cool completely.

7. Using a clean piece of parchment paper, invert the pink cake onto the paper and peel the bottom piece of parchment paper off. Flip the cake again, top side up, onto a parchment-lined baking sheet. Spread the surface edge to edge with a thin layer of jam. Repeat the steps for the yellow layer to invert it on top of the pink layer, and spread with a layer of jam. Top the yellow layer with the inverted green cake.

8. Weight the cakes down (to press the layers together) by placing a piece of parchment paper on the top layer and topping it with a baking pan filled with canned goods. Place the weighted cake in the refrigerator for at least 1½ hours.

9. In a microwaveable bowl, microwave the chocolate chips and coconut oil on high for 1 minute. Stir vigorously to hasten melting, and microwave for another 30 seconds.

10. Cut the layer cake into four 2-inch-wide strips and transfer them to a cooling rack set inside a baking pan. Spoon the melted chocolate over the tops, then turn each strip to one of its sides and spoon chocolate over it, then turn to the uncoated side and spoon chocolate over that as well as the ends (all sides, except the bottom will be chocolate covered). After the chocolate has set, place the cakes in the freezer overnight before cutting cleanly into ¾-inch-wide cookies.

SNICKERDOODLES ARE ONE COOKIE that has the culinary historians stumped. No one knows anything of their origin except that they first appeared in cookbooks at the turn of the twentieth century. I had never heard of them until I moved to New England, where nearly every parent brought them to an end-of-the-season party at the ski slopes. There I saw many ways to make them. There were puffy ones and flat ones, dry crinkly ones and moist ones. No matter what ingredients are used, if you love cinnamon and sugar, you'll love snickerdoodles.

Historically, snickerdoodle recipes included milk, but those older recipes produced pan cookies rather than drop cookies. The oldest recipes also used baking soda to leaven the cookies and cream of tartar as an acid to activate the baking soda reaction. Baking powder, a more modern invention than baking soda, includes an acid in its formulation, and it works just as well. For a gluten-free adaptation, I use dehydrated potatoes as the base to make the cookies moist and chewy. Balanced with brown rice flour and just a tad of tapioca starch, it makes a crinkly-on-the-outside, tender-on-the-inside cookie.

snickerdoodles

makes 2½ dozen cookies

FOR THE COOKIES:

2 cups (100g) dehydrated potato flakes

¾ cup (120g) brown rice flour

¼ cup (35g) tapioca starch

1 teaspoon baking powder

¼ teaspoon salt

4 tablespoons salted butter

2 tablespoons canola oil

1¼ cups sugar

2 large eggs

1 teaspoon vanilla extract

FOR THE CINNAMON SUGAR:

3 tablespoons sugar

1 tablespoon ground cinnamon

1. **Make the cookies:** In a food processor, grind the potato flakes until they are powder-like. Add the rice flour, tapioca starch, baking powder, and salt and process until well blended.

2. In a bowl, with a hand mixer, cream the butter, oil, and sugar. Add the eggs and vanilla.

3. Add the dry ingredients to the butter and egg mixture. Beat the dough until well blended. Refrigerate the dough for 30 minutes.

4. Meanwhile, position an oven rack in the center of the oven and preheat to 400°F. Line two baking sheets with parchment paper.

5. **Make the cinnamon sugar:** In a shallow bowl, blend the sugar and cinnamon.

6. Roll the dough into 1-inch balls and roll in the cinnamon-sugar mixture. Place the cookies 2 inches apart on the baking sheets. Bake the cookies for 8 minutes, rotating halfway through baking, or until the tops are set.

FLOURLESS RECIPES always get my attention and stimulate my creative juices. Such was the case when I first spotted a recipe for Flourless Chocolate-Walnut Cookies in François Payard's *Chocolate Epiphany*, using primarily powdered sugar and cocoa powder in lieu of flour. But the recipe had a frustratingly short shelf life. Although the directions specified that the cookies could be stored for up to 3 days, they were only okay on the second and not great on the third. That is when I decided that these cookies really wanted to be ice cream cookies—staling wouldn't be an issue, and they would make positively decadent ice cream cookies. Once you try them, I'm sure you will agree.

These cookies, which are crinkly on the top and fudgy inside, are the perfect size for an ice cream sandwich cookie. They have the taste and texture of a moist and chewy brownie. The dairy-free ice cream, which is whipped chocolate coconut cream, is one that you can make with a hand mixer and a bowl; no need to wrangle with an ice cream maker. It will drive you crazy waiting an hour for the ice cream to freeze between the two fudgy cookies, but the wait will totally be worth it.

chocolate mint ice cream cookies

makes 8 sandwich cookies

FOR THE COOKIES:

1³/4 cups powdered sugar

2 teaspoons tapioca starch

1/2 cup unsweetened cocoa powder

2 large egg whites

1 teaspoon mint extract

1/2 cup finely chopped hulled pumpkin seeds

FOR THE ICE CREAM FILLING:

3/8 cup coconut cream (skimmed from the top of a 13.5-ounce can of full-fat coconut milk), chilled

2 tablespoons powdered sugar

1 tablespoon unsweetened cocoa powder

1/2 cup dairy-free mini chocolate chips (such as Enjoy Life)

1. **Make the cookies:** Position an oven rack in the center of the oven and preheat to 300°F. Line a baking sheet with parchment paper.

2. In a medium bowl, stir together the powdered sugar, tapioca starch, and cocoa powder. Gradually work in the egg whites and mint extract and blend by hand until totally smooth and shiny. Stir in the pumpkin seeds until they are evenly distributed.

3. With damp hands, form the dough into 16 balls and place them 2 inches apart on the baking sheet. Wash out the bowl and put it in the freezer to chill.

4. Bake for 17 to 19 minutes, or until puffy and cracked. Allow the cookies to cool completely on the pan before preparing the filling; they will flatten as they cool.

5. Make the filling: Remove the bowl from the freezer and, using a hand mixer, whip the coconut cream, powdered sugar, and cocoa powder until it reaches a mousse-like consistency. Fold in the chocolate chips.

6. Pipe the filling in a spiral motion on the bottoms of 8 cookies. Press another cookie on the top. Wrap each cookie individually in plastic wrap and place in the freezer to harden. Serve frozen.

THESE COOKIES are an adaptation of an old *Yankee Magazine* recipe. Classic ginger snaps are crispy; these are chewy and utterly addictive ginger cookies. The chewiness in these cookies comes from the fat in the canola oil. Oil also has the advantage of limiting spread, which is typically a major problem in gluten-free cookies made with butter. Corn syrup and white sugar, typical of classic Southern ginger snaps, produces crispy cookies, whereas molasses attracts moisture and contributes to chewiness. My guess is that the Yankee in the name of these cookies reflects the fact that historically molasses was more accessible than sugar in the North, and the sugar-growing regions of the United States were located in the South.

This is one of my family's favorite cookies, so much so that it is the only recipe I have written into my copy of *Joy of Cooking*. In part due to the molasses, an excellent natural preservative, these cookies stay fresh and chewy long after most gluten-free baked goods would go stale.

yankee ginger snaps

makes 3 dozen cookies

1²⁄₃ cups (200g) light buckwheat flour

1 cup (140g) tapioca starch

½ teaspoon salt

2 teaspoons ground ginger

1 teaspoon ground cinnamon

2 teaspoons baking soda

½ cup canola oil

1 large egg

1 cup sugar, plus 2 tablespoons for rolling

¼ cup molasses

1. Position an oven rack in the center of the oven and preheat to 350°F. Line two baking sheets with parchment paper.

2. In a large bowl, blend the buckwheat flour, tapioca starch, salt, ginger, cinnamon, and baking soda. Set aside.

3. Using a hand mixer, combine the oil, egg, and 1 cup sugar in a medium bowl until the batter is light yellow. Beat in the molasses. Working by hand—the dough will be quite stiff—stir in the dry ingredients until the dough is fully blended.

4. Form the dough into 1-inch balls and roll them in the remaining 2 tablespoons of sugar. Place the balls about 2 inches apart on the baking sheets.

5. Bake the cookies for 10 to 12 minutes, rotating the sheets halfway through. The cookies will spread a little and be soft and fragile when you remove them from the oven. Allow them to cool for about 5 minutes, then use a flexible metal spatula to transfer them to a cooling rack.

I NEVER MET my husband Tom's grandmother, but I feel like I know her after inheriting her recipe collection and old cookbooks. She was a rural Texas math teacher, born to several generations of schoolteachers, and was widowed at an early age. She also spent her life typing hundreds of scrawled recipes, making precise notes and alphabetizing everything. It probably would disappoint her to know that she died before she had those last dozen recipes typed and filed away.

I found this recipe scribbled on the back of one of her student's homework from October 7, 1967. Tom's grandmother had nearly a dozen oatmeal cookie recipes in her collection, but this was the one she prized. All I had to do was convert the wheat flour to gluten-free flours. Oatmeal cookies can be fickle—sometimes they're thin, lacey layers and sometimes dry dense balls, depending on the type of shortening. This one uses both canola oil and butter: The butter makes the cookies tender, whereas the higher melting point of the canola keeps the cookies from spreading too much. Family lore is that Grandmother wasn't the best cook, but she definitely knew a good oatmeal cookie recipe when she saw one.

old-fashioned oatmeal cookies

makes 3 to 3½ dozen cookies

1⅓ cups (185g) tapioca starch

1⅓ cups (160g) light buckwheat flour

⅓ cup (65g) potato starch

1 teaspoon ground cinnamon

1 teaspoon baking soda

½ cup canola oil

8 tablespoons salted butter

1 cup packed brown sugar

1 cup granulated sugar

2 large eggs

1 teaspoon vanilla extract

3 cups rolled oats

1 cup raisins (or 10 ounces dark chocolate chips or chunks)

1. Position an oven rack in the center of the oven and preheat to 325°F. Line three baking sheets with parchment paper.

2. In a medium bowl, blend the tapioca starch, buckwheat flour, potato starch, cinnamon, and baking soda.

3. In a large bowl, with a hand mixer, combine the oil, butter, sugars, eggs, and vanilla and mix on high until the batter is light yellow. By hand, stir in the dry ingredient mixture until it is fully blended. Fold in the rolled oats and raisins.

4. Roll the dough in small balls, just under the size of a Ping-Pong ball. Place the balls about 2 inches apart on the baking sheets. Bake the cookies, one sheet at a time, in the center of the oven for 15 minutes.

IT IS SAID that the first taste is with your eyes . . . but with M&M's, it's just the opposite. Although they are rainbow-colored, they are all the same flavor. It is just that not everyone agrees: Some think the red ones taste better, and my son Alex prefers the greens. Just like I did as a kid, he sorts his M&M's into piles by color, and he saves the greens for last.

Mars, Inc., used color to turn M&M's into the number one selling candy in the world, with sales greater than the gross domestic products of some countries. Put two cookies side by side, one with brightly colored M&M's, in front of most anyone, and they will choose the one with the brightly colored candies. My son Alex is no exception. In his mind, everything tastes better with M&M's. I developed these cookies for Alex using toasted gluten-free oat flour. They are designed to spread just the right amount to make a chewy, buttery, brightly festive cookie.

m&m cookies

makes 2 dozen cookies

4 tablespoons salted butter

1/4 cup canola oil

1 cup packed brown sugar

1/2 cup granulated sugar

2 large eggs

1 teaspoon vanilla extract

1/2 teaspoon ground cinnamon

1 3/4 cups (175g) toasted oat flour

1 1/4 cups (175g) tapioca starch

1/2 teaspoon baking soda

1 cup M&M's

1. Position an oven rack in the center of the oven and preheat to 325°F. Line a baking sheet with parchment paper.

2. In a large bowl, with a hand mixer, cream the butter, oil, and sugars until light and fluffy. Beat in the eggs, vanilla, and cinnamon. Mix in the toasted oat flour, tapioca starch, and baking soda until fully incorporated. Fold in the M&M's.

3. Roll the dough in small balls, just under the size of Ping-Pong balls, making sure that 5 to 6 M&M's get into each. Place the balls on the baking sheet, spaced about 2 inches apart.

4. Bake the cookies for 15 minutes, or until kind of puffy and very lightly browned. They will become chewier as they cool. Allow the cookies to cool for 5 minutes on the pan before transferring them to a cooling rack.

I'M NOT SURE when something so simple as peanut butter got complicated, but there is a dizzying array of peanut butter products to choose from. The Aztecs made a paste from nothing but roasted peanuts. In the ensuing years, peanut butter has been transformed, marketed, flavored, blended, "improved" . . . but at least you can still buy peanut butter made of nothing but salted, roasted peanuts, my favorite kind. Peanuts played a major role in my life: From elementary school through the end of graduate school, I lived on peanut butter, so for years thereafter I didn't even want to look at it. That was until I discovered that peanut butter was one of the best flourless substitutes in a host of gluten-free baked goods.

These are a very traditional peanut butter cookie, with lots of whole-grain buckwheat goodness. These cookies are also chewy and sandy, like a good peanut butter cookie should be, without an oily taste. In this recipe, I used an organic peanut butter, which contained nothing but salted, roasted peanuts and none of the other commercial additives. I believe you can taste the difference.

classic peanut butter cookies

makes 20 cookies

4 tablespoons salted butter

1/4 cup coconut oil

1/2 cup packed brown sugar

1/2 cup granulated sugar

2 teaspoons vanilla extract

1 large egg

1/2 cup organic natural peanut butter

3/4 teaspoon baking soda

1/2 teaspoon salt

1 1/2 cups (180g) light buckwheat flour

1/2 cup (70g) tapioca starch

1. Position an oven rack in the center of the oven and preheat to 350°F. Line a baking sheet with parchment paper.

2. In a bowl, use a hand mixer on high to cream the butter, coconut oil, sugars, vanilla, and egg until the dough is light and creamy. Mix in the peanut butter until thoroughly blended. Beat in the baking soda and salt.

3. Beat in the buckwheat flour and tapioca starch. The dough will become very stiff; use your hands to gather it into a ball.

4. Roll the dough into 1 1/2-inch balls and place them on the baking sheet. Using the tines of a fork, press down each ball until it is between 1/4 and 1/2 inch thick. (The cookie will spread some as it bakes.) Turn the fork 90 degrees and press down the tines again to create a crosshatched pattern on the top.

5. Bake the cookies for approximately 15 minutes, or until the bottoms are lightly browned. Allow the cookies to cool for 5 to 7 minutes on the pan before transferring them to a cooling rack. The cookies will be soft and fragile when removed from the oven, but will set and harden as they cool.

WHEN THE BOYS WERE LITTLE, we enrolled them in a local preschool. Late one spring, the kids sprouted various vegetable seeds indoors, and by the end of the school year they were ready to be planted in the garden. Each child chose a pumpkin seedling to take home, and when I picked up my son Marty, he was proudly cradling a healthy-looking seedling. We talked on the way home about how he was going to grow a pumpkin, make a jack-o'-lantern, and roast pumpkin seeds. Marty carefully planted his seedling in our garden, and not long after, it sported a couple of little gourd-size pumpkins. On the first day of school, I joked with the director that he didn't tell me that I was growing miniature pumpkins. Another parent looked perplexed and said that his son's pumpkin was huge—and grew up to 120 pounds!

I particularly like pumpkins because they are native to the Americas, and you can eat the entire plant—the flesh, the seeds, and the blossoms. I love roasting pumpkin seeds; and pumpkin seeds and pumpkin seed products are wonderful additions to gluten-free baking. They have the properties of other seeds and seed butters and can be use to add balanced proteins and nutrients to less nutritious gluten-free flours and starches.

pumpkin seed butter spice cookies

makes 2 dozen cookies

4 tablespoons salted butter

¼ cup coconut oil

½ cup packed brown sugar

½ cup granulated sugar

2 teaspoons vanilla extract

1 large egg

½ cup roasted pumpkin seed butter (see Note)

1 teaspoon baking soda

1 teaspoon salt

1 teaspoon ground allspice

1 teaspoon ground cinnamon

½ teaspoon ground cloves

½ teaspoon ground ginger

1½ cups (180g) light buckwheat flour

½ cup (70g) tapioca starch

1. Position an oven rack in the center of the oven and preheat to 350°F. Line 2 baking sheets with parchment paper.

2. In a bowl, with a hand mixer, cream the butter, coconut oil, sugars, vanilla, and egg, beating on high until the dough is light and creamy. Mix in the pumpkin seed butter until thoroughly blended. It will be an army green color at this point; the spices will correct that.

3. Beat in the baking soda, salt, and spices. Stir in the buckwheat flour and tapioca starch. The dough will be crumbly, a little oily, and will not come together into a ball unless you knead it with your hands. This is the consistency you want for forming cookie-size balls.

4. Roll the dough into balls 1½ inches in diameter. Place them on the baking sheet, 2 inches apart; they will spread to approximately 2½ inches wide.

5. Bake the cookies, one sheet at a time, for approximately 12 minutes, until the tops set. Allow the cookies to cool for 5 to 7 minutes on the pan before transferring them with a spatula to a cooling rack. The cookies will be soft and fragile when removed from the oven, but will set and harden as they cool.

NOTE: I'm not sure why pumpkin seed butter and pumpkin seed flour aren't more popular, but you can make your own pumpkin seed butter. Roast several cups of hulled pumpkin seeds for 12 to 15 minutes on a baking sheet in a 375°F oven. Use a food processor to blend them until they are finely ground, release their oil, and become liquid like peanut butter. Roasted pumpkin seed butter is delicious for many things besides cookies.

IN THEORY, it shouldn't be that hard to make gluten-free shortbread. After all, it is named "shortbread" because of its crumbly texture. The typical ratio is 1:2:3 sugar to butter to flour, and the significant amount of butter is what makes the cookie crumble. In wheat-based cookies, the fat surrounds the flour particles and hinders the formation of gluten, which makes them tender. But in gluten-free formulations, the fat surrounds the flour particles and with nothing at all to hold them together, the shortbread disintegrates.

Of course, I decided there ought to be a gluten-free *and* dairy-free version of shortbread. These biscuit cookies have a very different sugar to fat to flour ratio from standard shortbread, and they do contain eggs, but they have that same rich taste and crumbly texture. The cacao nibs give them an added crunch. They are called Alex's Chocolate-Covered Shortbread Cookies because it was my son Alex who declared, "You ought to dip these in chocolate." His instincts were right: The chocolate coating seals in a rich and crunchy interior.

alex's chocolate-covered shortbread cookies

makes 2½ dozen cookies

FOR THE COOKIES:

½ cup granulated sugar

½ cup powdered sugar

⅓ cup coconut oil

1 large egg

1 teaspoon salt

⅔ cup (93g) tapioca starch

1 cup (120g) light buckwheat flour

1½ teaspoons baking powder

⅓ cup cacao nibs

2 teaspoons almond extract

FOR THE DIPPING CHOCOLATE:

1 cup dairy-free chocolate chips (such as Enjoy Life)

2 tablespoons cocoa butter

1. Make the cookies: Position an oven rack in the center of the oven and preheat to 350°F. Line 2 baking sheets with parchment paper.

2. In a food processor, cream both sugars, the coconut oil, egg, and salt. Add the tapioca starch, buckwheat flour, and baking powder and pulse until the mixture becomes sand-like. Scrape down the sides frequently to ensure a smooth dough. Add the cacao nibs and almond extract. Pulse until the dough forms a ball. If the dough seems a little dry, sprinkle a tiny amount of water on it and knead it by hand until it comes together as a ball.

recipe continues

3. Roll the dough into balls the size of large marbles (about ¾ inch diameter). Space the balls of dough at least 1 inch apart on the baking sheets as these cookies will spread.

4. Bake the sheets of cookies, one at a time, for 17 minutes, until they begin to brown. Allow the cookies to cool completely on the pan.

5. **Make the dipping chocolate:** In a microwave or a heatproof glass bowl set in a heated skillet with 1 inch of water, melt the chocolate chips and cocoa butter, stirring occasionally, until the consistency is right for dipping.

6. Using a fork, lower each cookie into the chocolate, cover it completely, tap it on the side of the bowl to remove any excess chocolate, and gently slide it off onto a cooling rack set over wax paper. (To keep the chocolate from hardening as you work, heat a plate and set it under the bowl of chocolate dip.) Allow the cookies to cool fully to harden the chocolate.

MY HUSBAND TOM'S GRANDMOTHER loved dates, or so it would seem judging from her recipe collection that I inherited because there were sweet date recipes, date pudding recipes, and savory date recipes. I grew up on Dromedary Dates, and I always thought they were a type of date like Medjool dates until I realized it was a brand of imported dates named after a camel. In the early twentieth century, date consumption was pretty much restricted to Thanksgiving and Christmas. In order to expand the market, the main importer, the Hills Brothers Company, waged an aggressive ad campaign to convince homemakers that dates were better than candy and healthier than bread. The ad campaign worked, and women like my mother-in-law and her mother baked lots of date recipes. Since I love dates and agree that they are healthier than bread, I was thrilled to have a window into her recipe collection.

One of the recipes I adapted was for these date cookies. Dates are not only sweet, but lend a chewy texture to cookies and bars. They also work well in flourless recipes because they serve as binders. This is a light but chewy flourless cookie with the added richness of walnuts and dates.

date cookies

makes 2 dozen cookies

1 cup pitted dates, chopped

1¾ cups finely chopped walnuts

1 tablespoon tapioca starch

2 large egg whites

1 teaspoon vanilla extract

1 cup sugar

1. Position an oven rack in the center of the oven and preheat to 350°F. Line a baking sheet with parchment paper.

2. In a medium bowl, toss the chopped dates and walnuts with the tapioca to coat. Set aside.

3. In a bowl, with a hand mixer, beat the egg whites and vanilla on high until soft peaks form. Gradually beat in the sugar, then continue beating the whites until glossy and stiff peaks form.

4. Fold the dates and walnuts into the egg whites, taking care to retain as much loft in the egg whites as possible. Drop the dough by teaspoons about 2 inches apart on the baking sheet. With wet fingers, lightly pat down each cookie until it is approximately ½ inch thick.

5. Bake the cookies for 15 minutes, or until the bottoms begin to brown and the cookie surface puffs up. Allow the cookies to cool and set on the pan for 10 to 15 minutes before transferring them to a cooling rack to cool completely.

WHEN I WAS IN FIFTH GRADE, the rule on Valentine's Day was that if you give anyone a valentine, you had to give one to everyone. I figured out that I could slip candy hearts with messages into my valentines to customize them for my intended recipient. All the girls in the fifth grade, including me, thought that we were in love with Alvin. I sifted through my box of candy hearts and found the perfect "I LOVE YOU" to put in his valentine. What I hadn't figured out was how I was going to gauge his reaction, so I stood in front of him and asked him to open it. He did and immediately started laughing. So did the gaggle of girls surrounding him.

You'd think after that humiliation I would have an aversion to messages in food for the rest of my life. I didn't. In the pre-gluten-free days, one of my favorite parts of eating at a Chinese restaurant was the message in the fortune cookie at the end of the meal. I always found them tremendously entertaining. These fortune cookies are great for entertaining and gifts (although I wouldn't recommend a fortune that reads I LOVE YOU unless you've thought out the consequences). The ingredients are so simple that you wonder why all fortune cookies aren't gluten-free.

fortune cookies

makes 6 to 8 fortune cookies

1 large egg white

½ teaspoon almond extract

¼ cup (35g) tapioca starch

⅛ teaspoon salt

3 tablespoons sugar

1 teaspoon canola oil

1. Use your imagination to write 6 to 8 brilliant fortunes on strips of paper about 3 × ½ inch. Set aside but have them at the ready for when you bake the cookies.

2. Position an oven rack in the center of the oven and preheat to 300°F. Grease 2 baking sheets.

3. In a bowl, with a hand mixer, beat the egg white and almond extract until they are thickened and foamy, but not stiff. On low speed, blend in the tapioca starch, salt, sugar, and oil until the batter is totally smooth (it will be somewhat runny). Let it sit for 10 minutes for the air bubbles to settle.

4. Making 2 cookies at a time, spoon about a teaspoon of batter for each cookie on opposite sides of a baking sheet. Tilt the pan over and down to allow the batter to form 3-inch rounds. It takes a little practice—they might have a couple of ears sticking out, but you can snip them off with kitchen shears before they solidify.

5. Bake for about 10 minutes, or until the edges turn a golden color but the center remains white (it will be really white because you are using tapioca starch). Check the cookies several times to be sure they don't go too far.

6. Working as quickly as you can, open the oven door and use a metal spatula to remove 1 cookie and flip it upside down on a wooden cutting board. Place your fortune in the center and fold the cookie over into a half-moon. Gently press the edges together and bend the folded edge over the rim of a coffee mug, pulling the two pointed ends down, to produce the traditional fortune cookie shape. You have to work quickly; if the cookie cools off too much, it will lose its flexibility and break when you fold it. Repeat with the remaining batter to make more cookies. Alternate between 2 baking sheets to ensure that the baking sheet is cool for the next batch.

MY MOM READ A LOT TO US when we were kids, and I loved books so much that I taught myself to read. My younger son, Marty, did the same thing. Early on, it became a Christmas tradition in my family to read *The Gingerbread Man* and make gingerbread men with cinnamon Red Hots and raisins. We used an old aluminum gingerbread man cookie cutter with a pointy head, and passed it from kid to kid. But it was decorating the gingerbread people that brought them to life, and it is no wonder that a story about a gingerbread man became a children's classic.

I've made my share of gingerbread people with my kids. Then I saw a craft decorating project for which ginger people were turned upside down and decorated as reindeer. Even though I'm not a terribly crafty person, I had to try. Talk about the potential of bringing personalities out in cookies! I developed this twist on gingerbread cookies specifically for the reindeer. These crisp and spicy gingerbread cookies are chocolate covered. They are dotted with cacao nibs, which give the gingerbread just a hint of chocolate and unite the cookies with their chocolate coating. The dough is surprisingly easy to prepare and roll out. Just be sure that you have plenty of time to release your inner decorating self.

chocolate gingerbread reindeer cookies

makes twenty to twenty-four 4-inch cookies

FOR THE COOKIES:

½ cup granulated sugar

½ cup powdered sugar

⅓ cup coconut oil

1 large egg

1 teaspoon salt

1 cup (120g) light buckwheat flour

¾ cup (105g) tapioca starch

1½ teaspoons baking powder

1 tablespoon ground ginger

1 teaspoon ground cinnamon

Scant ¼ teaspoon ground cloves

⅓ cup cacao nibs

2 teaspoons molasses

½ cup finely chopped crystallized ginger

FOR THE CHOCOLATE COATING:

2 cups dairy-free chocolate chips (such as Enjoy Life)

2 tablespoons (25g) grated cocoa butter (or coconut oil)

8 drops ginger oil (optional)

FOR THE ROYAL ICING:

2 cups powdered sugar

1 tablespoon pasteurized powdered egg whites

½ teaspoon vanilla, almond, or lemon extract

Food coloring, for coloring the icing

1. Make the cookies: Position an oven rack in the center of the oven and preheat to 325°F. Line a baking sheet with parchment paper and bake one batch at a time.

2. In a food processor, cream both sugars, the coconut oil, egg, and salt. Add the buckwheat flour, tapioca starch, baking powder, and spices. Pulse until the mixture becomes sand-like. Scrape down the sides frequently to ensure a smooth dough.

recipe continues

Add the cacao nibs and molasses. Pulse the mixture until the dough forms a ball. By hand, knead in the crystallized ginger.

3. Divide the ball into thirds and refrigerate the dough you are not working with. Roll the dough out between two pieces of plastic wrap to an ⅛-inch thickness. Cut out ginger people with a 4-inch cookie cutter and transfer them to the baking sheet. These cookies spread, so space them at least 1 inch apart—8 to 9 cookies will fit on a standard baking sheet.

4. Bake the cookies for 15 minutes until set. Allow the cookies to cool on a cooling rack before dipping in chocolate.

5. **Make the chocolate coating:** Use a microwave, or a heatproof glass bowl set in a heated skillet with 1 inch of water, to soften the chips and cocoa butter (and ginger oil, if using), alternating stirring and melting until the consistency is right for dipping.

6. Using a fork, lower each cookie into the chocolate to cover it completely, tap it on the side of the bowl to remove any excess chocolate, and gently slide it off onto wax paper. (To keep the chocolate from hardening as you work, heat a plate and set it under the bowl of chocolate dip.) Allow the cookies to cool fully to harden the chocolate.

7. **Make the royal icing:** In a small bowl, combine the powdered sugar, powdered egg whites, and flavor extract. Add 1 tablespoon at a time of water until you get the desired thickness (or if you go too far, add more powdered sugar to thicken). Color with food coloring as desired.

8. Pipe designs onto the cooled, chocolate-covered gingerbread people. To make reindeer, turn the gingerbread man upside down and decorate his face as a reindeer, his arms as ears, and his legs as antlers.

EVERY YEAR, my son Alex's therapeutic horseback riding stable has a holiday benefit party and silent auction. The big draw is a cookie swap, with cookies piled every which way on an 8-foot-long table. We always bring gluten-free cookies for that moment when Alex looks at the table, then looks at me, and I tell him the one thing he can eat—the cookies we brought.

Holiday cookies are such a ritual for many people. I believe that giving someone the gift of my time (in the form of homemade cookies) means a lot more than something I can buy. I've made all types of holiday cookies, but there is nothing like beautifully decorated sugar cookies for their WOW factor. Rollout cookies are usually more about the look than the taste, but these cookies are an exception. They are sweet and buttery, much like a shortbread, with a slightly exotic taste from the coconut oil. Without binders like xanthan gum, spreading can be a problem in gluten-free rollout cookies and blur the shape you hoped to achieve with cookie cutters. This is typically the case when you use an all-butter recipe, but in this recipe the coconut oil, which is 100% fat, is combined with the butter to limit spreading.

rollout sugar cookies

makes 4 dozen cookies

3/4 cup (105g) tapioca starch

1 cup (120g) light buckwheat flour

4 tablespoons salted butter

3 tablespoons coconut oil (substitute vegetable shortening if you don't want the coconut flavor)

1/2 cup sugar

1 teaspoon vanilla extract

1 large egg yolk

1. In a small bowl, blend the tapioca starch and buckwheat flour.

2. In a bowl, with a hand mixer, cream the butter, coconut oil, and sugar. Add the vanilla and egg yolk and beat on high until the mixture is light and creamy. Beat in the flour mixture. The dough will look like big curds. Using your hands, form it into a ball and refrigerate for 1 hour.

3. Meanwhile, position an oven rack in the center of the oven and preheat to 350°F. Line three baking sheets with parchment paper.

4. Divide the dough into three pieces, and return two to the refrigerator. Roll out the remaining dough on plastic wrap to a 1/4-inch thickness. Cut out the desired shapes with cookie cutters and transfer them with a spatula to a baking sheet, placing them at least 1 inch apart. Repeat with the remaining dough pieces.

5. Bake the cookies for 12 minutes, until they are firm and the edges are slightly browned. The cookies will be fragile when you first remove them from the oven, so let them cool for about 5 minutes on the pan. Then use a flexible metal spatula to transfer them to a cooling rack.

TRY AS I MIGHT, I could not figure out the true origin of Cowboy Cookies, except that it is an old recipe, dating back to the beginning of the twentieth century. Some say the cookie had its origins as a tasty, nutritious food cowboys made to ride the trail, but I doubt the chocolate in the cookies would have traveled very well. There are also early references to Ranger (or Texas Ranger) Cookies, made with breakfast cereal like cornflakes or crispy rice cereal blended in. Others refer to similar cookies as Kitchen Sink cookies, because they are essentially oatmeal cookies with "everything but the kitchen sink." Whatever the origins, vegan Cowboy Cookies would seem to be the best cookie to take on the trail, without any dairy or eggs to spoil.

I just love the idea that one can make a single cookie in a microwave. Sometimes you just want a few cookies without having to heat up the kitchen and make dozens at a time. And for those living in dorm rooms, this is a cookie you can fresh-bake. All those years Marty was unable to eat the college dining hall's cookies, he could have made his own late

microwave vegan cowboy cookie

makes one 5- to 6-inch cookie

1 tablespoon coconut oil

2 tablespoons packed brown sugar

1 tablespoon unsweetened applesauce

¼ teaspoon baking powder

¼ teaspoon salt

½ teaspoon vanilla extract

1 tablespoon tapioca starch

1 tablespoon oat flour

3 tablespoons rolled oats

1 tablespoon dairy-free mini chocolate chips (such as Enjoy Life)

1 tablespoon unsweetened shredded coconut

1 tablespoon chopped pecans

2 tablespoons crispy rice cereal, such as Erewhon (optional)

1. In a small bowl, use a fork to cream the coconut oil, brown sugar, and applesauce. Add the baking powder, salt, and vanilla. Mix in the tapioca starch, oat flour, and rolled oats. Finally work in the chocolate chips, coconut, pecans, and cereal (if using).

2. Cut out a 7 × 7-inch square of parchment paper and place it on a microwave-safe dinner plate. Dampen your hands and form the dough into a ball—it will be about the size of a tennis ball. Place it in the center of the parchment paper and flatten it until it is approximately 4 inches in diameter and ½ inch thick. It will look like a hamburger patty.

3. Microwave the cookie on high for 1 minute. You will see it puff all over. Check it. Microwave for another 30 seconds. If your microwave doesn't have a turntable, turn the plate 90 degrees and microwave the cookie for another 30 seconds.

4. Transfer the cookie on the parchment paper—very carefully, as the hot cookie will be fragile and very crumbly—to a cooling rack. For a perfectly round cookie, use a dampened butter knife to push in and even up the sides around the cookie. Let it cool thoroughly before eating.

at night while studying. Mix up the ingredients, pop it in the microwave, and let it cool. The result is a giant oatmeal cookie filled with chocolate, coconut, and pecans. It can't get any easier than having a scrumptious cookie on a plate in under 5 minutes. You can even enjoy the authentic crunch of Ranger Cookies simply by adding 2 tablespoons of gluten-free crispy rice cereal.

EVER NOTICED how soy seems to be in everything? Those of us with soy intolerances know all too well. Try to find chocolate without soy lecithin. That's a real challenge. Why is soy lecithin in most chocolates? Chocolate is a non-Newtonian fluid in which very fine solids (cacao, sugar, and sometimes milk solids) are dispersed in fat, and soy lecithin's function is to coat each of the tiny particles so they flow through the cocoa butter or fat to create the rich, melt-in-your-mouth sensation.

I got frustrated with commercial chocolate, and the geek in me decided to learn how to make my own—not fine eating chocolate, but chocolate suitable for baking, for a coating, or for a glaze. These granola bites are dipped in a chocolate made with just three ingredients and without refined sugar. The taste of the chocolate is directly related to the quality of the cocoa you use, so you don't want to scrimp there.

chocolate-covered granola buttons

makes 1½ dozen granola buttons

FOR THE GRANOLA BUTTONS:

½ cup pecans

¼ cup chopped banana chips

4 tablespoons salted butter

⅓ cup packed brown sugar

1 teaspoon vanilla extract

1 teaspoon baking powder

½ teaspoon ground cinnamon

½ teaspoon salt

1 large egg white

¼ cup (25g) oat flour

2 tablespoons tapioca starch

½ cup rolled oats

½ cup unsweetened shredded coconut

¼ cup cacao nibs

FOR THE CHOCOLATE COATING:

⅛ cup cocoa butter (see Note)

2 teaspoons honey

¼ cup unsweetened cocoa powder

1. **Make the granola buttons:** Position an oven rack in the center of the oven and preheat to 350°F. Line a baking sheet and a cooling rack with parchment paper.

2. In a food processor, coarsely grind the pecans and banana chips. Set aside.

3. In a large bowl, with a hand mixer, cream the butter, brown sugar, and vanilla until light and fluffy. Add the baking powder, cinnamon, salt, and egg white and beat until fully incorporated. Beat in the oat flour, tapioca starch, and rolled oats. The dough will be pretty stiff. By hand, stir in the coconut, cacao nibs, and banana-pecan mixture.

recipe continues

4. Form the dough into 1¹/₂-inch balls (a little smaller than a Ping-Pong ball). Place on the baking sheet and press down slightly with damp fingers until they are about ¹/₂ inch thick. They won't spread much, so they can be spaced within an inch of one another.

5. Bake the buttons for 15 minutes, rotating the sheets halfway through baking, or until they are set and the bottoms are lightly browned. Allow the buttons to cool for 5 minutes on the pan before carefully transferring them to the cooling rack. Allow them to cool completely before coating with chocolate.

6. Make the chocolate coating: In a small microwaveable bowl, melt the cocoa butter in the microwave. Or set a heatproof glass bowl in a heavy-bottomed skillet with 1 inch of water over low heat. Whisk in the honey until it is fully integrated into the cocoa butter. Stir in the cocoa powder until smooth.

7. One at a time, dip one side of a button into the chocolate coating and place it on wax paper to dry. Allow the chocolate coating to set for at least 2 hours (or longer depending on temperature and humidity). Store in the refrigerator during warm months.

NOTE: Cocoa butter, which is necessary for making the coating, is available in health food stores in major cities. If like me you live in a rural area, you may have to order it online. Just make sure to buy food-grade cocoa butter since it is also sold for cosmetic applications. You may also substitute the same amount of coconut oil.

MY PARENTS RETIRED TO CHARLESTON, South Carolina, over forty years ago, and my mom still lives there, as does my younger brother, Geoff. Every time I visit, I try to sample local cuisine, but it isn't always very easy being gluten-free in a place with long-held traditions like hush puppies as a side for just about everything. On one trip we ate out downtown with my brother at a local seafood institution. The restaurant had a gluten-free menu, which was a good sign. Housed in what was once an old warehouse of exposed brick walls, studded with the original oyster shell mortar, the eatery is a busy, noisy magnet for tourists and locals alike. We killed time waiting for a table by visiting their country store next door. There among the Fried Green Tomato Breader and Hush Puppy mixes were bags of Carolina Key Lime Cookies. We were very hungry, and my son Marty commented what he would give to eat one of those. So I developed this gluten-free adaptation of Key lime cookies, both puckery, sweet, and melt-in-your-mouth.

carolina key lime cookies

makes 3 dozen cookies

FOR THE LIME SUGAR:

2 teaspoons powdered lemonade mix (such as Crystal Light)

½ cup powdered sugar

FOR THE COOKIES:

½ cup granulated sugar

½ cup powdered sugar

⅓ cup coconut oil

1 large egg

Zest of 1 lime, finely grated

1 teaspoon salt

1 cup (140g) tapioca starch

¾ cup (90g) light buckwheat flour

1 teaspoon baking powder

2 tablespoons fresh lime juice

1. **Make the lime sugar:** Measure the powdered lemonade and powdered sugar into a 1-quart sealable bag. Shake to combine and set aside.

2. **Make the cookies:** In a food processor, cream both sugars, the coconut oil, egg, lime zest, and salt. Add the tapioca starch, buckwheat flour, and baking powder. Pulse the mixture until it becomes sand-like. Scrape down the sides frequently to ensure a smooth dough.

3. Add the lime juice. Pulse the mixture until the dough forms a loose ball. The dough will come together but be sticky. Transfer the dough to a bowl and refrigerate for at least 15 minutes to make it easier to handle. Wet your hands if necessary so that it does not stick to your hands.

4. Meanwhile, position an oven rack in the center of the oven and preheat to 325°F. Line two baking sheets with parchment paper.

recipe continues

5. Remove the dough from the refrigerator and roll it into balls the size of large marbles. Place them on the baking sheets 2 inches apart (these cookies will spread to 2¼ to 2½ inches in diameter, so allow them adequate space on the baking sheet). With damp fingers, flatten them to about 1¾ inches in diameter.

6. Bake the cookies for 18 minutes, rotating the sheets halfway through, or until the bottoms are lightly browned. Allow the cookies to cool for 5 minutes on the pan. While the cookies are still warm, but cool enough to handle, place several at a time in the sealable bag with the lime sugar and shake the cookies to coat them. Allow the cookies to cool fully on a cooling rack before stacking them and storing them in an airtight container (or the freezer).

variation

Although I may upset Charlestonians with this suggestion, this basic recipe lends itself to many variations. My favorite is a Nutmeg Orange Cookie: Use orange juice and zest instead of lime juice and zest, and dust the cookies with a combination of ½ cup powdered sugar and ½ teaspoon of ground nutmeg instead of the lime sugar.

WHEN IT COMES TO BROWNIES, there is no shortage of opinions, but they all seem to revolve around two black-and-white categories: cakey or fudgy. Some swear by a dark, moist, and dense texture. Others insist that a "real" brownie has a moist crumb with an airy interior. Basically, the cakey versus fudgy argument rests on the ratio of flour to egg. The more eggs, the fluffier, more cakey the brownie. But what if the brownies are flourless and don't include sugar? Here's a recipe that argues that maybe brownies can be both cakey *and* fudgy.

Of all baked goods, brownies probably lend themselves best to gluten-free adaptations. Brownies, like many cookies and bars, do not rely on gluten for their structure. In fact, the less gluten, the more tender the brownie—and the taste of chocolate has a way of masking nontraditional flour tastes and textures. The cocoa powder and sunflower butter serve as the flour, and the brownies are sweetened by honey and maple syrup. The brownie stays super-moist because the water-attracting honey also acts as an anti-staling agent.

flourless double-chocolate brownies

makes 9 brownies

1 cup sunflower seed butter (or nut butter of your choice)

½ cup honey

2 tablespoons maple syrup

2 large eggs

⅓ cup unsweetened cocoa powder

½ teaspoon baking soda

½ cup dairy-free chocolate chips (such as Enjoy Life)

1. Position an oven rack in the center of the oven and preheat to 350°F. Line an 8 × 8-inch baking dish with parchment paper.

2. In a medium bowl, with a hand mixer, cream the sunflower butter, honey, maple syrup, and eggs on high until light and fluffy. Fold in the cocoa and mix on medium until light and fluffy. Add the baking soda and mix again until well blended. Stir in the chocolate chips by hand.

3. Scrape the batter into the baking dish and spread the batter evenly in the pan. Bake the brownie for 20 minutes, or until the center of the brownie is set; the brownie will set further as it cools. Allow it to cool completely in the pan before cutting into squares.

CHOCOLATE AND CARAMEL go so well together, even though they are both strong flavors. Caramel not only balances the strong aromatic taste of chocolate, but its sweetness also magnifies the chocolate flavor. But trying to combine chocolate and caramel in a baked good can be problematic. Of course, it is easy to serve any chocolate confection with caramel sauce, and it is really good, but how do you integrate the two into something like brownies?

If you put pieces of caramel right into the batter, they melt during the baking process and pool at the bottom. If you spread caramel between two layers of batter, it still melts before the batter sets and turns into an ooey-gooey mess. Try swirling it in, same result. Finally, it occurred to me that the only way I could make it work was to create caramel chips that were caramel-like, but had enough substance to keep them intact long enough for the brownie batter to set. The major breakthrough came when I created my own caramel out of coconut cream and sugar only and I realized that I could thicken the caramel with coconut flour to make chips that wouldn't liquefy during baking. These brownies are moist, chewy, chocolaty, and are studded with bursts of caramel. No more scraping sticky caramel off of everything in sight.

caramel brownies

makes 9 brownies

1 cup sugar

½ cup coconut oil

½ cup unsweetened cocoa powder

1 teaspoon vanilla extract

2 large eggs

¼ cup coconut cream (skimmed from the top of a 13.5-ounce can of full-fat coconut milk)

¼ cup full-fat coconut milk

½ cup (56g) coconut flour

⅓ cup Coconut Caramel Chips (page 347)

1. Position an oven rack in the center of the oven and preheat to 325°F. Grease an 8 × 8-inch baking dish on the bottom and all sides. Line the bottom and two of the sides with parchment paper that hangs over the sides.

2. In a bowl, with a hand mixer, blend the sugar and coconut oil. Add the cocoa, vanilla, and eggs. Beat in the coconut cream and coconut milk until smooth. Beat in the coconut flour until well blended. Set the bowl aside and allow the coconut flour to absorb the liquid. Fold in the caramel chips by hand.

3. Bake the brownie for 45 minutes, or until the batter is set in the center. Allow the brownie to cool completely in the pan before inserting a sharp knife around the sides to loosen the brownie. Use the parchment paper to lift the brownie from the pan onto a cutting board. Cut into squares.

EVER SINCE I DISCOVERED how easy it is to make Coconut Butter at home, I have been thinking of ways to best use its almost magic properties—naturally sweet, high in fiber, low-glycemic, and solid at room temperature. The inspiration for these brownies came from chocolate-covered raisins, one of my longtime favorite candies. Mostly I associate them with movie theaters, big bright yellow boxes full of raisins that always seem sweeter and plumper when enrobed in chocolate. Coconut butter is naturally sweet, but when combined with bitter cocoa it requires an additional sweetener, such as dates. In these brownies the natural fats and oils in the coconut and cocoa powder carry the flavor and provide the binder for the more fibrous coconut and dates. The raisins add texture—bursts of natural sweetness—and remind me of chocolate-covered raisins, all without any refined sugars, artificial flavors, soy lecithin, or preservatives. No baking, either.

coconut raisin brownies

makes 16 brownies

³/₄ cup Coconut Butter, store-bought or homemade (page 143)

¹/₄ cup unsweetened cocoa powder

16 Medjool dates, pitted

¹/₂ cup raisins

1. In a food processor, combine the coconut butter, cocoa powder, and dates and process until the dates are incorporated into the other ingredients. (The mixture may be crumbly, depending on the moistness of the dates, but the dough will come together when pressed. Add a teaspoon of water, if necessary.)

2. Transfer the dough to a bowl and work in the raisins by hand. On a piece of plastic wrap, use your fingers to press the dough together to form a 5 × 8-inch rectangle, squaring the sides with a dough scraper or a knife.

3. Allow the brownie to solidify in the refrigerator for at least 30 minutes. Cut into 16 bars and serve.

TOURISTS FLOCK TO
VERMONT for the peak of fall
foliage; just as animals bulk
up for the winter, Vermont
nonprofit organizations use the
tourist season to raise needed
funds. I've done my share of
volunteering at roadside stands
selling baked goods during the
fall in Vermont, and the most
memorable one was the annual
cider sale for the Meetinghouse
School in Marlboro. One year,
I baked Maple Walnut Squares
and was opening up one really
cold morning when a couple
from Louisiana pulled up. They
asked for a hot cup of coffee,
bought two maple squares, and
retreated to their rental car.
All of a sudden, they were back
asking if they could buy the
entire pan of Maple Squares.
Why of course! When they
drove away, we high-fived
because we had only been open
less than fifteen minutes, and
we had already sold $20 worth
of baked goods. Two years
later, my kids had gone on to
elementary school and I was no
longer on cider sale duty, but
the couple came back looking
for my Maple Walnut Squares.
Amazing what one pan of bars
can do! These bars are that
good, and I have adapted them
to gluten-free with absolutely
no compromises. I can't think
of any baked good more fitting
of pure Vermont maple syrup
than these bars.

maple walnut squares

makes 9 squares

FOR THE CRUST:

½ cup (70g) tapioca starch

¼ cup (48g) potato starch

½ cup (80g) brown rice flour

¼ cup packed brown sugar

12 tablespoons cold salted
butter, cut into pieces

FOR THE WALNUT TOPPING:

1 large egg

1 large egg yolk

⅓ cup packed brown sugar

½ cup maple syrup

1 teaspoon vanilla extract

1½ tablespoons salted butter,
melted

¾ cup chopped walnuts

1. **Make the crust:** Position an oven rack in the center of the
oven and preheat to 350°F. Butter an 8 × 8-inch baking dish.

2. In a food processor, combine the tapioca starch, potato
starch, brown rice flour, brown sugar, and butter and pulse just
until it is the texture of sand (it should hold together when
squeezed).

3. Press the crust mixture evenly over the bottom and one-
quarter of the way up the sides of the baking dish. Bake the
crust for 10 minutes. Remove and set aside to cool slightly.
Leave the oven on.

4. **Make the topping:** In a bowl, with a hand mixer, beat the
whole egg and egg yolk until light and foamy. Beat in the brown
sugar, maple syrup, and vanilla until the sugar is dissolved. Stir
in the melted butter until uniformly blended. Pour the topping
onto the crust and scatter the walnuts over the top.

5. Bake for 20 to 25 minutes, or until the center looks set. Allow
to cool completely before cutting into squares. Refrigerating for
30 minutes after cooling will make it easier to make clean cuts.

AFTER A WORKOUT, your body needs protein. But while you are exercising or engaging in endurance activities, you need energy. These energy bars do just that, with lots of nutrition from the coconut, sesame, pumpkin, chia, and sunflower seeds, along with the powdered milk. Chock full of whole foods, they give you just the right amount of kick when you need it. My son Alex and I tried out these bars on our first tandem bike ride of the season. We decided on an ambitious first ride, out of Brattleboro, up and over Black Mountain, and back along the West River. By the time we reached the halfway point, that bar couldn't have come at a better time, and had just the right amount of crunch from the cacao nibs and a burst of sweetness from the raisins. It was as satisfying as a high-end chocolate bar. Fortified, we powered up to the peak and went screaming down the other side, through the long, cool covered bridge that spans the West River, and back to Brattleboro. Not bad for the first ride of the season. I'd like to think that the energy bars were responsible, but the sheer vitality of Vermont coming alive after so many months of snow and ice couldn't have hurt.

energy bars

makes 16 bars

1 cup Coconut Butter, store-bought or homemade (page 143)

¼ cup cocoa butter

½ cup honey

1 cup dried fat-free milk powder

½ cup unsweetened cocoa powder

½ cup chopped dates

½ cup chopped fruit-sweetened dried cranberries

½ cup sunflower seeds

½ cup chopped hulled pumpkin seeds

¼ cup sesame seeds

¼ cup chia seeds

½ cup golden raisins

½ cup cacao nibs

1. Position an oven rack in the center of the oven and preheat to 350°F. Grease a 9 × 13-inch baking dish and line with parchment paper.

2. In a heatproof glass bowl, soften the coconut butter and melt the cocoa butter using either a microwave or by placing the bowl in a skillet over low heat. Stir in the honey.

3. In a food processor, combine the milk powder, cocoa powder, dates, cranberries, sunflower seeds, pumpkin seeds, sesame seeds, and chia seeds. Add the cocoa-coconut butter mixture to the chopped ingredients and pulse to combine them. Transfer the mixture to a medium bowl and fold in the raisins and cacao nibs.

4. Spoon the mixture into the baking dish and bake for 30 minutes, or until it is set in the center. Allow to cool before cutting into bars. It may be placed in the refrigerator to cool faster.

IMAGE MY SURPRISE when I learned that Date Bars, a recipe I grew up with, was also known as "Matrimonial Cake." How in the world could date bars be the same as a matrimonial cake? What I found was a great article by Carol Wilson in the journal *Gastronomica* on the history of wedding cakes, where she explains that seventeenth-century "bride cakes" were the precursors of the modern-day wedding cake. She describes one recipe in which currants were sandwiched between two rounds of shortcake pastry sprinkled with sugar. How we got from humble, fruited bride cakes to towering, fondant-laden works of art is a bit of a mystery to me, but at least I now understand the peculiar name.

These date bars are an adaptation of a date bar made by my mom. Dried cranberries are combined with the dates to create a sweet filling. It is a surprising and pleasing texture in an otherwise meld-together type of bar. The rolled oats soak up much of the moisture, and the combination of toasted oat flour, light buckwheat flour, and tapioca starch binds it all together. This is a perfect dessert bar for the long winter months, served warm with a small scoop of vanilla ice cream.

cranberry-date bars

makes 20 bars

1½ cups rolled oats

½ cup (50g) toasted oat flour

¾ cup (90g) light buckwheat flour

½ cup (70g) tapioca starch

1 cup packed dark brown sugar

½ cup unsweetened shredded coconut (optional)

1 teaspoon salt

½ teaspoon baking soda

8 tablespoons salted butter, sliced

2 cups pitted dates (about 24 large dates)

¼ cup honey

1 cup fruit-sweetened dried cranberries

1. Position an oven rack in the center of the oven and preheat to 350°F. Grease a 9 × 13-inch glass baking dish with butter.

2. In a large bowl, combine the oats, oat flour, buckwheat flour, tapioca starch, brown sugar, coconut (if using), salt, and baking soda. Work in the butter until the mixture is crumbly. Sprinkle with 1¼ cups warm water to moisten it. Set aside.

3. In a medium saucepan, combine the dates, honey, and 2 tablespoons warm water and bring the mixture to a boil. Keep stirring until it is just thickened, about 3 minutes. Remove the mixture from the heat, stir in the cranberries, and allow it to cool for 10 minutes.

4. Press half of the oat mixture into the bottom of the prepared baking dish. Using a rubber spatula, spread the date filling over the base as evenly as possible. Sprinkle the other half of the oat mixture on the top and, with wet fingers, press down until the topping is integrated into the filling.

5. Bake the bar for 40 to 45 minutes, or until the top is lightly toasted. Allow the bar to cool at room temperature. Chill in the refrigerator before cutting into individual bars.

EVERY SUMMER, we meet up with a family from Rochester, New York, at our summer cottage on the St. Lawrence River. Half of the family, it seems, has spent their careers working for Wegmans, a well-regarded family supermarket chain in Rochester, New York. Lynn, the matriarch, is a huge fan of Wegmans and simply loves their brand of peanut butter. When she spends summers at the river, she brings a case with her. I learned about Lynn's peanut butter habit not long after I began experimenting with peanut butter as a flour substitute. I had been making peanut butter brownies for a while when I told Lynn about them, and her eyes got round. Just peanut butter in brownies? Could it be possible? So I did what any good neighbor would do: I baked her these peanut butter brownies, and she guarded them until the very last bite.

According to the National Peanut Board, Americans consume over 1.5 billion pounds of peanut butter and peanut products a year. If they all knew about these brownies, it wouldn't surprise me if that number doubled. There are a multitude of ways to customize these brownies with add-ins such as chocolate chips, crumbled banana chips, shredded coconut, and raisins.

peanut butter bars

makes 9 bars

1 cup smooth or chunky peanut butter

½ cup honey

1 large egg

½ teaspoon baking soda

¼ cup shredded coconut (optional)

1. Position an oven rack in the center of the oven and preheat to 350°F. Grease an 8 × 8-inch baking dish, then line it with parchment paper, allowing the parchment paper to overhang two sides of the dish.

2. In a bowl, with a hand mixer, blend the peanut butter, honey, egg, baking soda, and 3 tablespoons coconut (if using) until thick and creamy. Scoop the batter into the baking dish and use a rubber spatula to spread the batter until it is even.

3. Bake the bar for 18 to 20 minutes, or until set and the edges are just barely starting to brown (the center will be slightly lower than the edges when set). This batter has a tendency to overbake very quickly, so be sure to check for doneness at around 18 minutes. Remove the bar from the oven, sprinkle on the remaining tablespoon coconut for garnish, and allow to cool fully in the pan before cutting.

OF ALL THE PRODUCTS I MISS, I may miss fig bars the most. Opening the cellophane columns of cookies, prying several off the stack, and twisting the cellophane back is burned into my brain. I think the design is brilliant, from the taste and texture of the cookie and filling to the illusion that you are indulging responsibly. There is a reason that fig bars have been produced commercially for over 120 years.

Making fig bars at home is a multistep process, but the end result is worth the effort. Since you don't have a million-dollar cookie extrusion line, you have to roll out the dough, fill it, and fold it over to create a seamless bar. The individual cookies are cut and stored while the dough is still warm, to create the soft, moist exterior. Apple cider in the filling heightens the fig taste, and adds pectin as a binder. Just a little unsweetened apple butter in the cookie dough retains moisture and makes the dough pliable without altering the taste.

fig bars

makes 20 to 24 bars

FOR THE FILLING:

1 cup chopped dried figs, with stems removed

1 cup apple cider

1/4 cup packed brown sugar

FOR THE COOKIE DOUGH:

8 tablespoons cold salted butter, cut into pieces

1/2 cup packed brown sugar

1 teaspoon orange zest

1 large egg white

2 tablespoons unflavored, unsweetened apple butter

1 teaspoon vanilla extract

3/4 cup (105g) tapioca starch

1 cup plus 2 tablespoons (140g) light buckwheat flour

1. **Make the filling:** In a medium saucepan, combine the figs, cider, brown sugar, and 1 cup water and bring to a boil. Reduce the heat and simmer covered for 20 minutes, or until the figs are softened. Increase the heat, uncover, and boil the filling for approximately 50 more minutes, or until the liquids are reduced to a paste.

2. Blend the filling in a food processor until it is a smooth paste. Refrigerate the filling until ready to use.

3. **Make the cookie dough:** In a food processor, combine the butter, brown sugar, and orange zest and pulse to blend. Pulse in the egg white, apple butter, and vanilla. Then add the tapioca starch and buckwheat flour and blend until the dough comes together in a ball. Wrap the dough in plastic wrap and refrigerate for 2 hours.

4. Position an oven rack in the center of the oven and preheat to 350°F. Line a baking sheet with parchment paper.

5. Divide the dough into quarters and roll each one between your hands into a log shape. Work with one log at a time and refrigerate the others. Use your fingers to flatten the log a bit, lightly dust it with tapioca starch, and roll it out on a layer of plastic wrap to a thickness of between 1/8 and 1/4 inch (your preference) and a width of roughly 4 inches. Using a dough scraper, knife, or pizza wheel, trim the edges of the dough into a 4-inch-wide rectangle, squaring the ends.

6. Spread a layer of fig paste lengthwise down the center of the rectangle. (It should be about 1 1/2 inches wide and 1/4 inch thick.) Using the plastic wrap, fold one long side of the rectangle over the filling into the center and peel back the wrap. Then repeat the process for the other side, rolling it to the center and just overlapping the already folded side. Gently pat the seam to seal the fig bar. Use the plastic wrap to transfer the formed bar to the baking sheet and flip it onto the parchment, seam side down. Repeat the process for the remaining three logs.

7. Bake the fig bars for 20 minutes, or until they are just beginning to brown. While still warm, cut each bar crosswise into individual cookies about 2 inches long and use the parchment paper to transfer them to a cooling rack. While still slightly warm, store the bars in an airtight container, separating layers of cookies with parchment paper. (Storing the cookies before they are fully cooled will assist in moisture retention to keep the crust soft.)

IT'S 7 P.M., I just put dinner on the table, and my youngest son says, "I need to bring something to school tomorrow for a bake sale." Really? I ask him how long he's known this, and he answers, "Since last week." This was a scene repeated over and over when my kids were younger, and perhaps the reason I love simplicity: the fewer ingredients in a recipe, the better. I particularly love simplicity when I have to think on my feet to create a mouthwatering creation with whatever I have in my pantry.

I don't think there is any baked good recipe that beats this one for simplicity and impressive outcome. This recipe was inspired by the popular Cracker Candy or Saltine Toffee recipe that uses saltine crackers as the base, with a layer of brown sugar toffee, topped with melted chocolate chips. In this recipe, you significantly improve on the saltine crackers by creating your own buttery gluten-free base before topping it with melted chocolate chips. In just over a half hour, you'll have gourmet gluten-free bark in the freezer, guaranteed to be one of the first things to disappear from the bake sale table. Actually, it may take you a little longer since you'll want to make one sheet for you, and one for the bake sale.

chocolate-orange bark

makes 25 to 30 pieces

8 tablespoons salted butter (or substitute 100g coconut oil)

½ cup packed brown sugar

2 teaspoons orange extract

1 large egg yolk

½ cup (70g) tapioca starch

⅔ cup (80g) light buckwheat flour

1¼ cups semisweet chocolate chips

2 tablespoons chopped candied orange peel

1. Position an oven rack in the center of the oven and preheat to 350°F.

2. In a large bowl, with a hand mixer, beat the butter, brown sugar, orange extract, and egg yolk until well blended.

3. Fold in the tapioca starch and buckwheat flour until they are moistened, and then beat the dough again until it is well blended. The dough may seem crumbly, with the texture of oatmeal, but it will come together when spread and compressed.

4. Spread the dough evenly in an ungreased 10½ × 15½-inch rimmed baking sheet. Using a rolling pin and your fingers, press down while rolling out the dough until the dough is evenly spread over the entire pan. Make sure there are no holes. At first, it will seem like you have way more surface area than dough, but it will eventually cover the entire pan.

5. Bake for 12 to 15 minutes, or until the crust is set and lightly browned. It will look like a gigantic cookie.

recipe continues

6. Remove the crust from oven, sprinkle it evenly with the chocolate chips, and return it to the oven. Bake the bark for 3 to 4 more minutes, or until the chocolate chips are softened.

7. Remove the bark from the oven. Working quickly, spread the chocolate chips with a spatula until the surface is evenly and completely coated with chocolate. While the chocolate is still soft, sprinkle the top with candied orange peel; pat the pieces lightly into the chocolate to anchor them and allow the bark to cool fully.

8. Place the baking sheet in the freezer for 15 minutes to allow the bark to become brittle. Break it into uneven pieces of bark and store in a cookie tin or any airtight container.

variations

Although this recipe is for orange bark, there are many possibilities for flavor substitutions and garnishes. Some of my favorites include:

- Cherry bark: use 1 teaspoon almond extract and top with ½ cup chopped dried cherries.
- Peppermint bark: use 2 teaspoons peppermint extract and top with 1 cup of crushed candy canes or peppermint candies.
- Pecan bark: use 1 teaspoon vanilla extract and top with ½ cup chopped pecans.

CACAO NIBS are little chunks of pure cacao beans, and are chocolate in its purest form. They are produced during the lengthy chocolate-making process after the pods have been fermented, dried, and cracked open. In order to more efficiently remove the outer shell of the cocoa bean, the chocolate is broken into little chips rather than ground down to powder. If you've ever bitten into unsweetened baking chocolate, you'll be surprised by how different cacao nibs are in taste and texture. Although unsweetened, they're not nearly as bitter and acidic. Cacao nibs come roasted and unroasted—some believe that roasting reduces the bitterness a tad, whereas others tout the health benefits of raw nibs. Either way, cacao nibs draw out subtle flavor notes in anything they are paired with, particularly processed chocolate.

Cashews have a relatively high starch content of about 10%, making them more flour-like than many other nuts. The cacao nibs add a crunchy and bittersweet contrast to the cashew flavor. Although the cacao nibs are unsweetened, cashews give cocoa nibs the illusion of sweetness.

cashew chews with cacao nibs

makes 20 cookies

1 cup cashew butter

1 cup powdered sugar

1 large egg

½ teaspoon baking soda

½ teaspoon salt

½ cup cacao nibs (or mini dairy-free chocolate chips)

1. Position an oven rack in the center of the oven and preheat to 350°F. Line a baking sheet with parchment paper.

2. In a bowl, use a hand mixer to beat together the cashew butter, powdered sugar, egg, baking soda, and salt until the mixture is smooth (though still sticky). Fold in the cacao nibs by hand.

3. Roll the dough into balls the size of small marbles, wetting your hands if necessary. Place the balls 2 inches apart on the baking sheet. (They will spread significantly as they bake.)

4. Bake the cookies for 10 minutes, or until the tops are cracked and set. Allow the cookies to cool before lifting them from the baking sheet. As the cookies cool, they will flatten somewhat.

ONE DAY you're scraping your knees learning to ride your first two-wheel bike. The next thing you know, some of the things you've acquired have practically become vintage. That's the case with my wooden recipe box, which is retro in an age of online recipes, kitchen apps, and the like. But inside the box is a culinary trip through my life, harboring some of the best recipes I've ever encountered. I have similar recipe boxes assembled by my late mother-in-law, as well as by her mother. Some of the recipes in the latter box are nearly a hundred years old. I like fingering the worn recipes, deciphering their notes, taking a trip down their culinary paths, and making them my own.

This cranberry-pistachio recipe from a 1995 *New York Times* article by Suzanne Hamlin first caught my eye because I liked the festivity of the red and green colors in the biscotti, but I have made a half-dozen variations on it since that first inspiration. Making biscotti is a very rewarding process. Having family members ooh and aah over the biscotti is even more so. When we began eating a gluten-free diet, this was one of the first recipes I adapted and, honestly, because they are twice-baked, biscotti make an excellent gluten-free cookie recipe.

cranberry-pistachio biscotti

makes 30 biscotti

½ cup granulated sugar

½ cup powdered sugar

⅓ cup coconut oil

1 large egg

½ teaspoon salt

¾ cup (105g) tapioca starch

1 cup (120g) light buckwheat flour

1½ teaspoons baking powder

2 teaspoons vanilla extract

½ teaspoon almond extract

1½ cups coarsely chopped unsalted pistachios

½ cup chopped fruit-sweetened dried cranberries

1. Position an oven rack in the center of the oven and preheat to 325°F. Line a baking sheet with parchment paper.

2. In a food processor, blend the sugars, oil, egg, and salt until smooth. Add the tapioca starch, light buckwheat flour, and baking powder and blend until uniformly moistened. The dough will be crumbly. Add the vanilla and almond extracts and blend until the dough comes together in a ball.

3. Transfer the dough to a medium bowl and work in the pistachios and cranberries. Form into a ball, then divide and form 2 flat logs, 12 inches long by 2 inches wide. Set the logs side by side on the baking sheet, separated by 4 inches—they will spread during baking. Bake for 40 minutes.

4. Remove the logs from the oven and let the logs cool for about 10 minutes on the pan until you can handle them. While still on the pan, slice the logs crosswise into 1-inch-thick slices. Separate the slices from one another. Bake the slices (standing upright) for an additional 20 minutes. The biscotti should be dry and crumbly. Store in an airtight container.

LADYFINGERS AREN'T VERY LADYLIKE. But, oh my, are they delicate, sponge-like delicacies. In actuality, ladyfingers probably got their name from early recipes that directed the home baker to pipe out a strip of sponge cake batter the length of one's finger.

Gluten-free sponge cakes, which rely on air beaten into eggs for leavening and minimal amounts of flour, are virtually indistinguishable from wheat-based ones. Unlike breads and heavier baked goods, the idea in sponge cakes is to restrict gluten development. So this ladyfinger recipe is quick to assemble and bakes for a very short period of time. Like traditional ladyfinger recipes, the fingers are piped onto parchment paper. The result is a delicate, spongy cake to use in tiramisus, charlottes, and semifreddos (see Fresh Peach Semifreddo, page 325).

ladyfingers

makes 12 to 15 ladyfingers

2 large egg whites

½ cup granulated sugar

2 large egg yolks

1 teaspoon vanilla extract

⅓ cup plus 1 tablespoon (50g) light buckwheat flour

Powdered sugar, for dusting

1. Position an oven rack in the center of the oven and preheat to 400°F. Line a baking sheet with parchment paper.

2. In a medium bowl, with a hand mixer, beat the egg whites on high until soft peaks start to form. Gradually add 2 tablespoons of the granulated sugar and continue beating until glossy and stiff peaks form.

3. In a separate bowl, beat the yolks, the remaining 6 tablespoons granulated sugar, and vanilla on high until they are light in color and foamy, about 3 minutes.

4. Using a rubber spatula, fold half the egg whites into the egg yolks, then fold in the buckwheat flour. Finally, fold in the remaining egg whites. (The idea behind the folding is to minimize deflation of the batter.) Pour the batter into a pastry bag fitted with a ½-inch plain tip. (You can also use a quart-size sealable plastic bag with a corner cut off to pipe the batter.)

5. Pipe the batter into 4-inch-long strips onto the baking sheet. Place the fingers about 1 inch apart. Sift powdered sugar over the top of the fingers before baking to product a soft crust.

6. Bake the ladyfingers for 12 minutes. While they are still hot, slide a pastry knife under the ladyfingers to release them and transfer them to a cooling rack; they will be soft until they cool. Use the ladyfingers immediately after they cool, or freeze them. They will keep frozen for several weeks, but will soften over time in the freezer if kept longer.

variation

chocolate ladyfingers (DF)

Before incorporating the flour into the eggs, blend the flour with ¼ cup unsweetened cocoa powder and ¼ teaspoon baking soda.

ANYONE WHO HAS EVER WORKED with sesame seeds can tell you that they are pesky little devils. They are so tiny and light that they fly everywhere—except on the bread and pastry where you want them. Sesame seeds have an interesting history in this country. Also called *benne*, they were brought over from Africa by slaves to coastal South Carolina and Georgia. Sesame seeds grow in pods called capsules on 2- to 4-foot-tall flowering plants, and the early cultivars were as tricky to harvest as the seed is to work with. As a result, sesame seeds were never grown in the South as an agricultural crop. Instead, they were grown by slaves for their own use, a practice that was taken up by their white owners.

In antebellum times, benne were added to breads, soups, oyster stew, grits, and greens . . . and benne wafers, thin disks of brown sugar–sweetened sesame cookies. These cookies have been associated with the South Carolina Low Country for over 100 years. Benne wafers may be extremely thin or somewhat thicker, depending on the amount of flour. For a gluten-free adaptation, I developed a thin recipe, using as little flour as possible. The result is sweet and crunchy cookies, with a rich, nutty taste.

benne wafers

makes 80 thin wafers

⅓ cup white sesame seeds

¼ cup (35g) light buckwheat flour

¼ cup (35g) tapioca starch

½ teaspoon baking powder

¼ teaspoon baking soda

¼ teaspoon salt

4 tablespoons salted butter

¾ cup packed brown sugar

2 large egg whites

½ teaspoon vanilla extract

1. Position an oven rack in the center of the oven and preheat to 350°F. Line a baking sheet with parchment paper.

2. In a skillet, toast the sesame seeds over medium heat until they are browned, stirring them to prevent overheating. Remove them from the skillet and set aside to cool.

3. In a bowl, combine the buckwheat flour, tapioca starch, baking powder, baking soda, and salt and blend well.

4. In a separate large bowl, with a hand mixer, cream the butter and sugar until the mixture is light and creamy. Add the egg whites and vanilla and continue beating until the mixture is completely smooth. Add the dry ingredients to the dough and beat just until the batter is smooth. Fold in the sesame seeds.

5. Drop the dough by ½ teaspoon (like little buttons) onto the baking sheet. The wafers will spread to about three times their diameter so allow 2 inches between wafers.

6. Bake the wafers for 6 minutes, or until the cookies are golden brown and beginning to crisp around the edges.

7. Carefully slide the entire piece of parchment paper to a cooling rack and allow the wafers to cool for 5 to 8 minutes before attempting to peel them off the parchment paper; they will crisp as they cool. Once completely cooled, store the wafers in an airtight tin. They should last 1 to 2 weeks.

cakes

IN OUR FAMILY, birthday celebrations are fairly ritualized. I have always made birthday cakes from scratch, with a candle for each year and "one to grow on." Yes, I even make them for my own birthday, because who doesn't need an excuse to eat cake? The first birthday after beginning a gluten-free diet was my younger son, Marty's. That year, Marty was way into snowboarding and wanted a cake that looked like a snowboard jump. Okay, that didn't seem too hard since a few slip-ups could easily make my cake look like a jump when covered with white icing. I worked for days to get the right balance of loft and moisture, and while I produced a really tasty, moist cake, it had a sinking tendency. No problem, as my friend said, "it just gives you more spaces to fill with icing," which is what I ultimately did.

As I learned more about gluten-free baking I figured out how to fix my sinking cake problem (more eggs, less fluid) and I became interested in working with coconut flour. This naturally sweet and highly absorbent flour makes the lightest, moistest, and most flavorful yellow cake. It is the perfect platform for any type of icing.

basic yellow cake

makes one 9-inch 2-layer cake

1½ cups sugar

½ cup canola oil

1 cup sour cream

6 large eggs

1 cup (112g) coconut flour

1 cup (140g) tapioca starch

1 teaspoon baking powder

½ teaspoon baking soda

2 teaspoons vanilla extract

Basic Vanilla Buttercream Frosting (optional, recipe follows)

1. Position an oven rack in the center of the oven and preheat to 350°F. Generously grease two 9-inch cake pans and line with rounds of parchment paper.

2. In a large bowl, with a hand mixer, blend the sugar, oil, sour cream, and eggs. Beat the batter for approximately 4 minutes.

3. In a separate bowl, stir together the coconut flour and tapioca starch. Gradually beat them into the egg mixture. Beat several more minutes, making sure to scrape down the sides. Allow the batter to rest for 5 minutes to let the mixture thicken. Add the baking powder, baking soda, and vanilla, mixing them thoroughly into the batter.

4. Fill the cake pans approximately two-thirds full with batter. Bake for 30 to 35 minutes, or until the cake pulls away from the sides of the pan and the center springs back when touched. Allow the cake layers to cool in the pans on a cooling rack for 10 minutes before turning them out onto a piece of parchment paper on the cooling rack to cool completely before frosting.

basic vanilla buttercream frosting

makes enough to frost one 9-inch 2-layer cake

There are many variations of this classic vanilla buttercream frosting. My favorite is made with a combination of coconut oil and butter. I think it adds a natural sweetness from the coconut that pairs well with the delicate taste of coconut flour in the Basic Yellow Cake. Coconut oil has a low melting point, however, and becomes liquid on a hot summer day, so it is best used in colder temperatures. Icing consistency is a matter of preference, and I suggest that you add the cream 1 tablespoon at a time. If you find your icing is still thicker than you would like, try adding additional cream (or milk) in teaspoon increments. The flavor of this basic frosting can be changed by simply changing the flavor extract.

8 tablespoons salted butter

½ cup coconut oil (or ½ cup palm oil solid shortening, such as Spectrum)

2 teaspoons vanilla extract

1 pound (464g) powdered sugar

2 tablespoons heavy (whipping) cream

1. In a bowl, with a hand mixer, cream the butter and coconut oil until well blended. Add the vanilla and stir to combine. Add the powdered sugar 1 cup at a time, beating well between additions. At this point the frosting will be stiff and dry.

2. Begin adding the cream 1 tablespoon at a time, beating the frosting on high until the icing is light and creamy. If necessary, put the frosting in the refrigerator for a few minutes if it becomes too soft from the mixing.

THE FIRST CARROT CAKE I ever tasted was sent to me by my sister, Lynn, during my first week of college. Because my birthday falls at the end of August, it was the first of my life away from home. It was a touching gesture by my sister. It was also a chance to try out a really cool way she had read about to ship a cake to someone—smother it in popcorn, not those clingy Styrofoam things, but fresh, air-popped popcorn. She baked and iced the cake with a delicious cream cheese frosting, packed it up and sent it to New Orleans, where despite the heat and humidity it arrived in perfect shape. Since that time, I've always associated carrot cakes with birthdays. For Tom's last birthday, he requested a cake with no caffeine (so no chocolate), and it seemed to me to be the perfect occasion for a carrot cake

This is a pretty foolproof, moist, and delicious cake—the hardest and most time-consuming part is shredding the carrots. Since oranges are featured prominently in this cake, the recipe calls for both baking soda and baking powder, which interact with the acid in the oranges to produce a good rise. The combination of orange pulp and carrots is unbeatable for the flavor and texture it produces.

carrot cake

makes one 9-inch 2-layer cake

1 cup (140g) tapioca starch

1⅓ cups (160g) light buckwheat flour

1 teaspoon ground cinnamon

1 teaspoon baking powder

½ teaspoon baking soda

1½ cups sugar

4 large eggs

½ cup canola oil

¼ cup orange juice

1½ cups shredded carrots

½ cup orange pulp (see Note)

Cream Cheese Frosting (recipe follows)

1. Position an oven rack in the center of the oven and preheat to 350°F. Generously grease two 9-inch cake pans and line with rounds of parchment paper.

2. In a large bowl, blend together the tapioca starch, buckwheat flour, cinnamon, baking powder, and baking soda.

3. In a separate bowl, with a hand mixer, beat together the sugar and eggs. Beat in the oil and then add the dry ingredients, 1 cup at a time. Beat in the orange juice. Then beat in the carrots and orange pulp. Beat the batter for 2 additional minutes. Divide the batter between the two pans.

4. Bake the cakes for 35 minutes. Allow the cakes to cool in the pans for 10 minutes before turning them out onto cooling racks to cool completely before frosting.

NOTE: Orange pulp is the by-product of juicing an orange in a juicer. If you don't have any orange pulp lying around, you can substitute 1 tablespoon grated orange zest with ⅓ cup orange juice. Another alternative is adding the same amount of crushed, drained pineapple. Pineapple produces a different flavored cake, but carrots and pineapple are also a tasty and moisture-retaining combination.

cream cheese frosting

makes enough to frost one 9-inch 2-layer cake

This is a basic sweet and velvety cream cheese icing that pairs well with any type of cake, including red velvet and carrot, to name a couple. A tablespoon of freshly grated orange zest adds a distinctive counterpoint to the sweetness of the frosting.

4 tablespoons salted butter

8 ounces cream cheese

2 teaspoons vanilla extract

1 tablespoon grated orange zest

3 cups powdered sugar

In a bowl, with a hand mixer, cream the butter and cream cheese. Beat in the vanilla and orange zest. Beat in the powdered sugar 1 cup at a time until the frosting is smooth and fluffy.

WHEN MY SISTER, LYNN, and her husband, Joe, lived aboard their 40-foot sailboat, *Sunshine*, sailing from the Caribbean to the tip of Maine, it didn't take much for an excuse to have a party—like the running of the Kentucky Derby. My sister created this cake for just such an occasion, and it was such a sensation that the next year a guest showed up wearing a homemade hat that looked just like it.

Meringue cakes provide a nice, light follow-up to any dinner. This cake is inspired by the mint julep, the official Kentucky Derby drink, combining the crunchy sugar of the meringue with a hint of bourbon and a mint garnish. The recipe illustrates how eggs alone can provide a flourless structure for a rich and showy cake. Note also how the meringue is prepared; beating the egg whites to the soft peak stage before adding any sugar provides the meringue with greater stability and loft. Do not let the lengthy recipe be off-putting. Every step is very forgiving and the result is a stunning 5-star restaurant-quality dessert.

bourbon-laced kentucky derby cake

makes one 8-inch 3-layer cake

3/4 cup pecans

3/4 cup powdered sugar

4 large egg whites

1 tablespoon granulated sugar

1 cup heavy (whipping) cream

1/4 cup packed dark brown sugar

8 ounces cream cheese

1 ounce bourbon

Fresh mint, for garnish

1. Trace and cut out three 8-inch-diameter rounds of parchment paper.

2. In a heavy-bottomed skillet, toast the pecans over medium heat for several minutes, stirring to keep them from scorching. Remove them from the heat when they just start to turn brown. Transfer the toasted pecans to a bowl and allow them to cool.

3. Coarsely chop 1/4 cup of the toasted pecans, place them in a small bowl, and set aside to use as a decoration.

4. Transfer the remaining 1/2 cup toasted pecans to a food processor and coarsely chop. Add the powdered sugar and pulse until the nuts are uniformly covered and any lumps have been reduced to powder. Do not overprocess.

5. In a bowl, with a hand mixer, beat the egg whites on high until soft peaks form. Gradually add the granulated sugar and continue beating until glossy and stiff peaks form. Fold in the pecan and powdered sugar mixture, taking care not to deflate the meringue.

recipe continues

6. Position the oven racks in the upper and lower thirds of the oven and preheat to 225°F.

7. Fill a 1-gallon sealable plastic bag with the meringue and expel most of the air. Snip ¼ inch off one of the corners. Place a round of parchment paper on a cutting board and pipe one-third of the meringue onto the parchment round starting at the center and spiraling outward until you are within ½ inch of the edge of the round. Try to create a continuous layer without overlapping the piping; you can fix any holes using the back of a spoon. Slide the parchment paper and lining onto a baking sheet. Repeat this process two more times until you have three layers on 2 baking sheets.

8. Bake the meringue layers for 1½ hours. Turn off the oven and allow the layers to cool in the oven without opening the oven door, about 1 hour. Gently peel off the parchment paper. Store the layers in an airtight container if not using immediately.

9. In a medium bowl, with a hand mixer, whip the cream until it reaches the stiff peak stage.

10. In a medium bowl, and using the same beaters, cream the brown sugar, cream cheese, and bourbon until the brown sugar is no longer granulated and the cream cheese is whipped. Fold the whipped cream into the cream cheese mixture.

11. To assemble the cake, place a layer on a cake plate, flat side down. Spread one-third of the cream cheese filling over the layer. Do not frost the sides. Add a second layer, check for evenness, and spread another one-third of the filling. Add the third layer, this time with the flat side up, and spread with the final third of the filling. Sprinkle the top of the cake with the reserved chopped pecans and garnish with several sprigs of mint.

12. Refrigerate the cake for no longer than 1 hour for crisp layers. The filling and meringue will meld for a delicious effect if the cake is refrigerated longer. Slice with a serrated knife.

IN OUR EIGHTH YEAR OF BUSINESS, many of the original employees who began Against The Grain with us still work here. It was a really big deal when the first employee reached the one-year mark. I made a cake for the occasion, and we sat around the table in the break room and celebrated his anniversary. I had no idea at the time that I was establishing a tradition. For several years thereafter, I baked a unique gluten-free cake from scratch for each person's anniversary. Then we started growing so fast that I was baking cakes all the time, and I couldn't keep up.

But any event is always a good excuse to bake a cake. I'm not sure where I got the idea for this Italian cream cake, but I knew I wanted to make a cake with coconut, toasted pecans, and cream cheese icing. Unlike many Italian cream cakes, this one does not contain buttermilk. Rather, it includes sour cream, which works extremely well in gluten-free cakes to add tenderness and retain moisture. Like buttermilk, sour cream is acidic, so it also optimizes the leavening effect of the baking soda. The addition of coconut oil reinforces the taste of the toasted coconut, and the overall Italian-ness of the cake is enhanced by the amaretto liqueur.

italian cream cake

makes one 9-inch 2-layer cake

FOR THE CAKE:

1 cup chopped pecans

8 tablespoons salted butter

1/3 cup coconut oil

2 cups granulated sugar

4 large eggs, separated

1 cup sour cream

1/2 cup amaretto liqueur

1 cup (140g) tapioca starch

1 1/3 cups (160g) light buckwheat flour

1 teaspoon baking powder

1/2 teaspoon baking soda

1/2 cup unsweetened shredded coconut

FOR THE FROSTING AND GARNISH:

8 ounces cream cheese

6 tablespoons salted butter

1 pound powdered sugar

2 tablespoons amaretto liqueur

1 cup chopped pecans

1/2 cup unsweetened shredded coconut

1. **Make the cake:** In a heavy-bottomed skillet, toast the pecans over medium heat for several minutes, stirring to keep them from scorching, until they are lightly browned (or bake on a baking sheet for about 7 minutes in a 350°F oven, stirring several times). Set aside.

2. Position an oven rack in the center of the oven and preheat to 350°F. Generously grease two 9-inch cake pans and line with rounds of parchment paper.

3. In a bowl, with a hand mixer, cream the butter, coconut oil, and sugar. Add the egg yolks, sour cream, and amaretto. Add the tapioca starch and buckwheat flour gradually until they are well blended. Beat in 1/4 cup water to thin the batter, then beat in the baking powder and baking soda. Fold in the pecans and coconut by hand. Set the batter aside.

recipe continues

4. In a clean bowl with clean beaters, beat the egg whites until stiff peaks form. Gently fold the whites into the batter and divide the batter between the cake pans.

5. Bake for 35 to 40 minutes, or until the cake layers are set and spring back when touched in the center. Allow the cakes to cool in the pans for 15 minutes before turning them out on a parchment-lined cooling rack. Cool the layers completely before frosting.

6. Make the frosting: In a bowl, with a hand mixer, cream the cream cheese and butter. Gradually beat in the powdered sugar, alternating with the amaretto (1 tablespoon at a time). Frost the cake as desired. For garnish, press chopped pecans into the sides of the cake and sprinkle the top with the coconut.

variation

For a festive summer cake, add coarsely chopped cherries instead of the coconut garnish between the cake layers and on top of the icing.

I'M NOT SURE whether it is a curse or an asset, but I have a very sensitive sense of smell. When I was a child, the milkman delivered the milk once a week in clear glass bottles, and I used to drive my parents nuts at the dinner table because I would announce that the milk smelled sour to me. My siblings regarded me as the canary in the coal mine, and none of them would touch their glass of milk after my declaration. So I totally understand when wheat-eaters taste some gluten-free products and declare they taste "weird."

I must confess that I approached this recipe with a great deal of trepidation. For some time I had been reading about black beans as a "secret" ingredient in cakes, cookies, and breads. I first tried a black bean brownie recipe many people raved about. It was pretty good, but the chocolate taste was a tad dull, and the texture was kind of dense and chalky. But my breakthrough was pairing the black beans with coconut oil. Coconut oil, which by itself has a distinctive taste, enhances the chocolate flavor, and its mouthfeel and aroma alter your taste perception of the high-fiber black beans. For simple, gluten-free chocolate cupcakes, I always use this recipe.

cocobean cupcakes

makes 10 to 12 cupcakes

⅓ cup coconut oil

1 can (15 ounces) black beans, drained and rinsed

½ cup unsweetened cocoa powder

4 large eggs

1 cup sugar

½ teaspoon baking soda

White Chocolate Lavender Icing (recipe follows)

1. Position an oven rack in the center of the oven and preheat to 350°F. Line 12 cups of a standard muffin tin with paper liners (for taller cupcakes, line 10 instead of 12).

2. In a food processor, blend the coconut oil and beans until they are smooth and creamy. Blend in the cocoa powder. The batter will become stiff.

3. Blend in the eggs and sugar until the sugar crystals dissolve. The batter will become very creamy and look just like chocolate pudding. Scrape down the sides frequently as you blend. Blend in the baking soda.

4. Spoon the batter into the muffin cups until they are two-thirds full. Bake the cupcakes for 30 minutes, until the tops are set and firm. The cupcakes will rise about ½ inch above the paper liner. Allow the cupcakes to cool completely on a cooling rack before icing.

recipe continues

white chocolate lavender icing

makes enough to frost 12 cupcakes

This is a white icing with a hint of chocolate provided by chocolate extract. It is a light and refreshing topping for the Cocobean Cupcakes, the Decadent Chocolate Cake (274), or the Basic Yellow Cake (258). The cacao nibs provide an interesting contrast to the slight floweriness of the icing and add a surprising crunch.

3 tablespoons vegetable shortening (such as Spectrum All Vegetable Shortening)

1 cup powdered sugar

1 teaspoon chocolate extract (such as Nielsen-Massey)

1 teaspoon dried lavender blossoms

1 to 2 teaspoons cacao nibs, for garnish (or substitute chocolate sprinkles)

1. In a bowl, with a hand mixer, cream the vegetable shortening, powdered sugar, and chocolate extract.

2. Beat in the dried lavender and continue beating until the frosting is smooth. Add 1 teaspoon of warm water at a time until you reach a spreadable consistency.

3. After frosting your cupcakes, garnish with cacao nibs.

I'VE NEVER DECIDED whether it is the "red" or the "velvet" of Red Velvet Cake that makes it so alluring. When I was growing up in the South, it was considered the queen of all cakes. Most often, though, it was a disappointing devil's food cake mix with ounces of red food coloring. Being a whole-foods, bake-from-scratch kind of person, I decided to make a naturally colored version from beets (which would also help retain the cake's moisture). Instead of buttermilk, which is an acidic ingredient in many red velvet recipes, I sought to make this a dairy-free red velvet cake using coconut milk.

My first version of this recipe came out very tasty but hardly red velvet—it was perfectly chocolate in color. I then learned that beets have a reddish hue because they contain the plant pigment betanin (or beetroot red) which is sensitive to pH, temperature, and light. When baked in a red velvet cake, the acidic pigment is neutralized by an alkaline compound like baking soda and loses its color. But I couldn't totally eliminate the chemical leavener—so I used baking powder, which balances the acidity but still leavens the cake, and added lemon juice to significantly increase the acidity. I made this final version into cupcakes and brought them to work for the staff on Valentine's Day. They were iced with Simple Boiled White Icing,

red velvet cake

makes one 9-inch 2-layer cake or 20 cupcakes

1 can (15 ounces) whole beets, drained and blotted with paper towels

1½ cups sugar

½ cup canola oil

6 large eggs

1 cup (112g) coconut flour

1 cup (140g) tapioca starch

¼ cup unsweetened cocoa powder

½ cup full-fat coconut milk

1 teaspoon baking powder

3 tablespoons lemon juice

2 teaspoons vanilla extract

Simple Boiled White Icing (recipe follows)

1. Position an oven rack in the center of the oven and preheat to 350°F. Grease two 9-inch cake pans and line them with rounds of parchment paper. (Or grease 20 cups of 2 standard muffin tins or line with paper liners.)

2. Puree the beets in a food processor until they reach the consistency of applesauce.

3. In a large bowl, with a hand mixer, blend the sugar, oil, pureed beets, and eggs. Beat for approximately 4 minutes.

4. In a separate bowl, combine the coconut flour, tapioca starch, and cocoa. Gradually add the dry ingredients to the egg mixture and beat until fully blended, making sure to scrape down the sides. Add the coconut milk and thoroughly incorporate it into the batter. Beat in the baking powder, lemon juice, and vanilla, mixing them thoroughly into the batter.

5. Spoon the batter into the cake pans (or muffin cups). Bake for 28 minutes (or 22 to 25 minutes for cupcakes), or until the center of the cakes or muffins spring back when touched. Transfer to a cooling rack and let cool completely before icing.

recipe continues

simple boiled white icing

makes enough to frost one 9-inch 2-layer cake or 20 cupcakes

This is your basic fat-free icing, a recipe that has been around since my grandmother's time. You can make it chocolate-flavored by adding ¼ cup cocoa powder and increasing the sugar by ¼ cup and the water by 1 tablespoon. It is a very neutral and dairy-free icing that would highlight the colors and flavors of red velvet and chocolate cakes alike.

1 cup sugar

2 large egg whites

1½ teaspoons vanilla extract

¼ teaspoon cream of tartar

1. In a saucepan, stir together the sugar and ⅓ cup water and heat over medium heat until the sugar is dissolved and the mixture comes to a boil. Boil the mixture uncovered for 3 minutes (or to 240°F if you have a candy thermometer). Remove the pan from the heat.

2. In a medium bowl, with a hand mixer, beat the egg whites on high until soft peaks form. Beating constantly, gradually add the sugar syrup. Stiff peaks will form after about 7 minutes.

3. Beat in the vanilla and cream of tartar last. The cream of tartar will stabilize the egg white foam.

and the crumb was reddish-mahogany. One of my staff members, a self-proclaimed red velvet cake expert who insists on it for every birthday, deemed the cupcakes his best red velvet cake yet.

FOR MY TWENTY-FIRST BIRTHDAY in New Orleans, my husband, Tom, gave me a cornstalk dracaena plant. When we left New Orleans and moved to Philadelphia, the plant weathered the trip just fine, and four more moves after that. It grew and flourished until it was 12 feet tall and smashed against the ceiling of our Brooklyn brownstone. Tom outdid that present when he baked a cake for my fiftieth birthday: a rich, two-layer chocolate cake with a buttery chocolate ganache, topped by an insanely chocolaty glaze. No one had ever baked me such a wonderful cake.

Once we began following a gluten-free diet, that cake became the "gold standard" by which I measured all gluten-free cakes. I am happy to report that this cake finally measures up; it is a rich and moist cake in which the sensuality of the chocolate is the star. I have now baked it for all kinds of occasions and people uniformly tell me that it may be the best chocolate cake they have ever eaten. Who cares if it is gluten-free . . . it's chocolate. I just may have to strategically place the recipe somewhere obvious for my next birthday.

decadent chocolate cake

makes one 9-inch 2-layer cake or 20 cupcakes

1 cup (160g) brown rice flour

⅓ cup (64g) potato starch

1 cup (140g) tapioca starch

⅔ cup unsweetened cocoa powder

1 teaspoon baking soda

1⅔ cups sugar

4 large eggs

½ cup canola oil

⅔ cup orange juice

Chocolate Buttercream Ganache and Chocolate Glaze (recipe follows)

1. Position an oven rack in the center of the oven and preheat to 350°F. Generously grease two 9-inch cake pans and line with rounds of parchment paper. (Or grease 20 cups of 2 standard muffin tins or line with paper liners.)

2. In a separate bowl, blend the flours, cocoa powder, and baking soda. Set aside.

3. In a large bowl, with a hand mixer, cream the sugar and eggs. Beat in the oil, then add the dry ingredients, 1 cup at a time. Add the orange juice, and beat the batter for 2 minutes. Spoon the batter equally into the baking pans or muffin cups.

4. Bake the cake layers for 25 minutes (18 to 22 minutes for cupcakes) until the center of the cakes spring back when pressed. Allow the cakes to cool in the pans for 10 minutes before turning them out onto cooling racks. Cool the cakes completely before icing.

recipe continues

chocolate buttercream ganache and chocolate glaze

makes enough to frost one 9-inch 2-layer cake or 20 cupcakes

The cooled cake is first iced with the chocolate ganache, then the chocolate glaze is poured over the top. As the glaze cools, it finishes the cake with a silky smooth, semisolid topping.

FOR THE GANACHE:

4 ounces dark chocolate, chopped into small pieces

8 tablespoons salted butter

1 tablespoon heavy (whipping) cream

2 teaspoons vanilla extract

2 cups powdered sugar

FOR THE GARNISH AND GLAZE:

1 cup chocolate shavings, for garnish

1 cup (240g) semisweet chocolate chips

4 tablespoons salted butter

¼ cup amaretto or coffee liqueur

1. **Make the ganache:** In a heatproof bowl set in a skillet, heat the dark chocolate over medium heat until it is just melted. Remove the bowl from the skillet and allow the chocolate to cool for 5 minutes.

2. By hand, stir the butter and cream into the melted chocolate, then stir in the vanilla. Using a hand mixer, beat in the powdered sugar until the ganache is smooth and creamy.

3. Ice the bottom layer of the cake with the ganache. Then put on the top layer and ice the sides. The ganache left for the top will make a thin layer, but the glaze will cover the top. Press the chocolate shavings into the sides of the cake while the ganache is still soft.

4. **Make the glaze:** In a heatproof bowl set in a skillet, heat the chocolate chips over medium heat until they are just melted. Remove the bowl from the skillet. Quickly stir in the butter and then the liqueur, stirring until completely blended.

5. While the glaze is still warm and liquid, pour it on the top of the cake. Smooth it to the edges if necessary.

MEMORIES OF OUR WEDDING
are mostly a blur, but I'll never
forget the collective gasp of
our guests when we cut into
the cake and it was—drumroll—
chocolate, not a very traditional
cake for an East Coast wedding
in the early 1970s. I also
remember my going-away
outfit, a pair of white denim
short-shorts. As we ran through
a rain of rice I heard some
guests tut-tutting!

Here I've perfected a recipe
for an *entirely* gluten-free
wedding cake, and not just
the easy-to-make top layer.
This recipe will feed all your
guests—not counting the top
layer, which will be saved for
the bride and groom's first
anniversary. Getting married is
a joyous occasion for all, and so
there is no need to get stressed
out over dietary requirements.
Having a cake that is safe for
dietary-restricted guests and
tastes great for everyone is just
what you need. This gluten-free
wedding cake delivers on both
accounts. People often ask me
if we make wedding cakes (we
don't), and though there are
a growing number of regular
bakeries that make custom
gluten-free cakes, it is always
a bit dicey to ensure that there
is no cross-contamination with
regular flours. This recipe isn't
for a whopping 500-pound,
4-foot-tall gluten-free wedding
cake like Chelsea Clinton's, but
it won't cost you as much as
hers did either.

wedding cake

makes one 3-tiered (6-layer) wedding cake
(enough for 100 guests)

I based this gluten-free wedding cake on the Basic Yellow Cake
(page 258) and consulted Wilton's Wedding Cake Data Chart
on their excellent site (www.wilton.com). Careful planning has
to go into how much cake batter you can realistically make at
a time, how you apportion that batter into the cake pans, the
baking times, and the capacity of your home oven.

In order to create
a 3-tiered cake,
you need to use
3 different cake pan
sizes (each 2 inches
deep) and bake
2 layers for each size;
you will be baking a
total of 6 layers.

two 6-inch layers

two 10-inch layers

two 12-inch layers

Basically, you
will be baking
the 6 layers in 4 separate batches in order to fit the pans in
the oven. I have outlined below a plan that works with the
dimensions of a home oven. (I have also included a recipe for
the full amount of batter required to make the cake in the
event that you or someone making the cake has access to
professional baking equipment.) The completed, un-iced cake
will weigh almost 22 pounds.

recipe continues

NOTE: This is one cake where having specialty baking equipment on hand helps. You will need a heating core to use in the 10-inch and 12-inch pans. A heating core is a cone-shaped insert that is placed in the center of the cake pan and filled with batter. It is used to distribute the heat evenly over the entire layer. Without a heating core, you run the risk of having the bottom and edges brown before the center is baked. Heating cores are available online or at cake decorating stores.

FOR ONE BATCH:

3 cups sugar

1 cup canola oil

2 cups sour cream

12 large eggs

2 cups (224g) coconut flour

2 cups (280g) tapioca starch

2 teaspoons baking powder

1 teaspoon baking soda

4 teaspoons vanilla extract

FOR ALL LAYERS:

12 cups sugar (about 5.3 pounds)

4 cups canola oil

8 cups sour cream (about 4.2 pounds)

48 large eggs

8 cups (896g) coconut flour (about 2 pounds)

8 cups (1,120g) tapioca starch (about 2.5 pounds)

2 tablespoons plus 2 teaspoons baking powder

1 tablespoon plus 1 teaspoon baking soda

⅓ cup vanilla extract

BAKE PLAN ORDER (each batch will produce about 10 cups of batter):

Batch 1: 6 × 2-inch round pan and 10 × 2-inch pan

Batch 2: 12 × 2-inch round pan

Batch 3: 6 × 2-inch round pan and 10 × 2-inch pan

Batch 4: 12 × 2-inch round pan

WEDDING CAKE BAKING TABLE

PAN	BATTER	USE HEATING CORE	TIME AT 325°F	TOTAL COOLING TIME BEFORE REMOVING FROM PAN
6 x 2-inch round	2 cups	no	40–44 min	15 min
10 x 2-inch round	6 cups	yes	45–49 min	20 min*
12 x 2-inch round	9 cups	yes	48–52 min	25 min*

*Remove the heating core after 10 minutes of cooling time and unmold the cake plug inside the core.

1. Position an oven rack in the center of the oven and preheat to 325°F. Prepare the baking pans by greasing them well with butter and tracing the bottoms to cut out two sets of parchment paper rounds for each pan size. Place the parchment paper round in the bottom of the greased pan.

2. In a large bowl, with a hand mixer, blend the sugar, oil, sour cream, and eggs. Beat the batter for 4 minutes.

3. In a separate bowl, blend the coconut flour and tapioca starch together and gradually add them to the egg mixture. Beat 2 more minutes, making sure to scrape down the sides. Allow the batter to rest for 5 minutes. The mixture will thicken as the coconut flour absorbs the liquid.

4. Beat in the baking powder, baking soda, and vanilla, mixing them thoroughly into the batter.

5. Ladle the batter into the pans. Fill the pans approximately two-thirds full using the table opposite as a guide. (There will be leftover batter; save it to make cupcakes.) When using the heating core, fill it just over halfway full and place it in the very center of the pan before ladling the batter around it.

6. Bake the pans according to table Bake Plan Order (opposite), removing each layer from the oven after the prescribed baking time in the Baking Table (opposite). The layers are done when the center springs back when touched.

7. Allow the cake(s) to cool in the pan on a cooling rack for the listed amount of time before turning out of the pan onto a piece of parchment paper on the cooling rack to cool. (You may need to use an inverted pizza pan to cool the 12-inch layers if you don't have a rack large enough.) Cool the cake completely before icing. The un-iced layers will freeze and thaw well, if desired.

8. Wash and dry the pans, then re-grease them for the next batch.

9. Refer to the Wilton site for the icing recipes of your choice and detailed instructions on how to level, ice, and assemble your layers into tiers.

EVERY CHRISTMAS EVE it is a Vermont Public Radio tradition to have the author Willem Lange read his story *Favor Johnson*. It's about fruitcakes and small-town Vermont life. After gagging on a "fancy, boxed fruitcake" given to him by a flatlander doctor who saves his beloved hound, Hercules, Favor declares, "Pfah! I can do better'n that!" The old-time Vermont farmer shows his gratitude by baking and distributing homemade fruitcakes every Christmas to his entire town. It is such a Vermont story!

I've always thought that fruitcake gets unjustly maligned. Sure, we've all politely choked down dry fruitcake, used fruitcake gifts as doorstops, or eaten fruitcake with so much candied fruit that it made our teeth hurt. But fruitcake from a good recipe, in my opinion, can't be beat. This fruitcake is mostly about holding high-quality dried fruit together with just enough flour, butter, and sugar to make it a loaf. I added Triple Sec, an orange liqueur, for flavoring, but I also make some versions in which I use a homemade lavender liqueur (vodka, lavender blossoms, and sugar). Subtle variations in flavorings like these take an ordinary fruitcake and make it outstanding. I encourage you play around with the flavorings of your choice.

a fruitcake to be proud of

makes two 8-inch loaves

1 cup chopped dates

1 cup raisins

1 cup chopped apricots

1 cup chopped prunes

1 cup dried cranberries

1 cup chopped dried pineapple

3/4 cup (105g) tapioca starch

3/4 cup (90g) light buckwheat flour

1 1/2 teaspoons baking powder

1 teaspoon ground allspice

3 large eggs

8 tablespoons salted butter

3 tablespoons unflavored, unsweetened apple butter

1/2 cup packed brown sugar

1/2 cup granulated sugar

1/2 cup Triple Sec (or orange juice, for a nonalcoholic version)

1 teaspoon vanilla extract

1. Position an oven rack in the center of the oven and preheat to 300°F. Grease two 4 1/2 × 8-inch loaf pans.

2. Combine all the fruits in a large bowl and toss with the tapioca starch, buckwheat flour, baking powder, and allspice until completely coated.

3. In a separate bowl, with a hand mixer, beat the eggs and butter until smooth. Add the apple butter, sugars, Triple Sec, and vanilla and beat until well blended.

4. Pour the batter over the fruit mixture and toss until fully combined. The flours will thicken the liquid somewhat. Divide the batter between the loaf pans.

5. Bake for 1 1/2 hours, or until a toothpick inserted in the center comes out clean. Allow the loaves to cool fully in the pans before turning them out and wrapping them individually in foil. Store long-term in the refrigerator or freezer.

CAKE AND ICING GO TOGETHER. The best part of my birthday as a child was that I always got the piece of cake with the rose, or whatever extra icing decoration adorned the top. Growing up, we only had cake on birthdays, so I still remember some of them quite well. One I have never forgotten was a train cake that my mom made for my brother Martin for his sixth birthday. The boiler part of the train was a sponge roll cake smothered with coconut. That was my first sponge roll cake, and I couldn't believe there was a cake with icing in every bite, with a cake-to-icing ratio of 1:1.

Sponge cakes need to be both delicate and robust at the same time—moist and spongy, yet flexible enough to roll without cracking. I've been trying all my gluten-free life to perfect a light sponge that would roll with ease. This flourless sponge roll was yet another attempt at making a flexible sponge, but this time I was attracted by the idea of a flourless cake. In this recipe, the cocoa powder serves as the flour and lots of eggs provide the structure and make it easy to roll; balsamic vinegar stabilizes the egg whites. The icing seals in the flavor and keeps the sponge cake tender and moist. I call it my "experimental" birthday cake—cake with icing and amaretto-flavored whipped cream in every bite. You can't go wrong with that!

flourless chocolate sponge roll

makes one 10-inch roll cake

FOR THE SPONGE CAKE:

6 large eggs, separated

¼ cup plus 2 tablespoons granulated sugar

½ cup powdered sugar

¼ cup unsweetened cocoa powder

3 tablespoons canola oil

1 teaspoon vanilla extract

3 drops balsamic vinegar

FOR THE FILLING:

1 pint heavy (whipping) cream

2 tablespoons granulated sugar

2 teaspoons amaretto liqueur

FOR THE ICING AND GARNISH:

4 tablespoons salted butter

⅓ cup unsweetened cocoa powder

2 cups powdered sugar

2 tablespoons amaretto liqueur

4 tablespoons milk

2 tablespoons white nonpareils (optional)

1. **Make the sponge cake:** Position an oven rack in the center of the oven and preheat to 325°F. Butter a 10 × 15-inch rimmed baking sheet and line it with parchment paper.

2. In a large bowl, with a hand mixer, beat together the egg yolks and ¼ cup of the granulated sugar. Beat in the powdered sugar, cocoa powder, canola oil, and vanilla.

3. In a separate bowl, with clean beaters, beat the egg whites until soft peaks form. Add the vinegar and remaining 2 tablespoons granulated sugar and beat until glossy and stiff peaks form. Fold the egg white mixture into the yolk mixture and barely blend.

recipe continues

4. Lightly spread the batter in the pan. Bake the cake for 15 minutes. The cake will be puffy and deflate some as it cools. Remove the baking pan from the oven and cover the cake with a damp tea towel. Let the cake cool completely.

5. **Make the filling:** With a clean bowl and clean beaters, whip the cream, adding the granulated sugar and amaretto after it reaches soft peaks. Continue whipping the cream until it is thick and close to a butter consistency.

6. Remove the sponge cake on the parchment paper from the baking sheet. Use a spatula to spread the filling evenly over the sponge cake.

7. Using the parchment paper, gently roll up the log, peeling back the parchment paper as you roll. Position the roll seam side down on the baking sheet. Use two wide spatulas to transfer the roll to a serving platter.

8. **Make the icing:** In a clean bowl with clean beaters, beat together the butter, cocoa powder, powdered sugar, and amaretto until smooth. Add the milk 1 tablespoon at a time until you reach a spreadable consistency.

9. Ice the log, sprinkle with the nonpareils (if using), and put it in the refrigerator to cool for 1 hour before serving.

I'VE ALWAYS BEEN INTERESTED IN BRAZILIAN FOOD, particularly because tapioca is a staple in many Brazilian diets. This rolled sponge cake is a Brazilian favorite. It is traditionally filled with either guava marmalade or dulce de leche, a rich, caramelized milk sauce made from boiled-down condensed milk. *Rocambole*, unlike other sponge cakes (see Flourless Chocolate Sponge Roll, page 281), is based on a batter that begins with whipped egg whites, to which the other ingredients are added. In other sponge cake recipes, the egg whites are folded in last to prevent them from being deflated and to create a light and airy batter.

It is believed that this cake originated during the colonization of northeastern Brazil by the Portuguese, who brought with them a very thin-layered roll cake, or *bolo de rolo*. Although the Portuguese traditionally filled their cake with nuts, in Brazil they began filling it with a sweetened guava spread because of the abundance of guava and sugar factories. The rocambole layers are much thicker than the paper-thin layers of the bolo de rolo. And instead of equal proportions of sugar, butter, flour, and eggs, the rocambole is made with far more eggs and

brazilian roll cake (rocambole)

serves 8

5 large eggs, separated (see Note)

5 tablespoons granulated sugar

5 tablespoons tapioca starch (or 3 tablespoons tapioca starch and 2 tablespoons light buckwheat flour)

½ teaspoon baking powder

1 cup Coconut Dulce de Leche (recipe follows) or guava or quince jelly

Powdered sugar, for dusting

1. Position an oven rack in the center of the oven and preheat to 350°F. Grease a 10 × 15-inch rimmed baking sheet and then line with parchment paper.

2. In a bowl, with a hand mixer, beat the egg yolks until they are light and fluffy. Beat 5 tablespoons water into the egg yolks. Set aside.

3. In a large bowl, with clean beaters, beat the egg whites on high until soft peaks form. Beat in the granulated sugar until the mixture is glossy and stiff peaks form. The whites should double in volume.

4. Add the egg yolk mixture to the egg whites and beat well. Sprinkle the tapioca starch and baking powder on the top of the batter. Using a rubber spatula, fold in the flours without deflating the eggs. Lightly spread the batter in the pan.

5. Bake the cake for 18 minutes, or until the cake is golden brown and springs back when touched. Make sure the edges are loose by running a sharp knife along the edges of the baking sheet.

6. While it is still warm, lift the entire cake and parchment paper up and place it on a cutting board. Spread the dulce de leche on the cake and roll it up, peeling back the parchment paper as you roll it. Place the cake seam side down on a serving platter. Sprinkle the cake lightly with powdered sugar to serve.

NOTE: Egg whites that have been at room temperature for at least 30 minutes will increase at least sixfold in volume over cold egg whites when whipped.

coconut dulce de leche
makes 1 cup

This versatile gluten-free and dairy-free sauce can be used with sponge cakes, ladyfingers, and chocolate confections. Adapted from a *Bon Appétit* magazine recipe, it pairs particularly well with bananas, and makes an excellent ice cream topping. Make the sauce ahead of time and store it in the refrigerator for several weeks.

1 can (13.5 ounces) full-fat unsweetened coconut milk (such as Native Forest Organic)

½ cup (100g) coconut palm sugar

¼ teaspoon salt

1. Measure all the ingredients into a 12-inch skillet. Stir them together over medium heat until the sugar dissolves.

2. Bring the sauce to a boil (vigorous bubbling over the entire surface). Allow the sauce to boil uncovered for 15 minutes, stirring it several times to check the consistency. This process should reduce the volume to 1 cup and thicken the sauce. Remember, the sauce will seem thinner when hot.

3. Pour the sauce into a heatproof glass container and allow it to cool at room temperature for 30 minutes. Cover and refrigerate the sauce until needed.

water rather than butter. The resulting cake has somewhat fluffier or spongier layers and resembles more what we would think of as a jelly roll.

WHEN DOROTHY and the Cowardly Lion fall asleep in a field of poppies on their way to the Emerald City, they're soundly snoozing surrounded by the featured ingredient in this strudel: poppy seeds (*Mohn* means poppy in German). Mohnstrudel is a traditional rolled cake filled with a thick, sweet poppy seed filling that has been around since the eighteenth century in Austria and Hungary. I first learned about Mohnstrudel at the 2012 America's Best Raisin Bread Contest, where one individual's entry was a Mohnstrudel with raisins.

Poppy seeds are very aromatic, but their taste is often lost when we simply sprinkle them as seed toppings on breads, rolls, and bagels. In this sweet poppy seed filling, you can actually taste the poppy seeds; the filling is sweet and fragrant, with the characteristic crunch. I added a small amount of rum to bring out the flavor of the poppy seeds and raisins, but you may substitute another teaspoon of vanilla extract instead. The contrast of the black filling against the yellow strudel is both attractive and yummy-looking.

mohnstrudel

makes two 12-inch strudels

FOR THE POPPY SEED FILLING:

½ cup milk

2 tablespoons rum

¼ cup golden raisins

¾ cup poppy seeds

½ cup sugar

2 tablespoons salted butter

1 teaspoon vanilla extract

1 tablespoon honey

2 tablespoons lemon juice

FOR THE DOUGH:

1½ cups (210g) tapioca starch, plus ¾ cup (105g) for kneading in

1 cup (120g) light buckwheat flour, plus ½ cup (60g) for kneading in

½ cup milk

4 tablespoons salted butter

1 teaspoon salt

¼ cup plus 1 teaspoon sugar

1 tablespoon active dry yeast

3 large egg yolks

½ cup sour cream

1. **Make the filling:** In a small bowl, whisk together the milk and rum. Stir the raisins and poppy seeds into the liquid. Let them soak for 1 hour.

2. In a food processor, combine the soaked poppy seed mixture and sugar and process for about 5 minutes, or until the poppy seeds and raisins are chopped up.

3. Transfer the poppy seed mixture to a medium saucepan and add the butter, vanilla, honey, and lemon juice and bring to a slow boil, stirring frequently. Allow it to boil for 5 minutes. Remove from the heat and cool for 10 minutes, then refrigerate to continue cooling while you make the dough.

recipe continues

4. **Make the dough:** Clean out and dry the food processor and measure the 1½ cups tapioca starch and 1 cup buckwheat flour into the work bowl.

5. In a saucepan, combine the milk, butter, salt, and ¼ cup of the sugar and bring to a boil. Immediately pour the hot mixture into the food processor and pulse until the dough is completely combined. This will happen very quickly, and the dough will have a texture like hot icing. Allow it to cool for 20 minutes.

6. Meanwhile, in a small bowl, combine the yeast, remaining 1 teaspoon sugar, and ¼ cup warm water and allow it to proof for 15 minutes.

7. Whisk the egg yolks and sour cream into the yeast mixture until they are well blended. Pour the combined mixture over the dough in the food processor and process until the dough is smooth.

8. Transfer the dough to a medium bowl, cover with plastic wrap, and allow it to rise for 45 minutes. It will thicken some and double in size.

9. Using a rubber spatula, work in the ¾ cup tapioca starch and ½ cup light buckwheat flour. Let the dough rest for another 30 minutes to absorb the additional flour.

10. Divide the dough in half and roll each half out into a 12 × 10-inch rectangle on a piece of parchment paper dusted with tapioca starch. The dough should not be so sticky that it won't roll. If it is, dust it with a little tapioca starch. Divide the poppy seed filling in half and spread each rectangle with the filling to within 1 inch of the edges. Butter a 9 × 13-inch baking dish.

11. Pull up on the parchment paper and use it to roll the dough, starting at one of the longer ends, until you have a log 3 to 4 inches in diameter and 12 inches long. Trim the parchment paper around the log and transfer the log on the paper to the baking dish. Set the two logs seam side down and side by side in the baking dish. Cover the logs with plastic wrap and allow them to rise for 45 minutes.

12. Meanwhile, position an oven rack in the center of the oven and preheat to 350°F.

13. Unwrap and bake the loaves for 35 minutes, or until golden brown. Transfer the loaves on the parchment paper to a cooling rack.

NOTE: The greatest challenge here is creating a tender, moist bread that can be rolled out, yet retains its shape. This is accomplished by creating a well-hydrated dough that is given ample time to rest, absorb the liquids, and rise. Dry flour is kneaded in after the dough is fully hydrated to allow you to roll the dough into its signature poppy seed spiral. This dough also has a tendency to spread and flatten as it rises and bakes. To produce more rounded loaves, bake them in a 2-channel baguette pan lined with parchment paper.

I REMEMBER HOW LOST I WAS when my family members were first diagnosed with celiac disease, so I find it one of the most rewarding aspects of my job to teach about the science of gluten-free baking—introducing newbies to gluten-free flours and how proteins and starches create structure. Just at the point that their heads may be swimming with all the facts, I whip out my hand mixer and show them how to bake their knowledge into a cake.

This sour cream cake is the cake we make together to put all the information into action. Just as in the cooking shows on television, we go through the work of making the cake, and when we are done discussing how the process and ingredients come together in this recipe, we all have a piece of an already finished cake. I see the "Aha, I get it" looks on their faces. They may go home and bake this coffee cake for breakfast or dessert for the next month, but I know that I have made their lives easier. This recipe illustrates the fundamentals of gluten-free baking so well, and it is a really good, simple cake. It can be made with a mixture of gluten-free flours, or simply by measuring out a multipurpose gluten-free mix like the one made by King Arthur.

sour cream coffee cake

makes one 9-inch Bundt cake

FOR THE CINNAMON SWIRL:

2 teaspoons ground cinnamon

2 tablespoons salted butter

3 tablespoons sugar

FOR THE CAKE:

3/4 cup (120g) brown rice flour

1 cup plus 2 tablespoons (157g) tapioca starch

1 teaspoon baking soda

1 teaspoon baking powder

1 cup sugar

4 large eggs

1 cup sour cream

1 teaspoon vanilla extract

1/2 cup canola oil

1. Position an oven rack in the center of the oven and preheat to 350°F. Grease a 9-inch Bundt pan with butter.

2. **Make the cinnamon swirl:** In a small bowl, combine the cinnamon, butter, and sugar. Blend until fully incorporated. Set aside.

3. **Make the cake:** In a medium bowl, whisk together the rice flour, tapioca starch, baking soda, and baking powder.

4. In a large bowl, with a hand mixer, cream the sugar and eggs until they are well aerated and light yellow. By hand, stir in the sour cream, vanilla, and oil until the mixture is well blended. Fold in the dry ingredients until they are fully moistened.

5. Pour two-thirds of the batter into the Bundt pan. Sprinkle the cinnamon swirl filling on the batter. Top the cake with the remaining batter.

6. Bake for 40 to 45 minutes, or until the top springs back when lightly pressed. Allow the cake to cool in the pan for 5 minutes before turning it out (top side down) onto a parchment-lined cooling rack.

MY FAVORITE CAKE growing up was an applesauce cake—and the reason I probably liked the cake so much is that it was the only cake I ever had as a child that was made from scratch. Cake mixes were introduced as convenience foods in the 1920s, and though the mixes didn't produce a knock-off of a homemade cake, they were touted as modern conveniences for saving time. The biggest obstacle for manufacturers of early cake mixes was how to incorporate shortening in a boxed mix; but that changed in 1947 when Beatrice Creamery Company patented a powdered shortening. By the 1960s, cake mix advertisements touted a "wonderful new way to *pre-cream*" ingredients with "a new rich creamy shortening." Fast-forward to today and there are just about as many varieties of cake mixes as there are models of cars. You can even buy a basic applesauce cake mix, with 46 ingredients and enriched with factory vitamins, dough conditioners, and food coloring to make it all look normal and appetizing, and not even a single real spice. One of the biggest benefits of having to eat a gluten-free diet is that you can gracefully step off the packaged food carousel.

This applesauce cake recipe is shamefully simple: pretty much flour, sugar, eggs, oil, and applesauce with leaveners

applesauce cake with brown sugar caramel glaze

makes one 9-inch Bundt cake

FOR THE CAKE:

³⁄₄ cup (120g) brown rice flour

1 cup plus 2 tablespoons (157g) tapioca starch

¹⁄₄ cup (48g) potato starch

1 teaspoon baking powder

1 teaspoon baking soda

³⁄₄ teaspoon ground cinnamon

¹⁄₂ teaspoon ground allspice

¹⁄₂ teaspoon ground ginger

¹⁄₄ teaspoon ground cloves

1 cup granulated sugar

4 large eggs

¹⁄₂ cup canola oil

1 cup unsweetened applesauce

¹⁄₄ cup apple cider

FOR THE BROWN SUGAR CARAMEL GLAZE:

4 tablespoons salted butter

¹⁄₂ cup packed brown sugar

¹⁄₃ cup heavy (whipping) cream

¹⁄₂ teaspoon vanilla extract

1. **Make the cake:** Position an oven rack in the center of the oven and preheat to 350°F. Grease a 9-inch Bundt pan with butter.

2. In a medium bowl, blend the rice flour, tapioca starch, potato starch, baking powder, baking soda, and spices.

3. In a large bowl, with a hand mixer, beat together the sugar and eggs. Beat in the oil and applesauce. Beat in the dry ingredients, 1 cup at a time. Add the apple cider and beat the batter for 2 minutes.

recipe continues

and spices. This cake is sweet enough to serve with a simple dusting of cinnamon and powdered sugar, but the Brown Sugar Caramel Glaze makes it even more special. It also freezes and thaws nicely, so it is always a nice backup cake to have in the freezer.

4. Spoon the batter into the Bundt pan and bake for 50 to 55 minutes, until the top springs back when touched and the cake pulls away from the sides.

5. Allow the Bundt pan to cool enough so that you can handle it, then turn the cake out, top or flat side down, onto a parchment-lined cooling rack. Allow the cake to cool for about 30 minutes. It will still be warm.

6. **Make the glaze:** In a medium saucepan, bring the butter, brown sugar, cream, and vanilla to a boil. Once it reaches a boil, allow it to boil for 3 minutes. Remove it from the heat.

7. Pour the glaze on the cake while both are still slightly warm. The cake may be served warm or cooled to room temperature.

A HARVEY WALLBANGER CAKE was the first cake I made as an adult and brought to a party, and people went nuts over it. Now a retro drink, Harvey Wallbangers were popular in the 1960s and were made from vodka, orange juice, and Galliano liqueur. Actually, I've never tasted the drink, but at the time, to a twenty-something-year-old, it looked like a classy cake. The manufacturers of Galliano describe their secret recipe as "a medieval elixir of herbs, plants, roots, barks, spices and flower seeds" with 30 herbs, spices, and plant extracts. To say the least, it makes a unique-tasting cake.

The original recipe called for a package of instant vanilla pudding. It is not easy to make substitutions for instant puddings since they are "instant" because they contain modified food starches that have unique gelling properties. However, by increasing the proportion of tapioca starch relative to the other flours and increasing the amount of potato starch, these two starches can be used to the same effect. The starches retain moisture as well as contribute to a tight, velvety smooth crumb. This cake is plenty sweet and is served without any icing or glaze.

harvey wallbanger cake

makes one 9-inch Bundt cake

¾ cup (120g) brown rice flour

1¼ cups (175g) tapioca starch

¼ cup (48g) potato starch

½ cup canola oil

1¼ cups sugar

4 large eggs

1 cup orange juice

¼ cup Galliano liqueur

1. Position an oven rack in the center of the oven and preheat to 350°F. Grease a 9-inch Bundt pan.

2. In a large bowl, with a hand mixer, blend together the rice flour, tapioca starch, and potato starch. Add the oil, sugar, eggs, orange juice, and Galliano and beat on high until well blended, about 2 minutes.

3. Spoon the batter into the Bundt pan and bake for 35 minutes, or until the top springs back when touched and the cake pulls away from the sides. Allow the cake to cool in the pan for 10 minutes and then turn it out onto a cooling rack. Cool to room temperature to serve.

SOMETIMES MY HUSBAND, TOM, AND I eat dessert for breakfast. It's not that we wake up craving sugar; we wake up craving this creamy cheesecake—it is without a doubt my favorite dessert recipe in this book. There are some desserts that are probably far better for you than a bowl of cereal, and this cashew "cheesecake" is one of them. Made from only a few ingredients and no refined sugar, it is a sweet, protein-filled dessert that keeps us going most of the day.

With almost four times the starch content of most tree nuts, cashews meld with water and are highly effective as a thickener. Cashews are also lower in fat than most other nuts; their oil content is similar to that of heart-healthy olive oil. This is one dessert that you too will be eating for breakfast, and not just because it tastes so darn good.

cashew "cheesecake"

makes one 9-inch cake

2 cups raw cashews

4 large eggs, separated

1/8 teaspoon cream of tartar

1/2 cup maple syrup

1/2 cup coconut cream (skimmed from the top of a 13.5-ounce can of full-fat coconut milk)

2 teaspoons vanilla extract

1. To make the cashew "cheese," combine the cashews and 1 cup water in a food processor or high-speed blender and process until silky smooth (see Note). (Blend in several batches if you are having difficulty attaining a smooth texture.)

2. Position an oven rack in the center of the oven and preheat to 375°F. Grease the bottom and sides of an 8- or 9-inch springform pan with coconut oil.

3. In a medium bowl, with a hand mixer, beat the egg whites until stiff peaks form, adding the cream of tartar near the end. Set aside.

4. In a separate bowl, with the hand mixer, beat the maple syrup and yolks together. Add the cashew cheese and beat it until light and foamy; add the coconut cream and vanilla and beat for 2 minutes. Gently fold in the egg whites by hand.

5. Pour the batter into the pan and bake for 55 minutes, or until the center of the cake is set and the top is lightly browned. Allow the cake to cool for 10 to 15 minutes on a cooling rack before releasing the sides of the springform pan. Use a sharp knife to gently loosen the sides if you find they are sticking. Chill the cheesecake completely, preferably overnight, before serving.

NOTE: If you want to increase the cheese's tanginess, add either 2 teaspoons lemon juice or 4 capsules acidophilus.

MY MOM was part of the wave of Italian immigrants who urbanized Brooklyn and settled in multifamily homes along Flatbush Avenue. She grew up there in the 1920s and '30s when the Dodgers ruled Ebbets Field, and you could go to Nathan's in Coney Island and buy a frankfurter, hamburger, or roast beef sandwich for 5 cents. For years, I heard her rave about "Brooklyn cheesecake," so when we moved to Brooklyn in 1981, one of the first eating establishments we visited was Junior's to sample their famous cheesecake. Although Brooklyn cheesecake is synonymous with Junior's, my mom insisted that Junior's cream cheese–based cheesecake is not the cheesecake of her youth. To her, real cheesecake is made with ricotta cheese. I finally understood that my mom's memories were of classic Italian cheesecake, not New York cheesecake.

The combination of ricotta cheese and sour cream is astoundingly light and flavorful. There is no need to put a crust on this one. I finished this cheesecake with a homemade lemon curd, which plays extremely well with the lavender and ricotta. This one is for you, Mom, and I do believe that this may be the best cheesecake I have ever eaten.

lavender ricotta cheesecake with lemon curd

makes one 10-inch cheesecake

FOR THE CHEESECAKE:

4 large eggs, separated

1 cup sugar

15 ounces full-fat ricotta cheese

1/2 cup sour cream

1/2 teaspoon salt

1 teaspoon lemon extract

2 teaspoons dried lavender

FOR THE LEMON CURD:

4 tablespoons salted butter

3/4 cup sugar

2 large eggs

Grated zest of 2 lemons

1/4 cup lemon juice

1/4 teaspoon salt

1. Position an oven rack in the center of the oven and preheat to 375°F. Generously butter the bottom and sides of a 10-inch springform pan.

2. **Make the cheesecake:** In a bowl, with a hand mixer, beat the egg whites until stiff and shiny peaks form.

3. In a separate bowl, with the hand mixer, cream the sugar and egg yolks. Add the ricotta and beat it until it is light and foamy. Add the sour cream, salt, lemon extract, and lavender, and beat for an additional 2 minutes. Gently fold in the egg whites by hand, a portion at a time.

4. Pour the batter into the springform pan and place the pan on the center rack. Put a baking sheet on the rack under the cheesecake in case of leakage. Bake the cake for 1 hour, or until the center of the cake is set and the top is lightly browned. Remove the cake from the oven and let it cool for 10 to 15 minutes on a cooling rack before releasing the sides of the springform pan. Use a sharp knife to gently loosen the sides if you find the cheesecake is sticking to the pan. Allow the cake to cool fully—as the cake cools, the center will sink, leaving a higher rim around the edges (the sunken center will contain the lemon curd).

5. **Make the lemon curd:** In a bowl, with a hand mixer, cream the butter and sugar. Add the eggs, lemon zest, lemon juice, and salt. Pour the mixture into a medium saucepan and heat over low heat, stirring constantly for about 4 minutes, or until the mixture starts bubbling and thickens. Watch the curd closely since it is easy to scorch the bottom of the pan. Pour the thickened curd into a heatproof glass bowl and allow it to cool for 20 minutes.

6. Pour the lemon curd into the depression on the top of the cheesecake. Chill the cheesecake completely, preferably overnight, before serving.

SOME OF MY FAVORITE COOKBOOKS are Junior League cookbooks. The Junior League is one of the oldest and largest women's volunteer organizations, with over 150,000 members in four countries. These are women who are civic leaders, tireless volunteers . . . and often really good cooks and hostesses.

I discovered this recipe for Fresh Banana Cheesecake in *The Junior League Centennial Cookbook*, a compilation of over 750 regional recipes. This one came from the Junior League of Honolulu cookbook, *Another Taste of Aloha*. What caught my eye was not the fresh bananas but the oatmeal crust, calling for rolled oats, butter, brown sugar, and chopped pecans. I modified it to be more consistent with the tropical theme: I toasted the oats and substituted toasted coconut for the pecans and coconut oil for the butter. I was stunned by how well it paired with the filling and how beautifully it rose up inside the springform pan. Believe me, this is a cheesecake that will draw stares and leave mouths watering. It requires 24 hours in the refrigerator to realize its full flavor potential, but we could only wait until it was barely chilled. As is the case with many cheesecakes, it was even better the next day.

fresh banana cheesecake

makes one 9-inch cheesecake

FOR THE CRUST:

1½ cups rolled oats

1 cup unsweetened shredded coconut

½ cup packed brown sugar

¼ cup coconut oil

FOR THE FILLING:

2 8-ounce packages cream cheese

1 cup mashed ripe bananas (about 2 large)

¾ cup granulated sugar

2 tablespoons Kirsch (or lemon juice, for a nonalcoholic version)

4 large eggs

FOR THE TOPPING:

1 cup sour cream

2 tablespoons granulated sugar

1 teaspoon vanilla extract

1. **Make the crust:** Position an oven rack in the center of the oven and preheat to 350°F. Measure the oats and coconut onto a baking sheet and toast for 12 minutes. Set the pan aside to cool. Leave the oven on.

2. Transfer the oats and coconut to a food processor and pulse the mixture 4 to 5 times until it is coarsely chopped. Add the brown sugar and coconut oil. Blend it until the dough is fully moistened.

3. Using your fingers, press the crust into the bottom and ½ inch up the sides of a deep 9-inch springform pan (the crust will rise up along the sides of the pan as the cheesecake filling bakes and expands). The crust will not pack tightly, but will be sort of loose and crumbly.

recipe continues

4. Prebake the crust for 15 minutes. Allow it to cool completely. Leave the oven on.

5. **Make the filling:** In a large bowl, with a hand mixer, beat together the cream cheese, bananas, granulated sugar, and Kirsch until well blended and smooth. Beat in the eggs one at a time. Continue beating the filling until it is smooth and creamy and there are no lumps of cream cheese.

6. Pour the filling into the crust and bake the cheesecake for 55 minutes.

7. **Meanwhile, make the topping:** About 5 minutes before the cake is done, in a small bowl, beat together the sour cream, granulated sugar, and vanilla until well blended.

8. Remove the cheesecake from the oven, pour the topping over the cake and smooth it to the edges. Return the cheesecake to the oven and bake for 10 more minutes.

9. Remove the cheesecake from the oven and allow it to cool for 15 minutes. Loosen the sides of the springform pan, using the blade of a sharp knife to release the cake, and remove the ring. Cool the cake at room temperature for 1½ hours. Cover the cake with plastic wrap and refrigerate overnight before serving. The longer the banana melds into the filling, the creamier and more flavorful the cake becomes.

MY BEST FRIEND growing up was from a family of nine children. Her father had retired from the federal government to become a gentleman farmer, and his passion was strawberries. They grew acres upon acres of strawberries, and every one of her siblings who was old enough to handle a hoe had a summer job weeding, maintaining, and planting more strawberry beds. Living right down the road from their farm was such a treat—fresh-picked strawberries every day for nearly a month. As far as I'm concerned there is no fresh fruit as tasty as a sun-ripened strawberry, still warm from the sun and just plucked from the plant. Now I have my own strawberry patch, a small one, and the Vermont strawberry season is fleeting. But it really feels like summer has finally arrived when we pick our first berries and make strawberry shortcake.

Unlike my dad, who insisted on Bisquick, I like several kinds of shortcake. Sometimes it is biscuit-like with a hint of honey. Other times, I enjoy sweeter and simpler homemade sponge shortcake. You don't have to worry about making tough biscuits unlike wheat-based shortcake. This shortcake is a bit more involved than Bisquick's "90 seconds from package to oven," but not much more. Even my dad might have agreed that these were just as good or better than his old standard.

biscuit shortcake

makes 8 biscuits

1½ cups (180g) light buckwheat flour

1¼ cups (175g) tapioca starch

1 teaspoon baking soda

3 large eggs, separated

½ cup sugar

3 tablespoons salted butter

¼ cup light cream

1 tablespoon honey

1 teaspoon almond extract

1. Position an oven rack in the center of the oven and preheat to 375°F. Line a baking sheet with parchment paper.

2. In a bowl, combine the buckwheat flour, tapioca starch, and baking soda until they are fully blended. Set aside.

3. In another bowl, beat the egg whites on high until stiff and shiny peaks form. Set aside.

4. In a medium bowl, with the mixer, cream the sugar and butter until light and fluffy. Beat in the egg yolks, light cream, honey, and almond extract until light and foamy. By hand, stir in the flour mixture until it is completely moistened. Gently fold in the egg whites until they are fully incorporated.

5. Turn the sticky biscuit dough out onto plastic wrap dusted with tapioca starch. Dust your hands and the top of the dough with tapioca starch to handle, and gently pat down the dough to about ¾ inch thick and cut out biscuits. Reroll the scraps into biscuits, as necessary.

6. Use the plastic wrap to transfer the biscuits to the baking sheet. The biscuits will flatten and spread some as they bake, so place them 1 inch apart on the baking sheet.

7. Bake the biscuits for 18 minutes, or until they are lightly browned. Transfer to a cooling rack.

THIS IS ABOUT THE EASIEST and most versatile shortcake you can make. It is definitely sweeter and richer than the traditional shortcake, but it freezes and thaws extremely well. This shortcake also can be used as a platform for many other desserts in the same way that you might use ladyfingers. It holds up well to juicy strawberries and is ideal for soaking up simple syrups and liqueurs.

sponge shortcakes

makes 8 medium or 16 small shortcakes

1 cup sugar

8 tablespoons salted butter

1 teaspoon almond extract

4 large eggs

1 cup (140g) tapioca starch

1 teaspoon baking powder

1/2 teaspoon salt

1. Position an oven rack in the center of the oven and preheat to 375°F. Grease eight 2¹/₂-inch individual brioche molds (or 16 cups of 2 standard muffin tins for smaller cakes) with salted butter.

2. In a bowl, with a hand mixer, cream the sugar and butter. Beat in the almond extract. Beat in the eggs, one at a time, until the mixture is light and fluffy. Beat in the tapioca starch, baking powder, and salt until they are fully moistened.

3. Spoon the batter into the individual brioche molds (or muffin tins), filling them up about halfway.

4. If using brioche molds, place the filled molds on a baking sheet. Bake the shortcakes for 18 minutes. The shortcakes will initially rise way up, then fall back as they continue to bake, creating a depression in the center. (This is the "well" that you fill with berries when preparing berry shortcake.)

5. Transfer the individual molds (or muffin tins) to a cooling rack. Allow them to cool enough that you can handle the molds. Gently turn the shortcakes out onto a parchment-lined cooling rack. You may need to use a butter knife to loosen the edges around the fluting of the molds. Allow them to cool completely before assembling the shortcakes.

ABOUT A FIFTH OF OUR SUMMER GARDEN is my strawberry patch. The first year the plants produced fruit, but some chipmunks had a strawberry festival one night and cleaned out the entire patch. Luckily, this past year there were strawberries in abundance, so much so that we couldn't keep up with them. We ate strawberries for breakfast, strawberry shortcake for dessert, and I finally decided to make a fresh strawberry cake.

There are tons of recipes for strawberry cake using Jell-O, but hardly any with fresh strawberries. The reason may be that strawberries weep when they come in contact with sugar because of osmosis: a higher concentration of sugar on the outside of the berries draws out their internal moisture. Making a strawberry cake without sugar obviously doesn't work, so I use highly absorbent coconut flour combined with tapioca starch to soak up and thicken any extra strawberry juice. The result is a beautifully colored, fragrant cake that is sweet, yet not soggy. The sour cream pairs extremely well with the strawberries, creating a cake with a strawberries 'n' cream flavor. This strawberry cake can be iced with Cream Cheese Frosting (261), Simple Boiled White Icing (273), or Basic Vanilla Buttercream Frosting (259).

fresh strawberry cake

makes one 9-inch 2-layer cake or 20 to 24 muffins

1 cup fresh strawberries

1½ cups sugar

½ cup canola oil

½ cup sour cream

5 large eggs

1 cup (112g) coconut flour

1 cup (140g) tapioca starch

1 teaspoon baking powder

½ teaspoon baking soda

2 teaspoons vanilla extract

1. Position an oven rack in the center of the oven and preheat to 350°F. Generously grease two 9-inch cake pans and line with rounds of parchment paper. (Or line 20 to 24 cups of 2 standard muffin tins with paper liners.)

2. In a food processor, puree the strawberries until they are smooth. Set aside.

3. In a large bowl, with a hand mixer, blend the sugar, oil, sour cream, and eggs. Beat the mixture for approximately 4 minutes.

4. In a separate bowl, blend the coconut flour and tapioca starch. Gradually add the dry ingredients to the egg mixture and beat until fully blended, scraping down the sides as necessary. Add the strawberry puree and beat for 2 minutes. Let the batter rest for 5 minutes for the flours to absorb the liquid.

5. Beat in the baking powder, baking soda, and vanilla, mixing them thoroughly into the batter. Ladle the batter into the pans (or muffin cups) until they are two-thirds full.

6. Bake for 40 minutes (27 to 28 minutes for cupcakes), until the tops spring back when touched. Allow the cakes to cool in the pans for 10 minutes, then turn them out onto cooling racks. Cool the cakes completely before icing.

MADELEINES ARE SMALL, buttery French teacakes baked in a shell shape. Good madeleines are hard to come by in this country, great ones are rare, and gluten-free ones are virtually nonexistent. Traditionally made with nothing but flour, sugar, butter, and eggs, great madeleines are a perfect example of an artisan baker's passion for the finest ingredients and attention to detail. If you want great madeleines, you need to bake them yourself. Although you don't have to bake madeleines in their molds (you could use mini muffin tins), without them you won't get the delicate shell-shaped teacakes textured on one side with the characteristic hump on the other.

This recipe—adapted from Annemarie Conte's recipe for an authentic madeleine in the *New York Times*—bears a similarity to Julia Child's recipe in *From Julia Child's Kitchen*. Julia would be upset with a few liberties I took, including using baking powder in this recipe, but she never had to bake gluten-free. But she would be pleased that I adopted her technique for preparing the molds by painting them with a mixture of melted butter and flour. To achieve the classic madeleine hump, the batter is refrigerated to harden the butter, which produces a higher rise.

madeleines

makes 12 madeleines

½ cup plus 2 tablespoons sugar

½ cup (60g) light buckwheat flour

⅓ cup (50g) tapioca starch

½ teaspoon baking powder

2 large eggs

½ teaspoon orange extract

7 tablespoons salted butter, melted and cooled

For the madeleine pan:
1½ tablespoons melted butter, 2 teaspoons light buckwheat flour, 1 teaspoon tapioca starch

1. In a large bowl, stir together the sugar, buckwheat flour, tapioca starch, and baking powder. Slowly stir in the eggs and orange extract until all the flour is moistened. Add the melted butter and stir gently until the butter is evenly mixed throughout the batter. Cover and refrigerate the batter for at least 1 hour.

2. Position an oven rack in the center of the oven and preheat to 400°F. To prepare the madeleine pan, stir together the 1½ tablespoons melted butter, 2 teaspoons buckwheat flour, and 1 teaspoon tapioca starch. Using a small pastry brush, paint the insides of the molds, as well as a thin margin around the molds.

3. Spoon about 1 tablespoon of batter into each mold. (It will seem underfilled, but it will spread on its own to fill the mold.)

4. Bake the madeleines for 15 minutes, or until the edges of the madeleines turn golden brown and the rounded top springs back when lightly touched. Using a butter knife, gently release the madeleines from the molds and cool, rounded side down, on a cooling rack. The outsides will crisp slightly as they cool.

LAST YEAR, I GAVE MY HUSBAND, TOM, a juicer for his birthday, and I surprised him by making fresh orange juice for breakfast. It was our first juicer and, honestly, I had no idea it would produce so much pulp. Just before I whisked the pulp away to the compost bucket, I decided I was going to make an orange pulp–based baked good. Mini Orange Teacakes were the result.

For a while Starbucks offered an individually wrapped gluten-free Valencia Cake that was discontinued after several months in favor of a shelf-stable gluten-free offering. The ingredients included eggs, Valencia orange pulp, almonds, and sugar, in addition to flavorings and leavening agents. This is a similar orange cake, although it is based on coconut flour rather than almonds and is lighter and less calorically dense. It is a moist and tender cake, perfect with coffee and tea. And I've given you instructions here for making your own orange pulp, in case you don't have juicer pulp to spare. (Though if you do happen to have orange pulp, substitute 1 cup of pulp plus ¼ cup orange juice for the homemade pulp and skip step 1.)

mini orange teacakes

makes 8 teacakes

2 juice oranges

1 cup powdered sugar

¼ cup coconut oil

6 large eggs

½ cup (56g) coconut flour

1 teaspoon baking powder

1. To make the orange pulp, wash the oranges and cover them with water in a medium saucepan. Bring the water to a boil and simmer for 15 minutes. Remove the pan from the heat, run the oranges under cold water, and coarsely chop them, making sure to remove any seeds. Transfer the oranges to a food processor and blend them until smooth. Set aside.

2. Position an oven rack in the center of the oven and preheat to 350°F. Generously grease 8 mini-loaf pans.

3. In a bowl, with a hand mixer, beat together the powdered sugar and coconut oil until well blended. Add the eggs and beat on high until light and fluffy, about 2 minutes.

4. Add the orange pulp and beat an additional 2 minutes. Beat in the coconut flour and allow the batter to absorb for 5 minutes. Beat in the baking powder.

5. Spoon the batter into the prepared loaf pans. Bake the cakes for 35 minutes, or until the centers spring back and the cakes are lightly browned around the edges. Allow the cakes to cool for about 10 minutes in the pans, then turn them out onto a platter to continue cooling.

pies *and* desserts

WHEN YOU WANT A SOFTER, sweeter dough, this pastry is the perfect solution. The texture is softened by the addition of a whole egg and an egg yolk, and tenderized by adding sugar. The sugar and eggs also facilitate browning and produce a warm golden-color crust. Sweetcrust Pastry is a richer dough, perfect for cream pies and fruit pies.

sweetcrust pastry (pâte sucrée)

makes enough for a single 9-inch pie crust

¾ cup (105g) tapioca starch

1 cup (120g) light buckwheat flour

¼ cup sugar

½ teaspoon salt

8 tablespoons cold salted butter, cut into 10 to 12 pieces

1 large egg

1 large egg yolk

2 to 3 tablespoons cold milk

1. In a food processor, combine the tapioca starch, buckwheat flour, sugar, and salt and pulse together. Add the butter and pulse until the chunks of butter are no larger than peas.

2. In a small bowl, whisk together the whole egg and egg yolk. Add the eggs to the dough and pulse to combine until the yolk is completely blended and there are no streaks of yellow.

3. Add the cold milk 1 tablespoon at a time. The dough will start to come together, but it will still be loose and crumbly.

4. Follow the directions for rolling out the dough in Shortcrust Pastry (page 162).

SINCE 1875, FAMILIES HAVE BEEN COMING to Thousand Island Park, located on the tip of Wellesley Island in the St. Lawrence River. For the last fifteen years, the park library's major fund-raiser has been a pie sale. I'm not sure who thought of pie baking during the peak heat and humidity of July, but every year over a hundred pies are donated, and a line sixty people long forms a half hour before the sale begins. This past year, the pies sold out in a record three minutes. Fruit pies, apple in particular, are the number-one seller.

I decided to make what I thought would be a unique pie: a shoofly pie. "A what?" the lead organizer asked me when I delivered it. "It's a traditional Pennsylvania Dutch pie," I answered. He labeled it "gluten-free" and slipped it into the lineup with all the rest. I lived and worked in central Pennsylvania for three years and fell in love with this humble pie, which is a bit like a cake rather than a gooey pie. This recipe is adapted from a wet-bottomed shoofly pie by Wendy Jo Hess of the Central Market in Lancaster, Pennsylvania. Made from nonperishable pantry items like flour, brown sugar, and molasses, this pie has been a Pennsylvania Dutch staple since the early 1700s. Serve warm or at room temperature with vanilla ice cream or whipped cream.

shoofly pie

makes one 9-inch pie

Sweetcrust Pastry (opposite)

½ cup (60g) light buckwheat flour

½ cup (70g) tapioca starch

⅔ cup packed brown sugar

4 tablespoons salted butter

1 cup molasses

1 large egg

1 teaspoon baking soda

¾ cup boiling water

1. Make the pastry, roll out, and line a pie plate as directed. You can either flute the edges or trim the crust to the lip of the pie plate. Place the pie pan on a baking sheet.

2. Position an oven rack in the center of the oven and preheat to 375°F.

3. In a medium bowl, combine by hand the buckwheat flour, tapioca starch, brown sugar, and butter until the mixture is crumbly and well blended. Set aside ½ cup of the mixture to be used for the topping.

4. Add the molasses, egg, and baking soda and whisk to blend. Whisk in the boiling water until uniformly blended.

5. Pour the filling immediately into the prepared pie shell. Sprinkle the reserved topping mixture over the filling.

6. Bake for 18 minutes. Reduce the oven temperature to 350°F and bake for an additional 30 minutes, or until the crust is golden and the center of the filling is still a little jiggly.

ONE OF THE NEATEST THINGS about old cookbooks and recipes are the handwritten annotations made by the cook. My favorite annotations are the little stories that cooks sometimes tell. In this case, the recipe was from a friend of my late mother-in-law. She wrote a little "story" about a large pear tree in her yard and how she panicked when some surprise company arrived. She went out and picked some green pears for a pie, and not quite sure what to do, she grated them. The pie turned out to be a major hit, so thereafter she always raided the pear tree before the fruit was ripe.

When I saw some rock-hard Anjou pears on sale one day, I bought some to make this pie. But as time has a way of getting away, the pears ripened. I could no longer grate them, but I liked the flavor combination of the initial recipe—pears with a hint of orange and cloves. For this pie, I precooked the pears to determine the amount of juice I was dealing with. Then I thickened it separately and added back the thickened juice. Although this was intended to be an open-faced pie, I felt the precooked pears needed a little something on top. Sugared pie-crust cutouts on the top give it all the benefits of a lattice crust without struggling with weaving strips of unwieldy gluten-free dough. Besides, it makes it look special, and pies should be special. This one certainly is.

fresh pear pie

makes one 10-inch pie

Sweetcrust Pastry (page 314)

8 mostly ripe Anjou pears

Grated zest of 1 small orange or clementine

1 tablespoon orange juice

3 tablespoons sugar

4 whole cloves

1 tablespoon light buckwheat flour

1 tablespoon tapioca starch

1. Make the pastry and refrigerate. Measure off one-third of the pastry and return to the refrigerator. Roll out the remaining pastry and use it to line a 10-inch pie pan. The crust will be thin.

2. Peel and slice the pears, tossing them with the orange zest and juice as you work to prevent browning of the fruit. Add 2 tablespoons of the sugar and the cloves to the pears and toss.

3. Transfer the pears to a saucepan and cook over a low heat for 6 to 7 minutes, or until they start releasing lots of juice. Turn off the heat and set aside for 10 minutes. They will continue to leach juice—up to 1 cup, depending on how ripe they are.

4. Position an oven rack in the center of the oven and preheat to 450°F.

5. Drain the liquid off the pears into a bowl; discard the whole cloves and all but 1 tablespoon of the pear juices. In a small bowl, stir the buckwheat flour and tapioca starch into 1 tablespoon of the pear juices, pour it back into the pears, and heat until the pears are thickened. Pour the mixture into the pie shell.

6. Remove the reserved dough from the refrigerator and roll it out between two pieces of plastic wrap. Use a small cookie cutter to cut out enough shapes to overlap and create the surface of the pie (or simply use a glass to cut out rounds). Before placing the cutouts on the surface, dredge the pieces in the remaining 1 tablespoon sugar and flip them onto the surface sugar side up.

7. Place the pan on a baking sheet and bake for 10 minutes. Reduce the oven temperature to 375°F and bake for an additional 50 minutes, or until the crust is browned.

I HAVE A LONG HISTORY WITH BAKING PIES. I remember coming home in second grade and telling my dad that I needed to bring a cherry pie to school for a fund-raiser the next day. "Sure," he said, "and I'll tell you how to make it." *Me, make a pie?* I was eight years old, and that was the very first thing I ever baked. So, you think I'd be an expert at pie baking after starting out so young? Well, believe me, I was no prodigy. The Annual Columbus Day Cider Sale was a major fund-raising event at our sons' preschool when we first moved to Vermont, and I found myself recruited for an apple pie baking marathon with a half-dozen other moms. It took our host, Andrea, only seconds to whip up the dough, roll out a perfect crust, and fill the shell with apple slices. But when I rolled the dough, it either sprang back like a rubber band or stuck to my rolling pin. I had failed at the most basic task of making a country apple pie.

Gluten-free pie crusts changed all that for me. With no gluten to get rubbery and tough, apple pie baking is a fun fall ritual. My son Alex loves to crank the apple peeler, and together we make a deep-dish apple pie, chock full of apples and sweetened with Vermont maple syrup. You can use any variety of apples for this dish, but a combination of two types, one tart like Cortland and one sweet but crisp like

deep-dish vermont apple pie

makes one 9-inch deep-dish pie

Shortcrust Pastry (page 162)

2 tart apples, peeled, cored, and thinly sliced

2 sweet, crisp apples, peeled, cored, and thinly sliced

1 teaspoon ground cinnamon

½ teaspoon ground allspice

¼ teaspoon freshly grated nutmeg

2 tablespoons lemon juice

¼ cup packed brown sugar

½ cup maple syrup

2 to 3 tablespoons tapioca starch

2 tablespoons salted butter

1 tablespoon granulated sugar, for sprinkling the crust (optional)

1. Make the pastry as directed. Measure off one-third of the pastry and return it to the refrigerator. Roll out the remaining pastry and use it to line a 9-inch deep-dish pie pan. The shell will be thin.

2. In a large bowl, toss the apple slices with the spices, lemon juice, and brown sugar. Allow the apples to sit for 30 to 60 minutes, tossing them occasionally. This process is called *maceration* and will cause the apples to release their juices.

3. Meanwhile, position an oven rack in the center of the oven and preheat to 450°F.

4. Drain off the apple juices into a small bowl and add the maple syrup to the apples. Measure the amount of apple juices in the bowl and add the tapioca starch: The general rule of thumb for thickening with tapioca starch is 1 to 2 tablespoons per cup of liquid. Adjust your tapioca starch accordingly and stir it into the apple juices until all the lumps are eliminated.

recipe continues

Jonagold, gives the best flavor and texture. The juiciness of an apple varies depending upon when it was picked, so you may want to decrease the tapioca starch by a few teaspoons for apples that have been long stored away.

5. Toss the apples with the thickened juices and pour into the pie shell. Roll out the remaining dough between two pieces of plastic wrap and invert it onto the pie. Crimp and flute the edges of the pie crust using your thumb and forefingers. Using a sharp knife, cut out a circle in the center or simply cut steam vents. Sprinkle the crust with granulated sugar (if using).

6. Place an empty baking sheet on the rack underneath the pie in the event that the pie bubbles over. Bake the pie for 10 minutes. Reduce the oven temperature to 375°F and bake for an additional 50 minutes, or until the crust is lightly browned.

THERE ARE ESSENTIALLY TWO KINDS of pecan pies: those that use corn syrup and those that use brown sugar. The former comes out a little custardy, and the latter is more like a praline pie. I didn't even know what pecan pie was until I went to college in New Orleans, where authentic pecan pie making is considered an art. Once I tasted great pecan pie—the praline kind made with brown sugar—I knew I had to find a foolproof recipe. In the *Houston Junior League Cook Book* from 1968, given to me by my late mother-in-law, the top billing goes to the recipe for "Southern Pecan Pie," followed by the "Yummy Yankee Pecan Pie" underneath. The "Yankee" recipe is made with a combination of maple and corn syrup. I can just hear my mother-in-law grumbling from her grave about those "damn Yankees thinking they can come down here and improve things." A good pecan pie should be a Southern Pecan Pie. And this one isn't just good, it is the absolute best.

southern pecan pie

makes one 9-inch pie

Shortcrust Pastry (page 162)

8 tablespoons salted butter

1 cup packed brown sugar

1/2 cup granulated sugar

2 large eggs

2 teaspoons half-and-half

1 teaspoon vanilla extract

2 teaspoons tapioca starch

2 teaspoons light buckwheat flour

1 cup chopped pecans, plus 1 cup halved pecans (for top layer)

1. Make the pastry, roll out, and line a pie plate as directed. Place the pie plate on a baking sheet.

2. Position an oven rack in the center of the oven and preheat to 375°F.

3. In a bowl, with a hand mixer, cream the butter and both sugars on high until they are light and fluffy. Add the eggs, half-and-half, vanilla, tapioca starch, and buckwheat flour. Beat on high until all the ingredients are fully incorporated. The filling will be frosting-like. Fold in the chopped pecans.

4. Spread the filling mixture in the pie shell and, starting at the rim, cover the surface with pecan halves by arranging them in concentric circles, working toward the center.

5. Bake the pie for approximately 45 minutes, or until the pecans are lightly browned and the filling is firm. The filling will continue to set more as the pie cools.

A BOSTON CREAM PIE is a curious dessert, for it is not a pie at all, but a cake that allegedly had its origins in the mid-1800s. Pies, both savory and sweet, were everyday foods then, and Bo Friberg, in *The Professional Pastry Chef*, suggests that it was more common for colonists in New England to own pie pans than cake pans. He traces the Boston Cream Pie to an 1855 recipe published in a New York newspaper for a powdered sugar–topped "pudding pie cake." We do know that the chocolate-glazed Boston Cream Pie had its origins at the Parker House Hotel in Boston in 1856. Whatever its true origins, I'm completely okay with a cake that has a lot of features of an éclair and is called a pie.

For a number of years, Boston Cream Pie was a very popular flavor, spawning cake mixes, doughnuts, toaster strudels, yogurt, and ice cream. For this past Valentine's Day, I decided to make this Boston Cream Pie for Tom in one of my vintage heart-shaped cake pans. Unlike most Boston Cream Pie recipes, this one is gluten-, dairy-, soy-, and corn-free. It features coconut prominently in its many forms—flour, cream, milk, and oil—and I believe I like it better than the dairy version. There is a bit of cooling that goes on in this recipe: The cake layer must cool before filling it with the cooked pastry cream, which must be cooled as well. I

boston cream pie

makes one 9-inch pie

FOR THE CAKE AND FILLING:

¾ cup sugar

¼ cup vegetable oil

½ cup coconut cream (skimmed from the top of a 13.5-ounce can of full-fat coconut milk)

3 large eggs

½ cup (56g) coconut flour

½ cup (70g) tapioca starch

1 teaspoon baking powder

½ teaspoon baking soda

1 teaspoon vanilla extract

Pastry Cream (page 341)

FOR THE CHOCOLATE GLAZE:

1½ cups dairy-free chocolate chips (such as Enjoy Life)

2 tablespoons coconut oil

1. Make the cake and filling: Position an oven rack in the center of the oven and preheat to 350°F. Generously grease a standard-depth (1½-inch) 9-inch cake pan. Line the pan with a round of parchment paper.

2. In a large bowl, with a hand mixer, blend the sugar, oil, coconut cream, and eggs. Beat for approximately 4 minutes.

3. In a separate bowl, blend together the coconut flour and tapioca starch.

4. Gradually add the dry ingredients to the egg mixture. Beat for several more minutes, making sure to scrape down the sides. Beat in the baking powder, baking soda, and vanilla, mixing them thoroughly into the batter. Ladle the batter into the cake pan.

5. Bake the cake for 40 minutes, or until golden and the center springs back when pressed. Allow the cake to cool for 10 minutes in the pan before transferring to a cooling rack to cool thoroughly before assembling.

6. Meanwhile, make the pastry cream and chill as directed.

7. To assemble the "pie," slice the cake horizontally into two equal layers. Spread the pastry cream on the bottom half and top it with the other half.

8. **Make the chocolate glaze:** In a small microwaveable bowl, melt the chocolate chips and coconut oil in a microwave or use a double boiler, just until the chips soften. Stir the glaze vigorously until smooth. While still hot, pour the chocolate glaze over the "pie" and allow it to cool fully before serving.

took advantage of the sub-zero temperature on my front porch to cool the components with lightning speed. That night, nestled around the fireplace, we enjoyed a slice of the best pie. (Or was it cake?)

THE OPPOSITE OF MUD SEASON in Vermont is the "leaf-peeper" season in the fall, when tourists flock to our state in search of a piece of Vermont—beautiful scenery and authentic food and gifts. Roadside sales of homemade baked goods abound, and we never seem to have enough. When you just can't make enough apple pies, and when you need to make lots of them in a hurry, the Swedish Apple Pie is your ticket . . . and the purchasers won't even know or care that it is gluten-free. My friend Dottie gave me this recipe years ago when we were on apple pie baking duty for our kids' preschool. "Crusts?" she said. "Who makes crusts? This just can't fail, and it tastes lots better."

The beauty of this pie is its simplicity. It contains minimal ingredients, and the hardest thing is peeling the apples. It also can be sliced into neat squares and wrapped individually in plastic wrap, making it both a bake sale and lunch box favorite. The key to success with this pie is creaming the sugar with the butter, which traps air bubbles and creates a crusty loft. This recipe works just as well with seasonal fruits like blueberries, peaches, and even lightly sweetened rhubarb. It is a great recipe, for example, when you overdo PYO blueberries, and end up with more than you can eat before they spoil. This pie freezes well, and thaws tasting freshly baked.

swedish apple pie

makes one 8 × 8-inch pie

3 to 4 medium tart apples, peeled and thickly sliced

1 cup sugar, plus 1 tablespoon for sprinkling

1 teaspoon ground cinnamon

8 tablespoons salted butter

2 large eggs

½ cup (70g) tapioca starch

½ cup (60g) light buckwheat flour

Additional sugar and cinnamon, for sprinkling top (optional)

1. Position an oven rack in the center of the oven and preheat to 350°F. Grease the sides and bottom of an 8 × 8-inch baking dish.

2. Spread the apples evenly in the bottom of the baking dish. Sprinkle the apples with the 1 tablespoon sugar and the cinnamon.

3. In a medium bowl, with a hand mixer, cream the butter and the 1 cup sugar on high until the mixture is light and fluffy, about 2 minutes. Add the eggs and beat for 2 more minutes. Gently fold in the tapioca starch and buckwheat flour until just moistened.

4. Spoon the mixture over the apples and spread evenly to cover them. Sprinkle with additional sugar and cinnamon, if desired. Bake for 1 hour, or until the top is lightly browned and firm.

EVERY SUMMER WHEN I WAS GROWING UP, my parents planned our family vacation around their attendance at the Gordon Research Conference, the premier gathering of the world's leading scientists in New Hampshire. We would leave our home in Virginia in early August, "taking the scenic route," and camp along the way. Many years, our first stop was Kingsbury's Orchard just over the border in Maryland when the peaches were just beginning to ripen. We'd buy a half-bushel basket, with no place to set it other than the floor in the backseat amongst our skinny legs. We'd eat those sugary peaches for days, cradled in a paper napkin to keep the juice from running down our arms. I've been hooked on Southern peaches all my life, and there's nothing like peaches 'n' cream . . . except this semifreddo.

Peaches star in this semifreddo made of layers of peach-swirled ice cream and peach liqueur–flavored ladyfingers. Since the cream portion of this dessert is made with egg whites, the recipe includes a step to lightly heat and thus pasteurize them before they are whipped into a meringue. Alternatively, you can work with powdered egg whites or meringue powder, although fresh egg whites will produce the lightest and highest-volume layers.

fresh peach semifreddo

makes one 9-inch loaf

1 cup sugar

2 pounds peaches, peeled and cut into pieces

2 tablespoons peach liqueur

1 cup plus 1 tablespoon heavy (whipping) cream

12 Ladyfingers (page 252)

3 large egg whites

1 teaspoon vanilla extract

1. Line a 5 × 9-inch loaf pan with two pieces of plastic wrap, tucking one piece along the length of the pan and another across the width. Allow for overhang on all sides.

2. In a medium saucepan, combine 1/3 cup of the sugar and all but 1 cup of the peaches over medium-low heat. Cook the peaches for 10 to 12 minutes, or until they release their juices and start to thicken. Set the pan aside to cool, then refrigerate for 1 hour, or until the peaches are thoroughly chilled.

3. In a small bowl, whisk together the peach liqueur and 1 tablespoon of the cream. Using a pastry brush, paint the mixture on the flat sides of the ladyfingers. Cover them with plastic wrap and set them aside while you prepare the filling.

4. In a heatproof bowl, whisk together the egg whites and the remaining 2/3 cup sugar. Set the bowl in a saucepan over, but not touching, simmering water. Whisk the egg whites to dissolve the sugar while heating the mixture for 4 to 5 minutes, or until it is warm to the touch and is pasteurized (about 140°F).

5. Remove the bowl from the heat, add the vanilla, and use a hand mixer to beat the egg whites until they are tripled in volume and the meringue is completely cool.

recipe continues

6. In a small bowl, using clean beaters, whip the remaining 1 cup cream into soft peaks. Gradually fold the whipped cream into the meringue until blended. Fold in the chilled peach mixture without thoroughly blending it. (You want a marbled or swirled effect.)

7. Spoon and smooth one-third of the peach cream into the bottom of the prepared pan. Top with 6 ladyfingers, set flat side up and laid lengthwise in the pan. Spoon another one-third of the peach cream on top of the ladyfingers. Top that cream layer with another layer of ladyfingers. Smooth the remaining third of the cream on the top. Loosely fold the plastic overhang over the top and freeze for at least 8 hours. (You can also follow these steps in a semifreddo mold, as shown, placing the ladyfingers in a single layer.)

8. Remove the frozen semifreddo from the pan by using the plastic wrap to lift it. If necessary, run a thin, sharp knife under hot water and slip it down along the sides to loosen the semifreddo. Invert the semifreddo onto a platter and cut in slices to serve. Garnish with the reserved 1 cup peaches. The semifreddo is best when allowed to soften several minutes before serving.

RED RASPBERRIES grew all along the dirt road leading to our first home in Vermont. I'd go out with the kids and we'd pick for an hour or more and come home with only a little container, but they had to be the sweetest and most delicate fruit I had ever tasted. Our golden retriever quickly learned they were sweet as well. He would bound ahead of us and snatch berries right off the thorny canes. When we built our present home, blackberries soon began growing along the driveway and the edges between the yard and the woods, but no wild raspberries. But nearly twenty years later, wild red raspberries inexplicably appeared among the blackberries, every bit as sweet and tiny as the ones we picked years before.

Raspberries pair exceptionally well with chocolate, the sweetness of the berry offset by the smoky bitterness of the cocoa bean. For this tart shell, a chocolate graham cracker–like crust forms the shell, and the raspberry puree filling is thickened by nothing but coconut butter. This is a simple confection, perfect for tea and even better dressed up with freshly picked berries and whipped cream.

coconut raspberry chocolate tartlets

makes 9 to 12 tartlets

FOR THE CHOCOLATE SHELL:

½ cup (60g) light buckwheat flour

½ cup (70g) tapioca starch

¼ cup unsweetened cocoa powder

2 tablespoons (24g) potato starch

¼ cup brown sugar

¼ cup unsweetened shredded coconut

½ teaspoon salt

½ teaspoon baking powder

¼ teaspoon ground cinnamon

3 tablespoons coconut oil

2 tablespoons honey

½ teaspoon vanilla extract

FOR THE COCONUT RASPBERRY FILLING:

1 cup fresh raspberries (or thawed frozen)

2 tablespoons honey

1 teaspoon vanilla extract

1 cup Coconut Butter (page 143), softened

¼ cup dairy-free chocolate chips, melted, for drizzling (optional)

1. Make the chocolate shell: Position an oven rack in the center of the oven and preheat to 350°F.

2. In a food processor, combine the buckwheat flour, tapioca starch, cocoa powder, potato starch, brown sugar, shredded coconut, salt, baking powder, and cinnamon and pulse to combine. Blend in the coconut oil until the dough is mealy. Add the honey and vanilla and blend until the dough comes together. (If the dough gets too sticky to roll out, place it in a bowl in the refrigerator for at least 20 minutes.)

3. Divide the dough into 3 equal portions. Roll out one portion of dough on parchment paper as thinly as possible, 1/16 to 1/8 inch; keep the remainder of the dough refrigerated. Using a biscuit cutter or drinking glass, cut out 3 to 4 2½-inch rounds.

4. Turn a mini muffin tin upside down. Carefully transfer a dough round to the bottom of a muffin cup at one of the corners of the muffin tin. Center the dough over the cup and lightly press opposite sides against the muffin cup to create a 4-cornered tart shell. Repeat for 3 more cups at the corners of the muffin tin. Slide the upside down muffin tin onto a baking sheet and bake for 6 minutes. Allow the shells to cool on the muffin tin until set and then carefully transfer them to a cooling rack. They will be fragile until fully cooled. Roll out and bake the remaining shells and let them cool before filling.

5. Make the filling: In a small saucepan, combine the raspberries and 1 tablespoon water. Heat the raspberries over a low heat until the berries release their juices. Strain the berry juices into a bowl, using a fine-mesh sieve to remove the pulp and seeds. Add the honey, vanilla, and softened coconut butter to the raspberry juice and stir to combine.

6. Spoon the filling into the shells. Drizzle the tops with melted chocolate, if desired.

MACAROONS are one of the naturally gluten-free cookies that everyone likes, and they have a long shelf life so they are ideal for taking on road trips and planes. Not only are they convenient as cookies, they can be chopped up to make crusts and add texture to cream fillings. It never occurred to me for the longest time just to make my own and adjust the amount of sweetener, depending on whether we were going to eat them as cookies or use them in a dessert.

The shells of these cheesecake tarts are similar to macaroons, but not quite as sweet. They are attractive shells, a little like a bird's nest, that release easily from the pan and can be baked ahead of time. Cacao nibs in the shell give just a hint of chocolate and add texture and visual appeal. The cheesecake filling contains no eggs, so it need not be baked to be safe—only refrigerated to set. The filling, which tastes much like traditional cheesecake, is a bit lighter because the filling is half whipped cream. The lightness provides a distinct contrast to the chewier, earthier shell. These mini cheesecakes keep and freeze well. Just thaw to serve and top with fresh fruit. They are a delicious and showy handheld dessert, but try them frozen—that's Tom's favorite way to eat them.

fresh fruit cheesecake tartlets

makes 12 tartlets

FOR THE TART SHELLS:

2 large egg whites

2 tablespoons tapioca starch

2 cups unsweetened shredded coconut

1/2 cup sugar

1/2 teaspoon vanilla extract

1/4 cup cacao nibs

FOR THE FILLING:

1/2 cup heavy (whipping) cream

8 ounces cream cheese

3/4 cup (150g) sugar

1 teaspoon vanilla extract

2 cups chopped fruit or berries

1. **Make the tart shells:** Position an oven rack in the center of the oven and preheat to 325°F. Grease 12 cups of a standard muffin tin very liberally. Make sure there is plenty in the bottom to prevent sticking.

2. In a medium bowl, whisk together the egg whites and tapioca starch. Stir in the shredded coconut, sugar, and vanilla. Knead the mixture by hand until it is fully moistened and you can create a ball that holds together. Work in the cacao nibs by hand.

3. Roll the mixture into balls the size of golf balls and drop one in each muffin cup. Dampen your fingers and press each ball down into the bottom of the cup. Still with damp hands, press down on the dough and work it into and up the walls of the cup. The better you pack it, the more robust the tart shell will be.

recipe continues

4. Bake the shells for 23 minutes, or until the rims are golden brown and the insides are white. Allow the shells to cool enough to handle, but release them from the muffin tin while they are still warm and flexible. If you find them getting brittle, slide them back in the warm oven for a minute to soften. Let the shells cool completely.

5. **Make the filling:** In a bowl, with a hand mixer, whip the cream to soft peaks. Set aside.

6. In a separate bowl, with a hand mixer, beat the cream cheese until it is soft and fluffy. Beat in the sugar and vanilla. A little at a time, beat the whipped cream into the cream cheese mixture.

7. Fill the crusts immediately and refrigerate the tarts until the filling is firm. Top with fresh fruit to serve.

OUT HERE IN THE COUNTRY, we swap and gift plants. We start with a cutting or a clump, or just some excess when dividing perennials. Among the plants that have taken root in our garden, we have Liz's day lilies, Kathy's lupins, Virge's primrose, and Allie's gooseneck loosestrife. But the coolest plant of all is the rhubarb from Christopher's cuttings. Every year, it is the first spring sentinel of the garden.

There are two main varieties of rhubarb: red and green. Ours is of the green variety, with a tinge of red. Rhubarb, which is thought to have originated in Siberia, first appeared as an ingredient in tarts in Britain in the late 1700s. Rhubarb is a part of their pie heritage as apples are ours. Here in New England, almost everyone has a backyard rhubarb plant. The plant produces rhubarb for up to fifteen years. It is extremely cold-hardy and easy to grow with huge elephant ear–shaped leaves and long slender celery-like stalks. This tart showcases the beauty as well as the taste of the rhubarb. Rather than losing its identity in a sauce, the rhubarb lines the bottom of the tart shell and rises to the top during the baking process. The smooth, sweet cream filling contrasts with the tartness of the rhubarb in this quintessentially New England dessert.

rhubarb cream tart

makes one 10-inch tart

FOR THE TART:
Sweetcrust Pastry (page 314)
10.5 ounces fresh rhubarb
¼ cup sugar
1 tablespoon tapioca starch
1 tablespoon light buckwheat flour

FOR THE CUSTARD:
½ cup sugar
2 large eggs plus 1 large egg yolk
1½ teaspoons vanilla extract
1 cup light cream

1. **Make the tart:** Make the pastry, roll out, and use it to line a 10-inch tart pan with a removable bottom.

2. Cut the rhubarb into ¾-inch slices and toss it in a bowl with the sugar. Allow it to sit for 30 to 40 minutes. Drain the rhubarb in a colander and toss with the tapioca starch and buckwheat flour.

3. Meanwhile, position an oven rack in the center of the oven and preheat to 375°F.

4. Prebake the tart shell for 10 minutes. Remove the tart shell but leave the oven on and reduce the temperature to 325°F.

5. Arrange the rhubarb in the bottom of the prebaked shell. (It will rise to the surface as it bakes, so take care in how you arrange it. I like the look of a basket-weave pattern that alternates the direction of the rhubarb.)

6. **Make the custard:** In a bowl, with a hand mixer, beat the sugar, whole eggs, egg yolk, and vanilla on high until light and foamy. Add the cream and beat on high until well blended, about 2 minutes. Pour the filling over the arranged rhubarb.

7. Bake the tart for 45 minutes, or until the custard is firmly set.

ONE DAY, MY SON ALEX came home from school all excited about some jelly they had made. The jelly they made turned out to be quince, from a quince tree on the edge of the school's parking lot. A few weeks later I happened to be running near the farm school and noticed a bunch of bright yellow fruit on the ground under the tree. Of course I stopped and crammed as many as I could into the pouch of my hooded sweatshirt. By the time I got home, my car smelled otherworldly, sweet like honey, perfumed like a rose, yet tropical like a pineapple. Don't be fooled, though; the quince's perfume-like fragrance belies a puckery, tart fruit.

The quince is described as a cross between a pear and an apple, but I don't think that description does it justice—it is a pretty unique member of the rose family, which includes pears and apples. Although it is native to southwest Asia, it was commonly grown by the American colonists as a source of pectin for jams and jellies. In this galette, I pair roasted quince with tart cherries, which contrast nicely with a frangipane, or an almond paste–based pastry cream.

cherry and roasted quince galette

makes one 8- to 9-inch galette

FOR THE FRUIT FILLING:

2 large quinces

Juice of ½ lemon

¼ cup maple syrup

3 tablespoons salted butter

1 can (15 ounces) water-packed pitted tart red cherries, drained (such as Oregon Fruit Products)

Sweetcrust Pastry (page 314)

FOR THE FRANGIPANE:

⅓ cup Homemade Almond Paste (page 336)

4 tablespoons salted butter

½ cup sugar

2 large eggs

⅓ cup (40g) light buckwheat flour

1. Position an oven rack in the center of the oven and preheat to 350°F.

2. **Make the fruit filling:** Peel and cut the quinces into chunks and place them in an ovenproof bowl of water with the lemon juice to keep the fruit from browning as you work.

3. Drain the water, return the quince to the bowl and toss with the maple syrup. Dot it with butter. Roast the quince for 55 minutes, stirring about every 15 minutes. Remove the quince and let it cool. Toss in the drained cherries and set aside.

4. Meanwhile, make the pastry and refrigerate until you are ready to use it.

5. Position an oven rack in the center of the oven and preheat to 450°F. Butter a 9 × 13-inch or smaller baking dish. Line it with parchment paper. (Using a dish with sides will prevent the galette from spreading too much.)

6. **Make the frangipane:** In a bowl, with a hand mixer, beat together the almond paste and butter until well blended. Add the sugar and beat until the crystals are dissolved. Beat in the eggs, one at a time, until fully blended. Beat in the flour until well combined.

7. To assemble the galette, decide on the shape and size of the galette and the amount of crust you want to fold over on the top (I recommend about 2 inches for an 8- to 9-inch galette for the optimal top-crust-to-fruit ratio). Roll out the pastry ⅛ inch thick between two pieces of plastic wrap and transfer to your baking dish.

8. Spread the frangipane in the center of the pastry, leaving sufficient borders around the edge for folding up the pastry. Top the frangipane with the fruit filling and fold up and pleat the edges until you get a rustic-looking galette.

9. Bake for 10 minutes. Reduce the oven temperature to 375°F and bake for an additional 45 to 50 minutes, or until the filling is bubbling and the crust is lightly browned.

Although both fruits are tart, they represent a different quality of tartness and work extremely well together. A galette is a perfect gluten-free adaptation of pastry crust. Its freeform and rustic shape allows you to fold and pleat it any way you want, and imperfection is just fine.

A COUPLE OF YEARS BACK, we were driving on Interstate 95 not far from Florida. Up ahead we saw an 18-wheeler, loaded high, with some black netting flapping in the wind. Then we heard the sound. Despite the hum of the crowded interstate, we heard and then saw bees. Lots of bees. We were passing a pollinating rental truck, likely en route to the annual pollination of California's 800,000 acres of almond trees. Almond trees, curiously enough, are not self-pollinating; so every year, in February, nearly half of all the beehives in the United States—over a million hives—are trucked to California by over two thousand 18-wheelers. Almonds, almond flour, and almond paste are the basis of many cakes, cookies, and confections, not to mention frangipane, an almond cream filling. We can thank the migratory beekeepers for their existence.

You can always buy blanched almonds to make almond paste, but I find the transformation from a bag of wrinkled brown almonds to fresh, sweet, manila-colored paste for pastries and cookies is pretty amazing. I particularly like removing the skins by blanching the almonds and popping the nut out of the skin.

homemade almond paste

makes about 14.5 ounces (411g)

1½ cups raw almonds

1½ cups powdered sugar

2 teaspoons pasteurized powdered egg whites

½ teaspoon almond extract

1. To blanch the almonds, place them in a heatproof bowl and pour in just enough boiling water to cover them. Soak them in the boiling water for 1 minute, then drain and rinse several times with cold tap water.

2. Squeeze the skins off by pressing the pointed end of the nut between your thumb and forefinger. Scrape off the dark spot where the skin attaches to the nut with your fingernail. Spread out on a clean kitchen towel to dry. Make sure they are totally dry before proceeding with making the almond paste.

3. In a food processor, blend the almonds and ½ cup of the powdered sugar until the nuts are finely ground. They will look like sand. Add the remaining 1 cup powdered sugar and blend until thoroughly mixed into a uniform color. It should look like grainy flour. Try not to blend the almonds too much because the oils will release and cause clumping.

4. In a small bowl, whisk together the powdered egg whites and 1 tablespoon water. Add this mixture and the almond extract to the ground almonds. Process until the paste forms a smooth ball, adjusting the texture by adding a teaspoonful of powdered sugar or water as needed.

5. Double-wrap the paste in plastic wrap and then enclose that in a sealable plastic bag. You can keep it this way in the refrigerator for approximately 3 months or in the freezer for 6 months. When using almond paste in recipes, bring it to room temperature first. Because you have used pasteurized powdered egg whites, the almond paste is safe to use in unbaked recipes.

NOTE: Almond paste and marzipan have similar ingredients. Marzipan, which is used for candy and fondants, often has a higher ratio (up to 75%) of sugar. You can add about 2 cups (240g) of powdered sugar to this almond paste to make a good marzipan that can be dipped in chocolate, or tinted with food coloring and sculpted into marzipan candies.

THIS IS ONE OF THE EASIEST
gluten-free desserts to prepare
with only a few ingredients. It is
also guaranteed to impress your
family or guests. Sometimes
gluten-free baking requires a
leap of faith that the recipe
will come out as expected.
Consider this one a triple jump.
During the baking process, the
dough is literally transformed
from a semigelatinous glob
to the most attractive, best-
tasting, and uncompromising
éclair shell. You can simply
slice each shell open and fill it
with pudding, fruit, ice cream,
whipped cream, or whipped
coconut cream for a fantastic
dessert. Or you can dress it up
by dipping it in chocolate glaze
or drizzling it with a hard sauce
of your choice. People will be
talking about it for days.

What makes this work? The
answer is tapioca starch, a root
that can form a very rubbery
gel. Sometimes, in the absence
of gluten, rubbery is exactly
what you need. This éclair is a
prime example: What you're
doing is creating a paste capable
of ballooning up as it bakes.
It relies on the high moisture
content in the liquid and the
eggs to leaven the éclair shell
by steaming open the paste.
Initially, the éclairs are baked at
a high temperature in the lower
third of the oven to ensure
that the eggs act effectively as
emulsifiers, and the paste does
not separate.

coconut éclairs

makes 10 eclairs

½ cup full-fat coconut milk	1 cup (140g) tapioca starch
¼ cup coconut oil	2 large eggs
2 teaspoons sugar	Chocolate Glaze (page 276)
½ teaspoon salt	Pastry Cream (page 341)

1. Position an oven rack in the lower third of the oven and preheat to 450°F. Line a baking sheet with parchment paper.

2. In a saucepan, bring the coconut milk, coconut oil, sugar, salt, and ¼ cup water to a boil. Immediately stir in the tapioca starch. The mixture will be moistened and look kind of like gummy cauliflower. Transfer the mixture to a bowl and allow it to cool for 15 minutes.

3. Using a hand mixer, beat in the eggs one at a time. The goal is to get the dough to come together into a consistency that can be piped. It will first look like scrambled eggs. Add ¼ cup water and keep beating until the dough comes together. When it is both fluffy and rubbery (kind of like cooked dumplings) and the dough begins to climb the beater, it is done. You will notice almost wet pearls of tapioca in the dough; they will disappear in the baking process.

recipe continues

4. Use a piping bag fitted with a plain $1/2$-inch tip or cut a $1/2$-inch opening in the corner of a 1-quart sealable bag, and pipe straight logs (about the width of a hot dog and 4 inches long) onto the parchment-lined baking sheet, separating them by about 2 inches. (As the dough is piped, you may find that it clings to the bag at the end of the piping. Use a butter knife or a spoon to "cut" it loose.) After you have piped all the logs, wet your fingers to smooth any irregularities if you want perfect éclair shells.

5. Bake the éclairs for 15 minutes. Reduce the oven temperature to 375°F and bake for an additional 30 minutes until they are light golden in color. Turn off the oven, open the door, and allow the éclairs to cool in the oven.

6. Once the éclairs are fully cooled, use a serrated knife to cut them in half horizontally. Dip the top half of each éclair in the Chocolate Glaze and set aside. Fill the bottom half of each éclair with 1 to 2 tablespoons Pastry Cream and carefully set the glazed top back on. Keep refrigerated until ready to serve.

WHEN IT COMES TO DESSERTS, the real finishing touch is pastry cream, which adds flavor and a contrasting creamy texture to otherwise ordinary baked goods. This dairy-free pastry cream is based on Shirley Corriher's recipe for Crème Pâtissière in her book *BakeWise.* The unique flavor in this pastry cream comes from the coconut milk and particularly the coconut cream. The natural emulsifiers in the egg yolks hold the water and fat in the coconut milk together and give the cream its smooth texture. The tapioca starch becomes a gel as the cream is cooked and this gel, in combination with the eggs, allows the liquid to set. The tapioca also prevents the eggs from curdling. Vanilla is added at the end while the cream is still hot; once a gel has set, additional stirring will thin the pastry cream.

Pastry cream has so many applications and is used to fill pastries, cakes, and tarts. It can also be thinned to make a cream sauce or lightened with the addition of ½ cup whipped coconut cream. Pastry cream also can be flavored in as many ways as you can imagine, including plain vanilla, chocolate, coffee, liqueurs, and fruit purees. Interesting effects can be achieved by making the pastry cream either a complementary flavor, as in Boston Cream Pie (page 322), or a contrasting flavor.

pastry cream

makes 2 cups

4 large egg yolks

½ teaspoon salt

3 tablespoons (20g) tapioca starch

⅓ cup sugar

½ cup coconut cream (skimmed from the top of a 13.5-ounce can of full-fat coconut milk)

1 cup full-fat coconut milk

2 teaspoons vanilla extract

1. In a bowl, with a hand mixer, beat the egg yolks until they are thickened and light in color, 2 to 3 minutes. Set aside.

2. In a medium saucepan, stir together the salt, tapioca starch, and sugar. Stir in the coconut cream and then the coconut milk until completely blended. Turn the heat to medium and bring the mixture to a bubbling boil, stirring vigorously. The mixture will get thick and gelatinous.

3. Remove the pan from the heat. Take approximately ⅓ cup of the hot mixture and whisk it into the bowl of yolks. Then a little at a time, keep whisking the hot mixture into the eggs until the saucepan is emptied. The mixture will have thinned considerably.

4. Pour the blended mixture back into the saucepan and return it to medium heat. Constantly stirring, bring the mixture to a bubbling boil. Remove the pastry cream from the heat and stir in the vanilla.

5. Pour the pastry cream into a heatproof glass bowl, cover with plastic wrap on the surface (to prevent a skin from forming), and refrigerate until completely cooled.

WHEN WE DECIDED TO PRODUCE and sell our bread products commercially, we had no experience in the food industry. We were confident about the appeal of our products, but we were totally out of our league when it came to every aspect of food manufacturing. Luckily for us, Vermont has a highly regarded Food Venture Center that offers food business incubation and support services. One of the most helpful things was meeting another Vermont food manufacturer, Rhino Foods—a manufacturer of ice cream specialties and ingredients, and the developer with Ben & Jerry's of the first cookie dough for use in ice cream. Neither my husband, Tom, nor I will ever forget the day we walked onto their production floor— machines were pumping out chocolate chip cookies, rotating rack ovens were humming away, and a huge octopus-like machine was pumping frozen custard.

I remember thinking at the time, *Wow, we could make gluten-free ice cream sandwiches.* Ice cream sandwiches are a perfect gluten-free application because the wafer (or cookie) part of the sandwich doesn't really involve gluten, and shelf-stability isn't an issue because they are frozen. This is a rolled-out dough that can be made as thick or thin as you like. You can make traditionally

ice cream sandwiches

---

makes 10 to 12 rectangular sandwiches

---

1 cup (120g) light buckwheat flour

1 cup (140g) tapioca starch

1/2 cup unsweetened cocoa powder

1/4 cup (48g) potato starch

1 teaspoon baking powder

1/2 teaspoon salt

1/4 teaspoon ground cinnamon

8 tablespoons cold salted butter

1/3 cup packed brown sugar

3 tablespoons honey

1 tablespoon molasses

1 teaspoon vanilla extract

1/2 cup milk

1 pint ice cream

1. Position an oven rack in the center of the oven and preheat to 350°F. Line a baking sheet with parchment paper.

2. In a food processor, combine the buckwheat flour, tapioca starch, cocoa, potato starch, baking powder, salt, and cinnamon. Add the butter and pulse until the dough is mealy.

3. In a bowl, whisk together the brown sugar, honey, molasses, vanilla, and milk. Pour the wet ingredients into the food processor and pulse until the dough comes together. If the dough gets sticky, place it in a bowl in the refrigerator for 15 to 20 minutes.

4. Divide the dough into 4 portions. Working with one portion at a time, roll out the dough on parchment paper to a thickness of about 1/8 inch. Use a pizza cutter to cut 2 × 5-inch rectangles or any other shape of your choice. Transfer the sandwich wafers to the baking sheet. Using a wooden skewer, make docking holes in the top of the wafers.

5. Bake the wafers for 6 minutes. As soon as you can handle the baking sheet, slide it into the freezer to immediately cool down the wafers. This will not only cool the wafers but also soften them like a traditional ice cream sandwich cookie.

6. Once the wafers are frozen, spread each one with a 1/2- to 3/4-inch layer of your favorite ice cream. Depending on the ice cream, you may have to soften it slightly to work with it. Immediately wrap each sandwich in plastic wrap or a piece of parchment paper and return it to the freezer.

shaped rectangular ice cream sandwiches and round ones, and fill them with any ice cream flavor. Sometimes you just want a simple ice cream sandwich, and now you have one.

SOME TRADITIONS DIE HARD, but this one never died. I'm referring to our family's Annual Easter Egg Hunt. It all began one year when the kids were toddlers, and we read Rosemary Wells's delightful book, *Max's Chocolate Chicken*. In this particular story, Max and his bossy sister, Ruby, compete to find the most eggs, the prize being a chocolate chicken. That year, we found a chocolate maker in Brattleboro who actually owned a chocolate chicken mold and who made a chocolate chicken especially for us, and we held our first egg hunt. I'm not sure whether the parents hiding the eggs or the kids searching for them had more fun.

While the egg hunt hasn't changed in over twenty years, the contents of the eggs have. Now I make these chocolate-covered eggs that are valued as much as the final prize. I save the crumbs from leftover cake or failed cake recipes (yes, that happens sometimes) and freeze them. Making the chocolate eggs is a pretty simple task of shaping the eggs and dipping them. It is hard to believe that something so simple as coconut butter can transform a dry cake into a gourmet chocolate egg.

chocolate eggs

makes twenty 1- to 1½-inch eggs

2 to 3 cups crumbled yellow or chocolate cake, such as Basic Yellow Cake (page 258) or Decadent Chocolate Cake (page 274)

7 ounces Coconut Butter (page 143), softened (or substitute thick cake icing)

1⅓ cups chocolate chips

Scant 1 tablespoon coconut oil or vegetable shortening

1. In a large bowl, mix the cake crumbs and coconut butter by hand until it is uniformly moistened.

2. Wet your hands and form balls 1 to 1½ inches in diameter. Taper the ends to resemble a bird's egg. Place the eggs in a wax paper–lined baking dish and freeze.

3. In a microwaveable bowl, melt the chocolate chips in a microwave. Or set a heatproof glass bowl in a skillet with 1 inch of water and melt the chocolate chips over low heat. Stir to uniformly blend in the coconut oil. (If you need additional chocolate dip, you can prepare more with a ratio of 20:1 chocolate chips to coconut oil or vegetable shortening.)

4. Dip each egg in the chocolate and return to the baking dish. The chocolate should solidify quickly as it is cooled by the frozen egg.

I DIDN'T REALIZE I had a corn intolerance until late in life. It's now so strong that within minutes after ingesting anything with even a small amount of corn in it, I get a severe itching sensation. It is hardly life-threatening, but sometimes I think the inflammation will drive me crazy. Corn or some derivative seems to be in everything: It's in just about any candy, including caramels, which are so interesting to include in baked goods. A typical caramel ingredient label might include corn syrup, sugar, skim milk, palm oil, whey, salt, artificial flavors, and soy lecithin. So I learned to make my own caramels.

The best caramels, which are also dairy-free and vegan, can be made with just two ingredients: coconut milk and sugar. Honestly, you can make really great caramels in the time it takes to unwrap the cellophane from individually wrapped ones. These caramels taste almost like double caramels—during the cooking process, both the natural sugars in the coconut milk and the sugar caramelize. Not only are these great treats, but they make great caramel sauce and even caramel baking chips for Caramel Brownies (page 237).

coconut caramels

makes sixty 1-inch caramels

Coconut oil, for greasing the pan

2 cups coconut cream (skimmed from the tops of four 13.5-ounce cans of full-fat coconut milk)

2 cups sugar

1. Grease an 8 × 8-inch baking dish with coconut oil. Line it with a piece of parchment paper overhanging on two sides, and grease the paper with more coconut oil.

2. In a small saucepan, warm the coconut cream over low heat, but do not boil it. Turn off the heat, cover it, and set it aside for later. (You want the coconut cream to be warm so it combines more easily with the caramelized sugar in the next step.)

3. In a medium saucepan, melt the sugar over low heat. Heat it until all the solid crystals are dissolved and it is the color of maple syrup. If you are using a candy thermometer, this is 300° to 320°F. Stir as needed to break up chunks of sugar that form. Remove it from the heat.

4. Stir in the coconut cream. It will sputter and tend to clump but try to incorporate the cream in the sugar as best as possible. It will have a light, creamy color.

5. Return the saucepan to medium heat. Stir as little as possible, and only if necessary to melt the cooled caramel chunks. (You are trying to minimize creating crystals in the caramel. Should crystals form and get in the caramel, they can continue to grow and make your caramel gritty over time.) Allow the caramel to boil off 35% of its volume. As it boils, it will darken to a traditional caramel color. If you are using a thermometer, this will be 250°F, or what is known as the "hard

ball stage." Err on the side of underboiling. You can always reheat the mixture to make the caramel firmer, but you can't reverse overboiling.

6. Pour the caramel liquid into the prepared baking dish. Allow it to set before lifting it out of the pan by the overhanging parchment, and cutting into 1-inch squares with kitchen shears or a pizza wheel. Placing the pan in the refrigerator for 30 minutes or so helps making cutting easier.

7. If desired, wrap each piece in a small square of wax paper and twist the ends. Store the caramels in the refrigerator—they will keep for months without crystallizing.

coconut caramel chips · makes 1 to 1½ cups of chips

These chips should be made ahead of time so they can cool properly before adding them to baked goods. The cooled chips will be the consistency of taffy. They may be stored in the refrigerator for several months or frozen.

1 cup homemade Coconut Caramels, through step 5)

1 tablespoon coconut flour

Coconut oil, for greasing the pan

Tapioca starch, for dusting the chips

1. Microwave (or warm) the caramel for 15 seconds until it is softened. Stir in the coconut flour, then microwave the caramel for 15 more seconds to completely blend.

2. Grease an 8 × 8-inch baking dish with coconut oil. Line it with a piece of parchment paper overhanging on two sides, and grease the paper with more coconut oil.

3. Pour the caramel mixture into the prepared baking dish and allow it to cool fully. Cut the caramel into ½-inch (or larger) squares using kitchen shears. Dust the chips with tapioca starch to prevent sticking. Store in an airtight container in the refrigerator.

I make these caramels for gifts and I also use them as the creamy centers for chocolate-covered caramels. A candy thermometer is not essential for making these, but it will reduce the guesswork.

SINCE 1949, the Pillsbury Bake-Off has been the biggest cooking contest of its kind. In 1994, Mary Anne Tyndall won $50,000 for her Fudgy Bonbons, fundamentally a Hershey's Chocolate Kiss wrapped in a brownie. Her concept was brilliant, but her timing was off; Pillsbury upped the prize money to $1 million the next year. I began making her recipe when it was published, long before we followed a gluten-free diet. It was most definitely a winner and always received rave reviews.

The original recipe included chocolate chips, sweetened condensed milk, flour, vanilla, Hershey's Chocolate Kisses, and a white chocolate baking bar for decoration. My version of the recipe grew out of a need to figure out what to do with an extra 1-pound bag of Hershey's Kisses. I worked with the concept, tweaking the original ingredients a bit, and brought my bonbons to work the following day. The container was emptied within minutes of me walking in the door. I have tried lots of culinary experiments on my staff over the years, but this was the first one where they ganged up and sent a messenger to ask/beg me to make more. I didn't have enough of the "extra" kisses left, so I had to buy even more on the way home.

chocolate lava bonbons

makes 36 bonbons

2 cups powdered sugar

1/2 cup unsweetened cocoa powder

1/4 cup (35g) tapioca starch

1 cup hulled pumpkin seeds

2 large egg whites

36 Hershey's Kisses (to make the bonbons dairy-free, you can use any dark chocolate chunks instead of kisses), unwrapped

1/2 cup rainbow, 1/2 cup chocolate, and 1/2 cup white nonpareil sprinkles (optional)

1. Position an oven rack in the center of the oven and preheat to 325°F. Line a baking sheet with parchment paper.

2. In a food processor, combine the powdered sugar, cocoa, tapioca starch, and pumpkin seeds and process until the pumpkin seeds are reduced to fine pieces. Add the egg whites and process until the dough comes together. It will be a tad crumbly, but should come together like Play-Doh when squeezed and molded, and should not stick to your hands. (If the dough is either too dry or too wet, add a tad more tapioca starch or water in teaspoon amounts.) Knead the dough together and transfer it to a bowl. To keep it from drying out, cover the bowl with a damp kitchen towel as you work.

3. Roll a piece of dough (about 1 tablespoon) into a smooth ball the size of a large marble. Flatten the ball until it is a disk 1 3/4 to 2 inches in diameter. Place a kiss in the center of the disk and fold the sides up toward the pointed end of the kiss. Pinch the dough together at the top and smooth out any seams. Roll in the sprinkles, if using.

4. Place the balls 1/2 inch apart on the baking sheet and bake for 15 minutes, or until they are set. Allow the bonbons to cool completely on the baking sheet; they will be quite soft when you take them out of the oven and will set as they cool.

recipes
featuring
premade
breads

EVERY DAY I AM REMINDED that my company's products make a difference in the lives of many people who must follow a gluten-free or grain-free diet. When I started my company, I had a simple goal to make my products available to anyone who wanted them. From mothers who tell me I have made their teenager feel "normal," to customers who write me daily to say they have just discovered my pizzas or bread, I know I am getting closer to my goal. There is a lot to be said for the convenience of prepared foods, but I am also highly supportive of those who choose to bake from scratch. After all, that is how I got started in the first place.

All of the recipes in this book can be made ahead of time for great meals and treats, but

I'd like to close this book with some easy-to-prepare dishes that can be made using Against The Grain Gourmet premade products or recipes in this book. Against The Grain products can be found in the frozen foods section of your local natural foods store. Most of Against The Grain's products contain dairy, so for dairy-free substitutions in the following recipes, I suggest you use the Country White Sandwich Bread (page 67) for making bread-crumbs and the Rising Crust Pizza Dough (page 73) for pizza shells. Whatever way you make them, these dishes will allow you to share your gluten-free creation with your family and friends, as I've been lucky to do for the last eight years.

GLUTEN-FREE FOLKS have a love-hate relationship with onion rings. Who doesn't love big fat fried onion rings from time to time? But at a restaurant, the frying oil from the onion rings contaminates most French fries, and make both off-limits for the gluten-free. For years, I tried all kinds of batter, all of which just seemed to slide off once the onion ring hit the oil. Then I read a wheat-based recipe that dredged the onion rings in flour before dipping them in batter. That was the step I was missing. Dredging, dipping, and then breading the onion rings results in thick, succulent onion rings that are so good that you'll wish you didn't know how to make them.

onion rings

makes 12 large onion rings

¾ cup (100g) light buckwheat flour

½ cup (70g) tapioca starch

1 teaspoon baking powder

1 teaspoon salt

1 large onion, cut into ½-inch rings

1 large egg

½ cup milk

1 cup dried breadcrumbs made from 1 Sourdough Baguette (page 57) or 1 Against The Grain Original Baguette, finely ground in a food processor

1½ teaspoons Creole seasoning (or ½ teaspoon garlic salt, ½ teaspoon cayenne pepper, ½ teaspoon freshly ground black pepper)

4 cups vegetable shortening (or enough to come up 2 inches in a heavy-bottomed saucepan)

1. In a medium bowl, whisk together the buckwheat flour, tapioca starch, baking powder, and salt. Thoroughly dredge the onion rings in the flour mixture. Set aside.

2. Whisk the egg and milk into the flour mixture until it is smooth and well blended. Several at a time, dip the dredged onion rings in the batter until they are fully coated. Transfer them to a cooling rack set over a baking sheet to finish dripping.

3. Pour the breadcrumbs into a pie plate and blend in the Creole seasoning. Place the onion rings one at a time into the pie plate. Swirl the ring around, then flip it over and swirl again until breadcrumbs stick to all surfaces of the onion ring.

4. In a deep heavy-bottomed saucepan, heat the shortening until it reaches 375°F. Fry up to 3 rings at a time, turning them frequently, until they brown nicely. Transfer the onion rings to a plate lined with paper towels to drain.

THE AUTUMN LEAVES OF
VERMONT are spectacular,
but the real sensory treat is
Vermont apples. In the fall,
hand-pressed apple cider,
homemade apple pies, and
PYO orchards abound. Here's
a recipe that celebrates the
season and infuses your home
with divine smells. This is a
gluten-free adaptation of a
soup made by the Putney Inn,
in Putney, Vermont.

baked onion and apple soup

serves 6

1 Sourdough Baguette (page 57) or 1 Against The Grain Original Baguette, sliced into ³⁄₄-inch-thick rounds

Seasonings: ³⁄₄ teaspoon cracked black pepper, 1¹⁄₂ teaspoons whole cloves, ¹⁄₂ star anise, 1 bay leaf

4 tablespoons salted butter

4 large onions, thinly sliced

1 cup peeled and sliced apples

¹⁄₂ cup red wine

2 tablespoons apple brandy

2 cups vegetable stock

1 teaspoon dried thyme

1 cup apple cider

3 teaspoons balsamic vinegar

Salt

8 ounces Vermont Cheddar cheese, grated

1. Position an oven rack in the center of the oven and preheat to 375°F. Toast the baguette slices on a baking sheet for 15 minutes. Set aside. Leave the oven on.

2. Prepare a seasoning packet by placing the spices in the center of a disposable coffee filter. Gather the top of the filter and tie it securely using thread or kitchen twine.

3. In an ovenproof soup pot or a Dutch oven, melt the butter over medium-low heat. Add the onions and cook for about 10 minutes, or until lightly browned. Add the apples and sauté for 5 minutes.

4. Add the wine and brandy, scraping up any caramelized bits from the bottom of the pot. Add the vegetable stock and thyme and bring the soup to a boil. Add the seasoning packet to the boiling mixture and simmer for 30 minutes. Remove the seasoning packet and add the cider, balsamic vinegar, and salt to taste.

5. At this point, you can ladle the soup into individual ovenproof crocks, if you wish. Cover the top of the soup with a layer of baguette slices and top liberally with grated Cheddar. Brown the soup in the oven for 25 minutes until the cheese is bubbling and crusty. Serve hot.

variation

Using different cheeses changes the complexity of the soup: try adding crumbled blue cheese along with the Cheddar as a contrasting flavor accent. You can also substitute chipotle Cheddar instead of regular Cheddar to add an interesting kick to the crust layer.

STUFFED FLANK STEAK was a treat in my home growing up, but I had pretty much forgotten about it until recently. When I got my first share of grass-fed beef from a CSA, there were some flank steaks staring at me, and the memories of my dad making big pinwheels of stuffing-filled meat came back to me. The flank steak juices meld with the stuffing to create a moist, refreshing variation on a grilled steak.

stuffed flank steak

serves 4

1 (3-pound) flank steak

2 tablespoons salted butter

3 ribs celery, finely chopped

2 teaspoons chopped fresh rosemary

4 medium mushrooms, sliced

¼ cup red wine

1 Sourdough Baguette (page 57) or 1 Against The Grain Original Baguette, cut into ½-inch cubes and toasted

1 large egg

Freshly ground black pepper

1. Position an oven rack in the center of the oven and preheat to 350°F.

2. Cut the steak in half. Butterfly each half: Slice it horizontally, cutting almost through to the other side, but leaving the two slices attached on one side like a book. This doubles the surface area and creates 2 steaks.

3. In a skillet, melt the butter over medium heat. Add the celery and rosemary and sauté until the celery softens. Add the mushrooms and cook them until they begin to release moisture, 1 to 2 minutes. Add the wine and continue heating and stirring until the liquid is reduced by half, about 15 minutes. Remove the mixture from the heat and set aside to cool slightly.

4. In a medium bowl, toss together the sautéed vegetables, bread cubes, and egg until uniformly moistened.

5. Open the steaks up. Spread the stuffing on the steaks, dividing the filling between them, and roll them up as you would a jelly roll. Secure the roll with several toothpicks. Place seam side down in a baking dish. Grind pepper over each rolled steak.

6. Bake the steaks for 40 to 45 minutes for medium doneness.

THIS IS A MOIST, FLAVORFUL STUFFING that everyone—gluten eaters and avoiders alike—will enjoy. It can be made inside a turkey or outside in a covered baking dish and baked alongside the turkey.

rosemary stuffing

makes enough to stuff a 13- to 15-pound turkey

2 Sourdough Baguettes (page 57) or 2 Against The Grain Original Baguettes, sliced

4 tablespoons salted butter

3 celery ribs, finely chopped

1 medium onion, finely chopped

1 tablespoon fresh rosemary, chopped

Salt and freshly ground black pepper

1 large egg, lightly beaten

1. Position an oven rack in the center of the oven and preheat to 300°F. Toast the baguette slices on a baking sheet for 15 to 20 minutes and cut into ½-inch cubes.

2. In a skillet, melt the butter over medium-low heat. Add the celery, onion, rosemary, and salt and pepper to taste and cook for approximately 5 minutes. Remove from the heat.

3. Toss the sautéed vegetables with the bread cubes in a large bowl until well blended. Add the egg and toss until the stuffing is evenly moistened.

4. Either stuff a turkey cavity with the mixture and roast according to the directions on the turkey packaging, or bake the stuffing in a covered buttered baking dish at 350°F for 1 hour. For crisp stuffing, uncover the stuffing after 1 hour and bake for another 15 minutes.

AROUND THE HOLIDAYS we develop recipes for our retail stores to hand out or to prepare and sample for customers. This absolutely delicious salad, perfect either as a side dish or as a complete summer dinner, was developed by one of our staff members. To make this a gluten-free and dairy-free dish, you can substitute Country White Sandwich Bread (page 67) or Against the Grain Vermont Country Rolls for the bread and omit the Mexican cheese blend.

fiesta panzanella

serves 8

2 Sourdough Baguettes (page 57) or 2 Against The Grain Original Baguettes, cut into cubes

1 cucumber, peeled and cut up

1 head romaine lettuce, cut up

Chopped fresh cilantro, to taste

1/2 red onion, cut up

1 can (15 ounces) black beans, drained and rinsed

1 cup corn kernels (or substitute hulled sunflower seeds if avoiding corn)

1 package (8 ounces) shredded Mexican blend cheese

1 tub (16 ounces) fresh salsa

Oil and apple cider vinegar (or bottled vinaigrette), to taste

1 avocado

1. In a large bowl, toss together all the ingredients except the avocado.

2. Let the salad sit for a few hours before serving. Unlike other salads, this one improves with time as the yummy baguette soaks up the seasonings. Slice the avocados and arrange on top.

THIS RECIPE, developed by a staff member, is for those who need to avoid corn but have been missing nachos. With all the ingredients of nachos held together with a "U" of crusty baguette, this is a messy but very satisfying gluten-free appetizer that everyone will enjoy. For a variation, add chopped scallions, chives, or cilantro.

layered baguette boat dip

makes 12–16 slices

2 Sourdough Baguettes (page 57) or 2 Against The Grain Original Baguettes

1 can (15 ounces) refried beans with green chilies

1 jar (16 ounces) salsa (such as Green Mountain Gringo)

1 container (16 ounces) sour cream

16 ounces prepared guacamole

1 cup shredded sharp Cheddar cheese

Black olives, pitted and sliced

1. Position an oven rack in the center of the oven and preheat to 375°F.

2. Slice the baguettes horizontally. Spread half of the refried beans into the holes and grooves of each sliced baguette. Top the refried beans with a layer of salsa, then sour cream, then with a layer of guacamole.

3. Bake the baguettes in a 2-inch deep baking dish for 15 minutes, or until the crust of the baguettes is crisp and the dip layers warm up.

4. Remove the baguettes from the oven, top with the Cheddar, sprinkle with the olives, and return to the oven until the cheese is bubbling.

5. Using a serrated knife, slice each baguette crosswise into 1½-inch-wide slices. Serve with plenty of napkins.

I FIRST MADE THIS BLUEBERRY SALSA at the Townshend, Vermont, Farmers' Market as a guest chef. My task was to take what was available at the market and create a dish . . . without the ability to cook on-site. Served on toasted baguette rounds smeared with a layer of mascarpone and a hint of cinnamon, this is an attractive, fresh, midsummer appetizer.

bruschetta with blueberry salsa

makes 36 bruschetta

FOR THE SALSA:

4 medium heirloom tomatoes (4 colors, if possible), chopped

1 quart blueberries

3/4 cup chopped sweet onion

1/4 green bell pepper, chopped

1/2 Hungarian hot pepper, finely chopped

2 garlic cloves, minced

Juice of 2 limes

2 tablespoons chopped fresh basil

Salt to taste

FOR THE BRUSCHETTA:

2 Sourdough Baguettes (page 57) or 2 Against The Grain Original Baguettes, sliced into 1/2-inch rounds

8 ounces mascarpone cheese

1/2 teaspoon ground cinnamon

1. **Make the salsa:** In a large bowl, combine all the ingredients and toss them together. Set aside to let the flavors meld.

2. **Make the bruschetta:** Position an oven rack in the center of the oven and preheat to 375°F. Place the baguette slices in a single layer on a baking sheet. Bake for 15 minutes. Flip them over and bake them an additional 15 minutes, or until they are evenly toasted.

3. In a small bowl, combine the mascarpone and cinnamon and stir until fully blended.

4. Spread a thin layer of cheese on a baguette round and top with drained salsa.

MAKING A CAESAR SALAD?
Sometimes you just need some tasty croutons to go with it. Or you can use these croutons in our Fiesta Panzanella (page 359). These grain-free croutons crisp up beautifully, and can be made ahead of time and stored in an airtight container for several weeks.

simple grain-free croutons

makes 6 cups

4 tablespoons salted butter

2 teaspoons garlic salt

1½ teaspoons dried thyme

½ teaspoon dried parsley

1 teaspoon freshly ground black pepper

2 Sourdough Baguettes (page 57) or 2 Against The Grain Original Baguettes, cut into ½- to ¾-inch cubes

1. Position an oven rack in the center of the oven and preheat to 350°F. Line a baking sheet with parchment paper.

2. In a skillet, melt the butter over low heat and add the garlic salt, thyme, parsley, and pepper. Turn the heat off and stir to blend the seasonings completely in the butter.

3. Place the cubes in a sealable plastic bag. Using a rubber spatula to scrape the sides and bottom of the skillet, transfer the butter mixture from the skillet to the bag. Close the bag and shake it vigorously until all the croutons are covered with the seasoned butter.

4. Arrange the croutons in a single layer on the baking sheet and bake for 25 minutes, or until dried and crispy. If necessary, bake them for a few additional minutes until they are browned and the way you like them.

NOTE: These croutons may be made dairy-free by using a loaf of Country White Sandwich Bread (page 67) and a butter substitute.

WE MAKE THIS YUMMY PIZZA at work when the need for sweets hits us (or to celebrate someone's birthday, wedding, new apartment—we look for just about any excuse). This is also an ideal pizza to bring camping with you. Grill it carefully over a campfire and you have s'mores for all. No need to worry about marshmallows dropping in the fire or pulling gooey marshmallows off sticks! Of course, you can always make traditional s'mores with my delicious Graham Crackers (page 192), but that means baking the graham crackers first.

s'mores pizza

makes one 12-inch pizza

2 tablespoons salted butter

1 tablespoon brown sugar

1 teaspoon ground cinnamon

1 parbaked 12-inch Rising Crust Pizza Dough shell (page 73) or 1 Against The Grain Three Cheese Pizza Shell

1 cup chocolate chips

2 cups mini marshmallows

1. Position an oven rack in the center of the oven and preheat to 375°F.

2. In a small bowl, blend together the butter, brown sugar, and cinnamon.

3. Spread a thin layer of the butter mixture over the pizza shell. Sprinkle the chocolate chips and marshmallows over the top.

4. Bake directly on the oven rack (or a perforated pan) for 15 to 17 minutes, or until the chocolate is melted and the marshmallows begin to brown. Cut into wedges and serve warm.

To grill outdoors: Wrap the entire pizza loosely in foil, propping up the top layer of foil with strategically placed toothpicks. Set it over indirect heat for about 10 minutes (grills and conditions vary) until the crust and toppings are uniformly heated. Carefully remove the foil wrap and grill until the bottom is crispy and the top is beginning to brown.

WHAT DO YOU GET when you combine a pizza shell with baked apples? You get the most amazing gluten-free dessert—an apple pie in a pizza slice. And if you are using an Against The Grain Three Cheese Pizza Shell, you get a cheesy apple pie. The idea behind this recipe, best enjoyed with a dollop of vanilla ice cream, comes from the owner of one of the first all-gluten-free stores in New England.

baked apple pizza

makes one 12-inch pizza

⅓ cup packed brown sugar

½ teaspoon ground cinnamon

3 tablespoons salted butter

3 large Granny Smith apples, peeled, cored, and cut into ⅛-inch-thick slices

1 parbaked 12-inch Rising Crust Pizza Dough shell (page 73) or 1 Against The Grain Three Cheese Pizza Shell

1. Position an oven rack in the center of the oven and preheat to 400°F.

2. In a small bowl, blend the brown sugar and cinnamon. Set aside.

3. In a skillet, melt 1 tablespoon of the butter over medium-low heat. Add the apple slices and cook for 5 minutes, or until they are just beginning to soften.

4. Arrange the apple slices on the pizza shell. Sprinkle them with the cinnamon sugar and dot the top of the pizza with the remaining 2 tablespoons butter.

5. Bake directly on the oven rack (or on a perforated pan) for 15 to 18 minutes, or until the apples are soft and the top is melted and bubbling. Cut into wedges and serve warm.

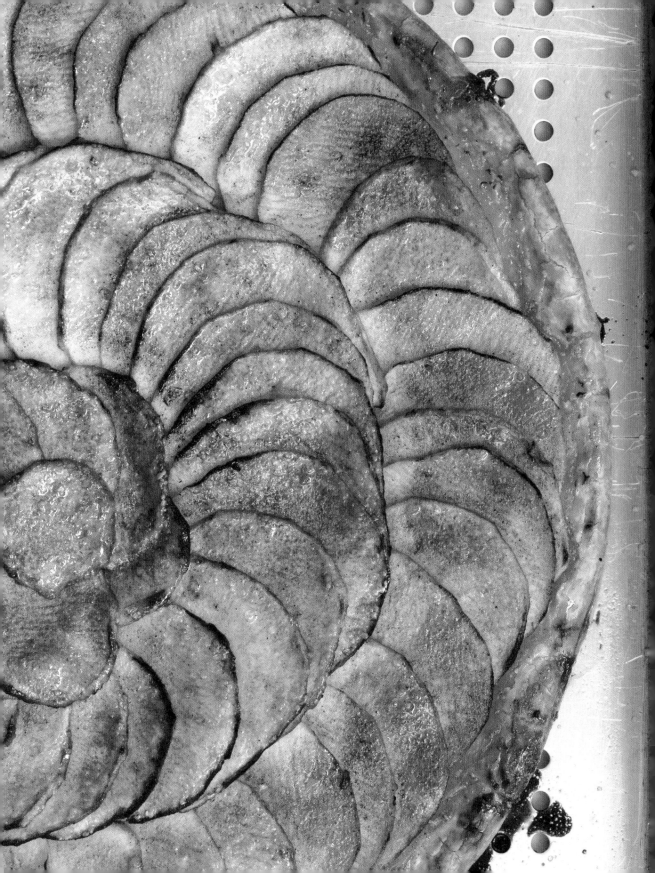

THIS PIZZA ORIGINATED as a group experiment at work. While we questioned eating a warm cheesecake, we couldn't resist and were rewarded with bursts of hot blueberries and strawberries tucked into a divine cheesecake layer. To our surprise, the cheesecake paired extremely well with the cheesiness of our pizza shells. Who says pizzas are for dinner? This pizza is a dessert you won't forget.

berry cheesecake pizza

makes one 12-inch pizza

1 package (8 ounces) cream cheese

¼ cup sugar

1 large egg

1 teaspoon vanilla extract

1 parbaked 12-inch Rising Crust Pizza Dough shell (page 73) or 1 Against The Grain Three Cheese Pizza Shell

1 cup strawberries, halved

1 cup blueberries

1. Position an oven rack in the center of the oven and preheat to 375°F.

2. In a small bowl, combine the cream cheese, sugar, egg, and vanilla and blend until smooth.

3. Spread the cheesecake filling over the top of the pizza shell. Arrange the strawberries cut side down on the filling. Sprinkle the blueberries over the top.

4. Bake directly on the oven rack (or on a perforated pan) for 18 to 20 minutes, or until the cheesecake filling starts to brown. Serve warm.

TUNA MELTS are comfort food to many. The combination of creamy, salty tuna and melted, stretchy cheese grilled on buttery slices of bread evokes memories of a simple Friday night dinner. Most gluten-free sandwich bread is either not big enough or not tough enough to take on tuna melts, but it works delightfully on a pizza shell.

tuna melt pizza

makes one 12-inch pizza

1 medium head broccoli, cut into small florets

1 can (5 ounces) water-packed solid albacore tuna

2 small kosher dill pickles, finely chopped

1 shallot, finely chopped

3 tablespoons mayonnaise

Salt and freshly ground black pepper

1 parbaked 12-inch Rising Crust Pizza Dough shell (page 73) or 1 Against The Grain Three Cheese Pizza Shell

2 tomatoes, thinly sliced

1½ cups shredded Swiss cheese

12 kalamata olives, pitted and chopped

1. Position an oven rack in the center of the oven and preheat to 375°F.

2. In a vegetable steamer, cook the broccoli until just tender. Remove from the heat and run under cold water.

3. In a small bowl, combine the tuna, pickles, shallot, mayonnaise, and salt and pepper to taste.

4. Spread the tuna salad lightly over the top of the pizza shell. Cover with tomato slices. Place the broccoli florets between the tomatoes and top with the Swiss cheese. Garnish with the olives.

5. Bake directly on the oven rack (or a perforated pizza pan) for 12 to 15 minutes, or until the cheese is melted.

THE FIRST GROUP OF FOLKS gets to our bakery at 5 a.m. to set up machines and begin dough preparation for the day. By the time I get into work many hours later, the opening staff has baked several different gourmet pizzas. They are sort of potluck pizzas, since no one knows just what bounty from his or her garden or creative toppings anyone will bring. On a cold winter day, they love to make breakfast pizza with the farm-fresh eggs we buy, and this is just one example. (If you prefer your eggs on the firmer rather than runnier side, you can fry the eggs separately and add them, the cream cheese, and the jalapeño after the pizza has baked for 10 minutes.)

breakfast pizza

makes one 12-inch pizza

½ cup refried black beans

1 parbaked 12-inch Rising Crust Pizza Dough shell (page 73) or 1 Against The Grain Three Cheese Pizza Shell

1 package (8 ounces) cream cheese

2 tablespoons chopped fresh chives

1 cup shredded mozzarella cheese

8 ounces fresh salsa

1 jalapeño pepper, thinly sliced in rounds

6 large eggs

1. Position an oven rack in the center of the oven and preheat to 375°F.

2. Spread a layer of refried beans on the pizza shell.

3. In a small bowl, blend the cream cheese and chives.

4. Sprinkle the mozzarella cheese across the pizza shell. Spread salsa over the cheese. Sprinkle the pizza with the jalapeño, and drop little dollops of cream cheese uniformly on the top. Crack the eggs, spacing them across the pizza shell.

5. Bake directly on the oven rack (or on a perforated pan) for 20 to 25 minutes, or until the egg whites are set.

THE FOURTH OF JULY comes just at the time in the summer when everyone needs a fun holiday, an excuse to have a picnic with red-and-white checkered tablecloths and to decorate with red, white, and blue. It is fun to decorate with food, too, but as it turns out, there aren't too many blue ones—but top a pizza with a homegrown sweet red pepper and blue cheese and you have a patriotic pizza.

red, white, and blue cheese pizza

makes one 12-inch pizza

3 to 4 tablespoons tomato sauce

1 parbaked 12-inch Rising Crust Pizza Dough shell (page 73) or 1 Against The Grain Three Cheese Pizza Shell

1 cup shredded mozzarella cheese

⅓ cup shredded Parmesan cheese

¼ fresh red bell pepper, cut into thin strips

2 ounces blue cheese

1. Position an oven rack in the center of the oven and preheat to 375°F.

2. Spread the tomato sauce evenly over the pizza shell and sprinkle it with mozzarella and Parmesan cheese. Arrange the pepper strips like fireworks bursts on the pizza shell. Crumble the blue cheese and put little mounds in the middle of the pepper bursts. Sprinkle the rest of the blue cheese around the pizza, like random fireworks.

3. Bake directly on the oven rack (or a perforated pan) for 15 to 18 minutes, or until the mozzarella cheese begins to brown.

I DON'T NECESSARILY think of our pizza shells as pizza bases. I think of them as platforms. To me, a pizza shell is an opportunity to make a quick, tasty, handheld dinner. This Southwestern-style pizza contains all the ingredients of my favorite burritos. And it is even better with homemade salsa and tender young lettuce leaves from your own garden.

southwestern pizza

makes one 12-inch pizza

2 skinless, boneless chicken breasts, grilled and cut into strips

1 parbaked 12-inch Rising Crust Pizza Dough shell (page 73) or 1 Against The Grain Three Cheese Pizza Shell

1 cup salsa

1 cup sour cream

1 cup shredded iceberg lettuce

1 avocado, sliced

1. Position an oven rack in the center of the oven and preheat to 375°F.

2. Spread the grilled chicken on the pizza shell. Top the chicken with a layer of salsa, then a layer of sour cream.

3. Bake the pizza directly on the oven rack (or a perforated pan) for 20 to 25 minutes, or until the toppings are heated all the way through and the sour cream is bubbling.

4. Remove the pizza from the oven and top with shredded lettuce. Arrange avocado slices on the top and cut to serve.

ANOTHER PATRIOTIC Fourth-of-July pizza features thinly sliced blue potatoes, which bake until just tender. The aroma is pleasing, the polka-dot effect is arresting, and fresh potatoes on pizzas are unusually yummy toppings.

blue potato pizza with red pepper confetti

makes one 12-inch pizza

6 small blue potatoes, very thinly sliced

1 garlic clove, crushed

Dash of salt

2 tablespoons olive oil

3 to 4 tablespoons tomato sauce

1 parbaked 12-inch Rising Crust Pizza Dough shell (page 73) or 1 Against The Grain Three Cheese Pizza Shell

1 cup shredded mozzarella cheese

1/3 cup shredded Parmesan cheese

1/8 red bell pepper, cut into small confetti-size pieces

1. Place the sliced blue potatoes and crushed garlic in a bowl, sprinkle with salt, and toss with the oil. Let the mixture marinate for approximately 30 minutes.

2. Meanwhile, position an oven rack in the center of the oven and preheat to 375°F.

3. Spread the tomato sauce evenly over the pizza shell and sprinkle it with mozzarella and Parmesan cheese.

4. Arrange the potatoes on top of the pizza shell and sprinkle with the red pepper. Bake the pizza directly on the oven rack (or on a perforated pan) for 15 to 18 minutes, or until the mozzarella cheese begins to brown.

NEW TO OUR GARDEN several summers ago was rainbow chard, a mix of red, orange, pink, yellow, and white with bold and streaked leaves. With all the bounty, we decided to make it into a pizza. We all agreed that it was one of our best veggie pizza combinations yet. Instead of a tomato sauce, the base for the pizza is small white onions sautéed with rainbow chard.

rainbow chard and kalamata olive pizza

makes one 12-inch pizza

2 tablespoons canola oil

6 small white onions, sliced

A good handful of rainbow chard (approximately 30 leaves with stalks), cut up

1 parbaked 12-inch Rising Crust Pizza Dough shell (page 73) or 1 Against The Grain Three Cheese Pizza Shell

½ cup shredded mozzarella cheese

½ cup freshly grated Parmesan cheese

½ cup chopped kalamata olives

1. Position an oven rack in the center of the oven and preheat to 375°F.

2. In a medium saucepan, heat the canola oil over medium heat. Add the onions and chard and cook for about 10 minutes, or until the stems are barely tender.

3. Spread the sautéed vegetables evenly on the pizza shell. Sprinkle the cheeses on the chard and top with the olives.

4. Bake directly on the oven rack (or on a perforated pan) for 25 minutes, or until the cheese is lightly browned.

south-of-the-border grilled flatbread, vermont style

---

serves 4

---

1 tablespoon chopped fresh cilantro

½ cup olive oil

¼ cup white balsamic vinegar

Salt and freshly ground black pepper

1 parbaked 12-inch Rising Crust Pizza Dough shell (page 73) or 1 Against The Grain Three Cheese Pizza Shell

2 tablespoons refried black beans

4 ounces chipotle cheddar cheese, grated

4 slices bacon, cooked and crumbled

1. In a screw-top pint jar, combine the cilantro, oil, vinegar, and salt and pepper to taste and shake until combined. Prepare the cilantro vinaigrette ahead of time for maximum flavor.

2. Heat a grill pan or cast-iron skillet over medium heat.

3. Cut the pizza shell into halves. Brush the surface of each half liberally with the cilantro vinaigrette. Spread the refried black beans on one half and top with the grated cheese and bacon crumbles. Close the flatbread sandwich and place on the grill pan.

4. Grill for 4 to 5 minutes, or until the cheese is melted and the shell is toasted with golden grill marks. Cut into quarters with a pizza cutter to serve.

DURING MY CHILDHOOD, late Sunday mornings meant competing with my siblings over who got first crack at the comic sections of the *Washington Post.* My favorite comic was *Blondie,* about a ditsy blonde housewife and her sandwich-obsessed husband, Dagwood. My entire life, I have found it entertaining to emulate Dagwood and create towering sandwiches with whatever I can find in the refrigerator. My son Marty inherited that gene because he too became a sandwich artist, layering fixings like turkey, bacon, Cheddar cheese, spinach, pepperoncini, mustard, and mayonnaise into 3-inch-tall sandwiches. When he was diagnosed with celiac disease, he lost his interest in sandwiches for a while . . . that is, until he found the perfect bread.

There aren't too many gluten-free breads that can handle Dagwood-style sandwiches without falling apart or becoming soggy, but the Pumpernickel Rolls are one of them. They can even be made into thick Reuben sandwiches oozing with Thousand Island dressing and melted cheese. Even with the juice of a thick layer of tangy sauerkraut, the roll maintains its integrity. These Reuben sandwiches are wrapped in foil and baked, but they could just as easily be grilled.

reuben sandwiches

makes 4 sandwiches

3 cups sauerkraut

4 Pumpernickel Rolls (page 96) or 4 Against The Grain Vermont Country Rolls

½ cup Thousand Island dressing (make sure it is gluten-free)

12 ounces sliced corned beef

6 ounces sliced Swiss cheese

1. Position an oven rack in the center of the oven and preheat to 325°F.

2. Drain the sauerkraut well and squeeze out any liquid using a paper towel.

3. Slice the pumpernickel rolls horizontally and open them up. Spread about 1 tablespoon Thousand Island dressing on the open sides of the rolls. Between the two sides of the roll, layer about ¼ inch of corned beef, 1 to 2 slices Swiss cheese, and as much sauerkraut as the sandwich will hold.

4. Place each sandwich in the center of a piece of foil and wrap the four corners up until the sandwich is completely enclosed.

5. Bake directly on the oven rack for 20 minutes. Be careful when opening the foil to let the steam escape.

THIS MAY BE MY FAVORITE SANDWICH of all time. It is a New Orleans Central Grocery original. There is a lot of meat and cheese on this sandwich and a lot of liquid in the olive salad. Our Against The Grain Original Rolls are the only commercial gluten-free bread that can handle these fillings, unless of course you choose to make your sandwich on a Rustic Boule.

muffuletta sandwiches

makes 2 large sandwiches (serves 4)

FOR THE OLIVE SALAD:

1 jar (6 ounces) marinated artichoke hearts, drained and cut up

2½ ounces pepperoncini, cut up

1 jar (16 ounces) giardiniera, drained and cut up

1 18-ounce jar roasted peppers, drained and cut up

1 ounce capers

6 ounces sliced pimiento-stuffed green olives

6 ounces sliced black and/or kalamata olives

¼ cup olive oil

FOR THE MUFFULETTAS:

2 Rustic Boules (page 101) or 4 Against The Grain Original Rolls, sliced in half horizontally

4 ounces hot capicola, sliced

4 ounces baked ham, sliced

4 ounces Genoa salami, sliced

4 ounces sharp provolone cheese, sliced

1. **Make the olive salad:** In a large bowl, combine all the ingredients and toss to thoroughly mix.

2. **Assemble the muffulettas:** Lightly toast the bread and spoon as much of the salad onto the bread as it will hold. (Store any extra salad mix in the refrigerator for more sandwiches.)

3. Top with slices of capicola, ham, salami, and cheese.

BAGUETTES are not only tasty bread, but they make the most flavorful, moist meatballs and stuffing mixtures. One of our favorite simple meals is a meatball hoagie on a baguette made with extra sharp Vermont Cabot Cheddar cheese or shredded mozzarella.

meatball hoagies

makes 3 hoagies (3 to 4 meatballs each)

2 Sourdough Baguettes (page 57) or 2 Against The Grain Original Baguettes

1 medium onion

1 pound very lean ground beef

1 tablespoon Worcestershire sauce

1 large egg

1 can (15 ounces) tomato sauce

1/2 cup shredded mozzarella

1. Cut one baguette in half crosswise. Save one half for the hoagies. Using a food processor, finely chop the other half baguette and onion into crumb-size bits.

2. In a large bowl, mix the beef thoroughly with the onion breadcrumbs, Worcestershire sauce, and egg. Shape the meat mixture into 9 to 12 meatballs.

3. In a 12-inch or larger oiled skillet, brown the meatballs. Once browned on all sides, add the tomato sauce, cover, and allow the meatballs to simmer for about 15 minutes.

4. Meanwhile, position an oven rack in the center of the oven and preheat to 300°F.

5. Cut the remaining baguette and a half horizontally and then into halves so you have 3 sandwiches, with tops and bottoms. Place the baguettes, cut side up, on a baking sheet and toast for 3 to 5 minutes.

6. Spoon the meatballs with sauce onto the bottom piece of each baguette and top with cheese. Return the bottom layer to the oven and toast until the cheese is melted. Place the tops on the hoagies and serve.

OUR BREADS are famous in the gluten-free world for their ability to soak up juices without disintegrating. You'll find the same can be said for the Sourdough Baguettes. What better bread for making French toast? Thick baguette slices make wonderful country-style French toast.

country-style french toast

serves 4 to 6

1 cup milk

3 large eggs

2 tablespoons maple syrup

1/2 teaspoon vanilla extract

1/2 teaspoon ground cinnamon

2 Sourdough Baguettes (page 57) or 2 Against The Grain Original Baguettes, sliced into 1½-inch rounds

4 tablespoons salted butter

Powdered sugar, for serving

1. In a medium bowl, whisk together the milk, eggs, maple syrup, vanilla, and cinnamon. Pour the mixture into a shallow baking dish.

2. Set the bread slices into the mixture, gently press down on them, and then flip them over and press the other side. Transfer the slices to a baking sheet.

3. In a 12-inch skillet, melt 1 tablespoon of the butter over medium heat. Add as many bread rounds as you can at a time and cook for 3 to 4 minutes per side, or until they are golden brown. Add additional butter to the skillet as needed. Dust with powdered sugar and serve warm.

WHEN YOU'RE IN THE MOOD FOR A QUICHE, but don't want to fuss with a crust, this strata is a perfect alternative. It is substantial enough for dinner or is a great dish to prepare ahead of time for brunch. Assemble and chill this strata for at least 8 hours before baking. Prepare it in the morning before you go to work, or the night before for brunch.

bacon and cheese strata

serves 8

1 pound uncured bacon, cut crosswise into 1-inch slices

1/2 teaspoon freshly ground black pepper

1/2 teaspoon freshly grated nutmeg

1 large onion, finely chopped

2 Sourdough Baguettes (page 57) or 2 Against The Grain Original Baguettes, cut into 1-inch cubes (about 8 cups)

2 cups grated Swiss cheese

1 cup freshly grated Parmesan cheese

8 large eggs

3 cups milk

1 tablespoon Worcestershire sauce

1 teaspoon mustard powder

2 tomatoes, thinly sliced

1. In a 12-inch skillet, cook the bacon over medium heat until it just begins to crisp. Pour off all but 1 tablespoon of the grease. Add the pepper, nutmeg, and onion and cook with the bacon slices for about 5 minutes, or until the onion is soft.

2. Spread one-third of the bread cubes in a well-greased 9 × 13-inch baking dish. Top the bread with one-third of the bacon and one-third of each type of cheese. Repeat this layering two more times, ending with the cheese.

3. In a large bowl, whisk together the eggs, milk, Worcestershire sauce, and mustard powder. Pour the mixture over the strata, cover with plastic wrap, and refrigerate for at least 8 hours.

4. Remove the strata from the refrigerator and top with the sliced tomatoes. Allow the strata to come to room temperature.

5. Meanwhile, position an oven rack in the center of the oven and preheat to 350°F.

6. Bake the strata for 45 minutes, or until browned, puffed, and set in the center. Let it sit for 5 to 10 minutes before slicing.

THESE ARE OLD-FASHIONED COOKIES first popularized in *Hershey's 1934 Cookbook* as a recipe for Cocoa Breadcrumb Cookies. They were from a time when bread didn't contain so many preservatives and actually staled. And before gluten-free bread, which can stale as you are waiting for your kids to come to the dinner table. (You can also make these cookies dairy-free by using Country White Bread on page 67 for the crumbs.)

cherry almond crumb cookies

makes 30 cookies

½ stale Sourdough Baguette (page 57) or ½ Against The Grain Original Baguette, cut into cubes

2 large egg whites

½ cup powdered sugar

½ cup granulated sugar

7.5 ounces almond paste, store-bought or homemade (page 336)

½ cup packed dried sour cherries, chopped

1. Position an oven rack in the center of the oven and preheat to 375°F. Bake the bread cubes on a baking sheet for about 15 minutes. Turn off the oven. Allow the cubes to cool.

2. Transfer the cubes to a food processor and process until they are small crumbs. If the crumbs are still somewhat damp, put them back in the oven for an additional 10 to 15 minutes, making sure that they don't brown too much.

3. In a bowl, with a hand mixer, beat the egg whites with both sugars until fully blended and the mixture thickens. Add the almond paste and beat the egg whites until the almond paste is fully incorporated and fairly smooth. Fold in the breadcrumbs and chopped cherries. Place the dough in the refrigerator for 30 minutes to 1 hour.

4. Preheat the oven to 350°F. Line a baking sheet with parchment paper.

5. Drop the dough by teaspoons about 1½ inches apart onto the baking sheet. Bake for 18 minutes, or until very lightly browned. Transfer to a cooling rack.

THIS LAYERED BREAD PUDDING with a hard sauce is from Mrs. Mary Randolph's cookbook, *The Virginia Housewife*, published in 1860. Besides being an interesting snapshot of pre–Civil War cuisine, it includes charming comments on the importance of refined and domesticated women to a household. The contemporary variation, which I have adapted to gluten-free, is from Colonial Williamsburg's *Historic Foodways*.

sippet pudding

makes one 9-inch bread pudding pie

FOR THE PUDDING:

3 large eggs

1/2 cup sugar

2 cups milk

1 teaspoon freshly grated nutmeg

1 1/2 Sourdough Baguettes (page 57) or 1 1/2 Against The Grain Original Baguettes, sliced into 1/4-inch-thick rounds

8 tablespoons salted butter, thinly sliced

1/2 cup dried currants or golden raisins

FOR THE HARD SAUCE:

1/4 cup sugar

1/4 cup white wine

4 tablespoons salted butter

1. Position an oven rack in the center of the oven and preheat to 375°F. Grease a 9-inch pie plate liberally with butter.

2. **Make the pudding:** In a medium bowl, beat together the eggs and sugar until well blended. Beat in the milk and nutmeg and set aside.

3. Layer the pie plate as follows: Line the bottom of the pie plate with bread slices, top with a few pats of butter, and sprinkle on some currants. Repeat that process until the pie plate is full and some currants and the last butter pats are on top. Gradually pour the egg mixture over the contents of the pie pan.

4. Bake for 25 to 35 minutes, or until the bread browns and the center is firm. Set aside and let cool slightly (it should still be warm when served).

5. **Meanwhile, make the hard sauce:** In a saucepan, combine the sugar, wine, and butter. Bring the mixture to a slow boil, stirring constantly, and allow the sauce to reduce and thicken.

6. Drizzle the warm sauce over the bread pudding to serve.

DATES ARE A VERY POPULAR ALTERNATIVE sweetener and binder today, but they were once foreign to the American homemaker. When Hills Brothers introduced packaged Dromedary Dates in this country, they ran a recipe contest in 1910 and published a little book of the recipes submitted to the contest. This charming booklet contains some quirky recipes, like Date Mush, Rice and Dates, and Date Dainties for Travelers. And it instructs you not to pit a date, but "stone" it. This Date Torte appeared in that book, but I have had to translate statements like "Bake slowly in a moderate oven."

date torte

makes one 9-inch torte

3 large eggs, separated

1 cup plus 1 tablespoon sugar

1 cup breadcrumbs from 1 Sourdough Baguette (page 57) or 1 Against The Grain Original Baguette, toasted

2 teaspoons vanilla extract

½ cup chopped walnuts

1 cup chopped Dromedary Dates

8 ounces heavy (whipping) cream

1. Position an oven rack in the center of the oven and preheat to 350°F. Butter a 9-inch tart pan with a removable bottom.

2. In a bowl, with a hand mixer, beat the egg whites until soft peaks form. Gradually beat in the 1 cup sugar until it dissolves and stiff peaks form.

3. In a separate bowl, beat the yolks until they are thickened and light in color. Beat in the breadcrumbs and 1 teaspoon vanilla. Fold the yolk mixture, walnuts, and dates into the egg whites, taking care not to deflate the whites.

4. Spread the batter in the tart pan. Bake for 25 minutes, or until the center of the torte is set. Transfer to a cooling rack.

5. In a medium bowl, with a hand mixer, whip the cream until it thickens. Add the 1 tablespoon sugar and remaining teaspoon vanilla and beat until it stiffens. Spread the whipped cream over the surface of the cooled torte.

NOTE: This recipe may be made dairy-free by substituting the Country White Sandwich Bread (page 67) for the breadcrumbs and whipped coconut cream for the whipping cream.

acknowledgments

When I began this project, I had no idea that the production of a cookbook would touch so many lives. It all began with the editor of *Cabin Life*, Mark R. Johnson, for whom I wrote an animal behavior column for many years. He introduced me to my agent, Sharon Bowers, whose enthusiasm, professionalism, and persuasion convinced me that this was a book that had to be written. Mark, I owe you a huge thanks! Thank you, Sharon, for leading a neophyte through this process and being such a knowledgeable and skilled negotiator.

Thanks to the entire staff of Against The Grain Gourmet. Your energy, passion for good food, and problem-solving abilities inspire me every day. You are without a doubt our most important ingredient. Thank you for tasting my creations and giving me honest feedback (well, most of the time). Above all, thank you, Tom, for running the place by yourself in addition to everything else you do. I know how hard it was when I was off developing and testing recipes instead of managing the production floor and writing performance reviews.

To those who tested various recipes, including Harry Borst, Marty Cain, Josh Grabel, Lynn Jelinski, Rosemary Kelly, Ruth Pearson, Emily Samet, Kina Viola, and Christopher Wesolowski, thank you for your time, insightful feedback, and helpful suggestions. Lynn, thank you for your moral support, scouring Goodwill for cake pans and other useful gadgets, and powering through recipe testing by day and sending me photographs by night. Only you could have reduced baking a gluten-free wedding cake to a science.

I knew I was in good hands when my editor, Jessica Freeman-Slade, and art director Jane Treuhaft led me to Jennifer May, a gifted photographer with the eye of a painter. Supported by prop stylist Raina Kattleson, food stylist Kendra McKnight, and her assistants Sarah Green and Kazio Sosnowski, we spent eight intense, snowbound days in Woodstock, New York, prepping, baking, and photographing. What we created together was literally an illustration of "the whole is greater than the sum of its parts." And, Jess, before the photos brought my manuscript to life, you skillfully chopped and edited my manuscript into a polished cookbook without losing my soul—definitely not an easy task!

Thank you to the rest of the team at Clarkson Potter, who embraced the concept of a gluten-free cookbook, debated its finer points, and professionally produced this book: Aaron Wehner, publisher; Doris Cooper, editorial director; Kate Slate, copy editor; Ashley Tucker, designer; Kim Tyner, production manager; Marysarah Quinn, head of design; and Kate Tyler, publicity director.

index